THE HERALD IN LATE MEDIEVAL EUROPE

As officers of the crown, ducal courts and noble families, heralds played central roles at a number of levels in medieval society, operating at high levels in diplomacy, chivalry and heraldry. They had an essential role in foreign and domestic relations and chivalric culture, and were increasingly to become the powerbrokers of heraldic symbols and genealogy. However, their roles have been hitherto little explored. This collection considers the place of heralds in late medieval and early modern Europe, from Florence to Scandinavia, from Burgundy to Scotland and England.

The Herald

in Late Medieval Europe

Edited by

Katie Stevenson

THE BOYDELL PRESS

First published 2009

The Boydell Press, Woodbridge
ISBN 978 1 84383 482 3

The Boydell Press is an imprint of Boydell & Brewer Ltd
PO Box 9, Woodbridge, Suffolk IP12 3DF, UK

and of Boydell & Brewer Inc.
668 Mount Hope Ave, Rochester, NY 14604, USA

website: www.boydellandbrewer.com

A CIP catalogue record for this book is available
from the British Library

This publication is printed on acid-free paper

Typeset by Word and Page, Chester

Printed in Great Britain by
CPI Antony Rowe, Chippenham and Eastbourne

CONTENTS

ILLUSTRATIONS

Colour Plates

Plates

CONTRIBUTORS

Adrian Ailes is principal records specialist in early modern records at The National Archives (UK).

Wim van Anrooij is a professor of Dutch literature at Leiden University.

Jackson W. Armstrong is a lecturer in history at the University of Aberdeen.

Bogdan Wojciech Brzustowicz researches late medieval knightly culture and is a member of the Polish Heraldic Society.

Laura Cirri is an associate member of the Académie internationale d'héraldique and researches Florentine heraldry.

Alexia Grosjean is an honorary member of the Institute of Scottish Historical Research at the University of St Andrews and acting director of the Strathmartine Centre, St Andrews.

Michael Jones, Correspondant de l'Institut, is Emeritus Professor of Medieval French History at the University of Nottingham.

Henri Simmoneau is a doctoral researcher in medieval history at the University of Lille III – Charles de Gaulle.

Katie Stevenson is a lecturer in late medieval history at the University of St Andrews.

Franck Viltart is doctoral researcher in medieval history at the University of Lille III – Charles de Gaulle.

ACKNOWLEDGEMENTS

THIS VOLUME is the result of a late-night conversation in the bar at Merton College, University of Oxford, during the Fifteenth Century Conference in September 2006. It was the first time I met Jackson Armstrong, then of Trinity Hall, University of Cambridge. He and I discussed at length the existing problems with the current understanding of late medieval officers of arms. We both agreed there was a need for a volume on the subject. Encouraged by Jackson, and the warm enthusiasm shown by Caroline Palmer of Boydell and Brewer, I set about finding and commissioning authors to contribute to the volume. This involved a great deal of research and, to my delight, I found many scholars in Europe and North America working on the subject. In the end some were unable to contribute to the project, including Maria Dobozy, Michael Jucker, Gert Melville, Harald Nissen and Torsten Hiltmann; I would like to extend my thanks to them for their continued support. Torsten Hiltmann deserves special mention for his generosity in sharing with many of the volume's contributors not only his own research findings but also the database of his major project on the officers of arms in France and Burgundy, based at the German Historical Institute in Paris.

I would also like to thank all of the contributors to *The Herald in Late Medieval Europe*, who have been patient with my demands and timely in meeting them. Particular attention should be drawn to those non-native English speakers who agreed to write (many for the first time) for an English-speaking audience. I appreciate their tolerance through the lengthy editorial process and the collection is much richer due to their efforts. The contributors, in turn, will have their own debts of gratitude to friends and colleagues who read and commented on their chapters; the editor's principal acknowledgement is to Boydell and Brewer, and particularly Caroline Palmer for her continued advice, guidance and support. My personal thanks go to my husband, Gordon Pentland, who has endured more conversations about medieval heralds than anyone should have to!

This volume would not have been possible without generous financial assistance from the Carnegie Trust for the Universities of Scotland. I would also like to thank the following for their permission to reproduce illustrations: the Trustees of the National Library of Scotland; Sir Francis Ogilvy; Biblioteka Jagiellońska, Kraków; Universitäts-Bibliothek Ruprecht-Karls-Universität, Heidelberg; Bibliothèque nationale de France; the Trustees of the British Library; Bibliothèque municipale de Valenciennes; Archives départementales du Nord, Lille; the Royal Library of Brussels; and the Stadsbibliotheek Antwerpen.

Katie Stevenson
University of St Andrews

ABBREVIATIONS

£	*livre* (and equivalents)
AD	Archives départementales
ADC	Thomas Thomson, ed., *The Acts of the Lords of Council in Civil Causes* (Edinburgh, 1839)
ADCP	Robert Kerr Hannay, ed., *Acts of the Lords of Council in Public Affairs 1501–1554* (Edinburgh, 1932)
ADLA	Nantes, Archives départementales de la Loire-Atlantique
ADN	Lille, Archives départementales du Nord
AM	Archives municipales
ASFI	Archivio de Stato di Firenze
BL	British Library, London
BnF	Bibliothèque nationale de France, Paris
Bodl.	Bodleian Library, Oxford
CA	College of Arms, London
CDS	J. Bain, ed., *Calendar of Documents Relating to Scotland A.D. 1108–1526* (Edinburgh, 1881–8)
d.	*denier* (or equivalents)
ER	J. Stuart *et al.*, eds, *The Exchequer Rolls of Scotland* (Edinburgh, 1878–1908)
FL	Landévennec, Abbaye Saint-Guénolé, Fonds Lebreton
NLS	National Library of Scotland, Edinburgh
n.s.	new series
RPS	K. M. Brown *et al.*, eds, *The Records of the Parliaments of Scotland to 1707* (St Andrews, 2007–8), online at <http://www.rps.ac.uk/>
s.	*sol* (and equivalents)
TA	T. Dickson and J. Balfour Paul, ed., *Accounts of the Lord High Treasurer of Scotland* (Edinburgh, 1877–1916)
TNA	The National Archives

Introduction

Katie Stevenson

IN THE SEVENTEENTH AND EIGHTEENTH CENTURIES, particularly in the British Isles, antiquarian scholars and heralds began to write about the history and science of heraldry. Men such as Edward Bysshe, Elias Ashmole, John Anstis, George Mackenzie of Rosehaugh and Alexander Nisbet produced significant annotated editions and collections of sources comprehending such diverse subjects as the genealogy and coats of arms of the nobility, the art and laws of heraldry, the court of chivalry, chivalric orders and the history of the officers of arms. Interest in these officers was further developed in the nineteenth century, as part of the European vogue for all things 'medieval', and into the twentieth century, when the first attempts at comprehensive histories of heralds were written. Most influential amongst these latter works were the two significant tomes written by Anthony Wagner, himself a herald: *Heralds and Heraldry* and the *Heralds of England*.[1] However, it was not until the 1980s that the study of officers of arms made an impact on mainstream academic scholarship, with research by Maurice Keen leading the way. Keen devoted an entire chapter of his Wolfson Award-winning *Chivalry* (1984) to the subject of heralds and heraldry, inaugurating a new phase in the way in which scholars viewed officers of arms. In Keen's view, heralds were significant because by the fourteenth century they had an established position and were dignified figures of the chivalrous world'.[2] However, Keen's work

[1] Anthony Wagner, *Heralds and Heraldry in the Middle Ages: An Inquiry into the Growth of the Armorial Function of Heralds*, 2nd edn (Oxford, 1956); Anthony Wagner, *Heralds of England: A History of the Office and College of Arms* (London, 1967).
[2] Maurice Keen, *Chivalry* (New Haven and London, 1984), p. 134. Keen further developed his ideas on late medieval heraldic culture in Maurice Keen, *Nobles, Knights and Men-at-Arms in the Middle Ages* (London and Rio Grande, 1996), ch. 4, and Maurice Keen, *Origins of the English Gentleman: Heraldry, Chivalry and Gentility in Medieval England, c.1300 – c.1500* (Stroud, 2002).

on medieval heralds remains very much an exploratory overview. It was never intended to be comprehensive and thus left much scope for research in this field. Continental scholars have been rather more quick off the mark than their English-speaking colleagues in identifying the potential for important research into the office of arms. The work of Gert Melville, for example, has been very influential.[3] The recent completion of Torsten Hiltmann's project at the Deutsches historisches Institut Paris on the officers of arms in late medieval Burgundy marks a significant advance in our knowledge and a prosopographic and fully searchable database will be available online from 2009.[4] Several contributors to this present volume have also shaped our understanding of the subject: in particular, Adrian Ailes, Michael Jones and Wim van Anrooij.[5] Indeed, the geographical range represented by current and

[3] See for example Gert Melville, 'Pourquoi des hérauts d'armes? Les raisons d'une institution', *Revue du Nord* 88 (2006), 491–502; Gert Melville, 'Hérauts et héros', in *European Monarchy: Its Evolution and Practice from Roman Antiquity to Modern Times*, ed. Heinz Duchhardt, Richard A. Jackson and David Sturdy (Stuttgart, 1992).

[4] For Hiltmann's forthcoming and published work see Torsten Hiltmann, *Zwischen Heroldsamt und Adel: die Kompendien des 'office d'armes' im französischen und burgundischen Spätmittelalter* (forthcoming); Torsten Hiltmann and Uwe Israel, '"Laissez-les aller": die Herolde und das Ende des Gerichtskampfs in Frankreich', *Francia* 34:1 (2007), pp. 65–84; Torsten Hiltmann, 'Vieux chevaliers, pucelles, anges: fonctions et caractères principaux des hérauts d'armes d'après les légendes sur l'origine de l'office d'armes au XVe siècle', *Revue du Nord* 88 (2006), pp. 503–25; Torsten Hiltmann, 'Information et tradition textuelle: les tournois et leur traitement dans les manuels des hérauts d'armes au XVe siècle', in *Information et société en Occident à la fin du Moyen Âge*, ed. Claire Boudreau (Paris, 2004). The database will be available from 2009 at <http://www.heraudica.org>.

[5] See for example Adrian Ailes, 'Le développement des "visitations" de hérauts en Angleterre et au Pays de Galles', *Revue du Nord* 88 (2006), 659–79; Adrian Ailes, '"You know me by my habit": Heralds' Tabards in the Fourteenth and Fifteenth Centuries', *The Ricardian* 13 (2003), pp. 1–11; Michael Jones, 'Malo et Bretagne, rois d'armes de Bretagne', *Revue du Nord* 88 (2006), pp. 599–615; Michael Jones, 'Servir le duc: Remarques sur le rôle des hérauts à la cour de Bretagne à la fin du Moyen Âge', in *À l'ombre du pouvoir: les entourages princiers au Moyen Âge*, ed. Alain Marchandisse and Jean-Louis Kupper (Geneva, 2003); Michael Jones, 'Vers une prosopographie des hérauts bretons médiévaux: une enquête à poursuivre', in *Académie des Inscriptions et Belles Lettres, Comptes rendus des séances de l'année 2001* (Paris, 2001); Wim van Anrooij, 'Hendrik van Heessel, héraut à la cour impériale et à la cour de Bourgogne', *Revue du Nord* 88 (2006), 709–27; Wim van Anrooij, 'Heralds, Knights and Travelling', in *Medieval Dutch Literature in its European Context*, ed. Erik Kooper (Cambridge, 1994); Wim van Anrooij, 'Gelre Herald and Late Medieval Chivalric Culture', *Coat of Arms*, n.s. 9:160 (1992), pp. 337–44; Wim van Anrooij, 'Maerlant, Heraut Gelre en de "Korte kroniek van Holland"', *Tijdschrift voor Nederlandse taal- en letterkunde* 108:4 (1992), pp. 289–323; Wim van Anrooij, 'Heraut Beyeren en de sterfdatum van Albrecht van Beieren', *Spiegel der letteren: tijdschrift voor Nederlandse literatuurgeschiedenis en voor literatuurwetenschap* 31:4 (1989), pp. 301–11; Wim van Anrooij, 'Het Haagse handschrift van Heraut Beyeren: de wordingsgeschiedenis van een autograaf', *Tijdschrift voor Nederlandse taal- en letterkunde* 104:1 (1988), pp. 1–20; Wim van Anrooij, 'Heraut Beyeren en heraut Gelre: oude theorieën in nieuw perspectief', *Bijdragen en mededelingen betreffende de*

ongoing research made the European framework of this volume indispensible as well as providing the kind of comparative breadth that might allow us to suggest where research into the office of arms might be taken in the future.

Much of the research into officers of arms to date has followed the careers of specific heralds or considered the relationship between a particular herald and the manuscripts that he produced or owned. This collection of essays aims to place officers of arms in a range of other contexts both 'domestic' and 'international'. It seeks to place the officers of arms of Europe in their political, diplomatic and administrative contexts, as well as exploring their better-known role in chivalric culture. In doing so, the picture that emerges from these essays is one of broadly similar and comparative experiences across Europe, but with some remarkable differences, which were for the most part dictated by the peculiar political and cultural worlds in which these men operated. The collection is not exhaustive (if collections of this type ever can be) and there is notable under-representation of areas including Ireland, Spain, Portugal, Hungary and much of Italy and France. This does not imply that heralds were not active in these areas and from time to time this collection does offer glimpses of their activities.[6]

In spite of these omissions the geographical spread of the contributions to this volume is wide. Taken as a whole the essays suggest representative patterns in the development of the office of arms, which are discernible throughout Europe. Jackson W. Armstrong and Adrian Ailes explore the development of the office of arms in England and Katie Stevenson concentrates on the same in Scotland; Michael Jones considers Breton heralds; Franck Viltart and Henri Simmoneau investigate city heralds in the Burgundian Low Countries; Wim van Anrooij discusses the unusual hierarchy of officers of arms in the German Empire; Laura Cirri uncovers the heralds working in the Republic of Florence; Bogdan Wojciech Brzustowicz and Katie Stevenson consider the evidence for heralds at the Polish royal court; and Alexia Grosjean explores the complex web of heraldic offices in the three Scandinavian kingdoms of the Kalmar Union.

The late Middle Ages, here defined as the fourteenth, fifteenth and early sixteenth centuries, was a significant period in the development of the office of arms across Europe. Indeed, all the essays in this collection remark that the late fourteenth century or early fifteenth century was a time of marked changes in the office. Across Europe there was an almost simultaneous

geschiedenis der Nederlanden 101:2 (1986), pp. 153–76; Wim van Anrooij, 'Herauten in de middeleeuwen', Spiegel historiael 21 (1986), pp. 270–9, 309–10; Wim van Anrooij, 'Dichter, kroniekschrijver en wapenkundige Heraut van Gelre en zijn werk', Literatuur: tijdschrift over Nederlandse letterkunde 2:5 (1985), pp. 244–51.

[6] See for example the Portuguese herald, Coimbra, in ch. 5 below, and the discussion of Hungarian heraldic and chivalric interactions with Poland in ch. 9 below.

3

swelling in the ranks of the officers and an increasing move towards professionalisation. This manifested itself uniquely in France and England by the
foundation and incorporation of colleges of heralds during the fifteenth
century. The most significant of the late-fourteenth-century developments
was the granting of titles to previously anonymous heralds. Often these
titles were of symbolic importance to the king, duke, town or family to
which the herald belonged. For example, the English heraldic titles derived
from names of the royal house (ch. 2 below), the Scottish titles came from
royal territories and an emerging royal iconography (ch. 4 below), the
Burgundian city heralds took their names from the civic rituals to which
they were tied (ch. 6 below), and Michael Jones suggests that many of the
Breton titles had connections to the orders of chivalry founded in Brittany,
including the heralds A ma vie, Ermine and Espy (ch. 5 below). The use
of named offices soon brought about a more sharply focused demarcation
of rank within the heraldic hierarchy and, with that, the introduction of
kings of arms to oversee heraldic operations, such as King of Arms of the
Ruwieren in the German Empire by 1362 (ch. 7 below), Lyon King of Arms
in Scotland by 1412 (ch. 4 below), Garter King of Arms in England by 1417
(ch. 2 below), and Bretagne King of Arms in Brittany by 1419 (ch. 5 below).

The officers of arms appear to have had their 'golden age' in the fifteenth
century but were abandoned, in decline or completely reformed during the
sixteenth century. In both England and Scotland the sixteenth century was
the period when the numbers of officers of arms were reduced while their
practices were increasingly monitored and controlled more carefully by
centralised government institutions. This century also witnessed a reduction in their duties and a focus on the armorial aspects of their profession
(ch. 2, 3 and 4 below). In Continental Europe, by the sixteenth century
the office of arms had almost ceased to exist. Wim van Anrooij detects a
lack of use of the King of Arms of the Ruwieren during the period of the
emperorship of Maximilian of Habsburg (1508–19) (ch. 7 below). Alexia
Grosjean has mapped the terminal point in the history of Scandinavian
heralds to the collapse of the Kalmar Union in 1523 (ch. 10 below). Likewise,
Laura Cirri determines that the office of herald of the Florentine signoria
was abandoned at the end of the republican system of government in 1532
(ch. 8 below). Michael Jones finds that as the ranks of the officers of arms
in Brittany were so depleted by the sixteenth century, they were evidently
no longer integral to the operation of communications; by the 1540s only
Bretagne King of Arms operated in Brittany, whereas more than forty officers had been in (at least temporary) existence in the ducal period. After
1547 there is no trace of a Breton herald (ch. 2 below). Franck Viltart and
Henri Simmoneau account for the disappearance of heralds in the towns
of Burgundy by the mid-sixteenth century, after long death throes, to the

4

decline of civic chivalric festivals (ch. 6 below). In Poland, the abandonment of the office had taken place even earlier. Bogdan Wojciech Brzustowicz and Katie Stevenson find the last recorded act of a Polish herald in 1454: by the mid-sixteenth century they were already curiosities of a bygone age (ch. 9 below).[7]

Thus it would seem that the political contexts in which our heralds found themselves had a significant impact upon the development of the office of arms. Seven of the essays contained herein consider heralds under royal, Imperial or ducal authority (those by Armstrong, Ailes, Stevenson, van Anjooij, Jones, Brzustowicz and Stevenson, and Grosjean) and two focus on heralds in a civic context (those by Viltart and Simmoneau, and Cirri). In Lille and Valenciennes, according to Viltart and Simmoneau, the heralds' principal duties were to superintend civic tournaments and record the coats of arms granted to the urban elite; in Florence, according to Cirri, the Palazzo Vecchio functioned as a quasi-court and the city's elite shared the same values as the nobility elsewhere (ch. 6 and 8 below). These 'civic' heralds, it would appear, were employed by the city bourgeoisie, who were attracted to the ideas and values of the nobility. The pictures that emerge in the German Empire and Scandinavia are even more complex. Wim van Anjooij finds that in the German Empire, Imperial heralds had no specific authority over other heralds operating in regions of the empire that retained individual power. Instead, the emperor granted one particularly skilled herald, drawn from any Imperial territory, the additional and special status of King of Arms of the Ruwieren (ch. 7 below). Alexia Grosjean concludes that the heralds employed in Scandinavian service were almost all foreigners (and mostly Scots). As Grosjean points out, this had particular advantages in the regular Scotto-Scandinavian diplomacy that was a feature of the late fifteenth and sixteenth centuries (ch. 10 below). But it also points to an enterprising solution to a sometimes fraught political situation in the three kingdoms of the Kalmar Union. The neutrality of foreign officers of arms in this context was evidently highly valued.

Most of the essays in this collection explore the relationship between late medieval heralds and heraldry. Contrary to the commonly held view that heralds were in charge of all things armorial, the essays herein find overwhelmingly that officers of arms did not grant armorial achievements. Of course, there are exceptions: there is some evidence for grants of arms in England from the fifteenth century and two isolated instances in Scandinavia in 1418 and 1420 (ch. 2 and 10 below). On the whole, arms were granted by the political authority under which a nobleman lived; a king, parliament, a duke or a town council. In the late Middle Ages this was not

---

[7] See also M. Bielski, *Kronika* (Kraków, 1564, facsimile Warsaw, 1976), p. 205.

a function of European officers of arms. However, one armorial activity in which heralds did extensively engage was the collection and collation of information about coats of arms. This was part of their wider function as historians, genealogists and commentators on the social elites. Thus a roll or book of arms might be compiled by a herald to record military participation, to commemorate a joust or, by the fifteenth century, to act as a record of those men in a principality who might offer administrative service. Some of the most beautiful survivals in medieval manuscript tradition are rolls of arms and although they have been studied by armorists, they still offer much potential for historical research.[8]

Indeed, the manuscript compilations in which these rolls are often found also warrant attention from modern scholars. These collections might be seen as 'heraldic handbooks' and often contain a vast array of tracts, treatises, poems and aides-memoires on all manner of subjects that might assist the officer of arms in his professional capacity. Whereas armorists have tended to home in on the blazons and spectacularly illuminated coats of arms, the compilations do need to be considered as a whole in order to understand the full range of a herald's interests. Many of the essays herein focus on this type of manuscript, which contain rolls of arms nestled amongst treatises on military law, practical advice on marshalling ceremonies, and extensive and detailed advice for men involved in top-end international diplomacy.[9] Discussed in context, rolls of arms thus become another tool that might be utilised by an officer of arms in the range of his daily duties.

These heraldic handbooks also demonstrate the international nature of being a herald. Many, for example, contain copies of important texts that were widely circulated throughout Europe, such as Bartolus of Saxoferrato's *Tractatus de Insigniis et Armis* and Nicholas Upton's *De Officio Militari*. Some contain explanations of ceremonial practices and rituals in neighbouring kingdoms. Late medieval officers of arms evidently had an international lifestyle and developed essential skills to support this. They were part of an international community, lodging with each other when visiting foreign courts and exchanging information with each other as they met on their travels. We learn from the essays contained herein that many

---

[8] The collection edited by Peter Coss and Maurice Keen, *Heraldry, Pageantry and Social Display in Medieval England* (Woodbridge, 2002), is, in part, an attempt to draw historians' attention to the significance of the visual world of the Middle Ages; similarly, Susan Crane's *The Performance of Self: Ritual, Clothing, and Identity During the Hundred Years War* (Philadelphia, 2002) puts forward a convincing account of the role of heraldry in the creation of late medieval identity.

[9] See for example the discussion of the *Ceremonie notate in tempi di Francesco Filarethe Heraldo* by Cirri (ch. 8 below); of the *Gelre Armorial* by van Anrooij (ch. 7 below); and of the Loutfut manuscript by Stevenson (ch. 4 below).

spoke several languages (ch. 4, 9 and 10 below), and that they acquired knowledge of local customs and topography to act as guides to visiting dignitaries (ch. 6 below).

The men offered posts as officers of arms were clearly drawn from the ranks of the well-educated. Aside from the extensive evidence we have of their literary capabilities (for example, histories, translations, rhetoric and poems), they were often in receipt of formal training in law, either at university or through apprenticeships (ch. 2, 4, 5, 10 below). Education in civil law was of premier importance in those kingdoms where officers of arms were involved in the administration of justice, and particularly in cases of treason. Courts of chivalry, under the authority of constables and marshals, were also in operation to deal with all manner of military matters, including treason and armorial disputes (principally in France, England, and possibly Scotland and Scandinavia) (ch. 2, 4, 10 below). In these courts the officers of arms also had a role.

Another development that we see throughout Europe is the connection between officers of arms and the orders of chivalry that emerged from the middle of the fourteenth century and gained exponential popularity throughout Europe in the fifteenth century. Much research has been done on Garter King of Arms and his office's relationship to the Order of the Garter,[10] but similar work might be carried out for the dozens of orders that were founded in the late Middle Ages.[11] Indeed, connections are drawn in many of the essays contained herein between officers of arms and the foundation and operation of orders of chivalry (ch. 2, 3, 5, 7, 10 below; for more on the connection between the Order of the Teutonic Knights and Prussia King of Arms see ch. 9).

From this collection of essays the impression one gets of the officers of arms in late medieval Europe is that they were flexible, educated, of increasingly high status (often knighted and landed, especially from the second half of the fifteenth century) and of good moral character. They were adaptable, literate and astute diplomats, often entrusted with tasks of a delicate nature, and consummate representatives of their masters. The officers of

---

[10] J. Anstis, *Register of the Most Noble Order of the Garter*, 2 vols (London, 1724); Hugh E. L. Collins, *The Order of the Garter, 1348–1461: Chivalry and Politics in Late Medieval England* (Oxford, 2000); H. S. London, *The Life of William Bruges: The First Garter King of Arms*, Harleian Society, old ser., pp. III–12 (London, 1970); Peter J. Begent, 'The Creation of the Office of Garter King of Arms', *Coat of Arms*, n.s. II, no. 172 (1995), pp. 134–40; Adrian Ailes, 'The Creation of the Office of Garter King of Arms: A Postscript', *Coat of Arms*, n.s. II, no. 182 (1998), pp. 239–40; Peter J. Begent and Hubert Chesshyre, eds, *The Most Noble Order of the Garter: 650 Years* (London 1999).
[11] For more on the orders of chivalry in late medieval Europe see D'Arcy Jonathan Dacre Boulton, *The Knights of the Crown: The Monarchical Orders of Knighthood in Late Medieval Europe, 1325–1520* (Woodbridge, 2000).

arms were so much more than just the 'acknowledged experts on armorial bearings' and the essays herein attest to the diversity and breadth of their functions in late medieval Europe.[12] It is hoped that this collection might play some modest role in opening up the study of these important and multifaceted men to students and researchers alike.

[12] Wagner, *Heralds of England*, p. 27.

The Development of the Office of Arms in England, *c.* 1413–1485[*]

Jackson W. Armstrong

W ITH THE DISSEMINATION AND SYSTEMATISATION of heraldic coat armour throughout the European nobility in the late twelfth and early thirteenth centuries, the opportunity arose for those claiming expertise in armorial matters to offer their services in noble and royal households. Heralds first appear in English records in the reign of Edward I (1272–1307). Those named in the king's household accounts are evidently principal servants using personal names together with the title of 'king of heralds', suggesting that a hierarchy of armorial agents was already in place, closely associated with minstrels.[1] In addition to offering expert service in heraldic matters, they acted as marshals of ceremonies for their masters. 'Private' heralds retained in a noble household might enter the service of the crown after their master's death. By the reign of Edward III (1327–77), royal heralds were taking on broader military and diplomatic duties, as messengers of war and peace and as supervisors

---

[*] This paper derives from an essay originally produced in 2002 as a preliminary component for the M.Phil. in medieval history at the University of Cambridge, diligently supervised by Christine Carpenter, to whom I am indebted for her guidance and comment. I also wish to thank Katie Stevenson for more recent conversations on officers of arms, and related matters, and for comment on various aspects of this essay.

[1] Payments of 20s. each to Robert Parv[us] 'regi heraldorum' and Nicholas Morell, 'regi haraldorum, roi dez haraz', are recorded in 1290 (18 Edward I), London, National Archives, E 101/352/24, cited in J. Anstis, *Register of the Most Noble Order of the Garter*, 2 vols (London, 1724), i, pp. 302 n. 'h', 319 n. 'n'. See A. R. Wagner, *Heralds and Heraldry in the Middle Ages* (Oxford, 1939), pp. 27, 39; N. Denholm-Young, *History and Heraldry 1254 to 1310: A Study of the Historical Value of the Rolls of Arms* (Oxford, 1965), pp. 54–63, appendix, p. 166, both also discussing the appearance in a charter of 1276 of Peter 'rex hyraudaorum citra aquam de Trente ex parte boriali'. BL, MS Harley 54, g. 44.

of chivalric tournaments.[2] If chivalry was 'the secular code of honour of a martially oriented aristocracy',[3] heralds in the fourteenth century became the king's chivalric administrators.[4] Collectively, the heraldic agents of the royal household comprised the 'office of arms', and became clearly subdivided during the fourteenth century into three levels of seniority: pursuivants, heralds and kings of arms.[5] The officers of arms came to be supervised by the Lord High Constable and the Earl Marshal of England who, from at least 1348, also held a joint court of chivalry to administer the law of arms as used in England. Here the heralds could act before the court (much like lawyers) as experts on armorial matters.[6]

The role of armorial officials was constantly evolving throughout the later Middle Ages, and in this regard the turn of the fifteenth century was a time of particular acceleration.[7] Between 1415 and 1417, Henry V (1413–22) created a new officer of chivalry, Garter – 'Principal' King of Arms – whose role in part was to oversee the operation of the armorial office. Almost seven decades later, in letters patent dated 2 March 1484, Richard III (1483–5) formally incorporated the office and all its members.[8] The Ricardian patent,

---

[2] Wagner, *Heralds and Heraldry*, pp. 26–7, 33–4; M. H. Keen, *Chivalry* (New Haven and London, 1984), pp. 133–7; Anstis, *Register*, i, p. 288; A. R. Wagner, *Heralds of England: A History of the Office and the College of Arms* (Oxford, 1967), p. 55; A. R. Wagner and H. S. London, 'Heralds of the Nobility', in *The Complete Peerage*, ed. V. Gibbs *et al.* (London, 1910–59), xi, appendix C, pp. 39–104, at 44.

[3] Keen, *Chivalry*, pp. 251–2. For a list of the diverse duties of heralds, see ibid. pp. 134, 142.

[4] See also T. Twiss, ed., *The Black Book of the Admiralty*, 4 vols, Rolls Series (London, 1871–7), i, p. 295; and Wagner, *Heralds and Heraldry*, pp. 100–20.

[5] G. D. Squibb, ed., *Munimenta Heraldica 1484–1984*, Harleian Society, n.s. 4 (London, 1985), p. 1; Anstis, *Register*, i, pp. 281–4. In this paper, as in common usage, the term 'heralds' will sometimes be used to refer collectively to all members of the office of arms, and not just the specific rank described here.

[6] G. D. Squibb, *The High Court of Chivalry: A Study of the Civil Law in England* (Oxford, 1959), pp. 1–28; see also Wagner, *Heralds and Heraldry*, pp. 18–24; Wagner, *Heralds of England*, pp. 125, 130; R. Dennys, *Heraldry and the Heralds* (London, 1982), pp. 130–7. See also M. E. James, 'English Politics and the Concept of Honour, 1485–1642', in *Society, Politics and Culture: Studies in Early Modern England*, ed. M. E. James (Cambridge, 1986), p. 334, drawing a comparison between sixteenth-century English heralds and judges. However, unlike Lyon in Scotland, it seems that only in unusual cases might officers of arms act in a judicial capacity where the English king was concerned: M. H. Keen, *The Laws of War in the Late Middle Ages* (London and Toronto, 1965), pp. 48–50, 53, discusses the peculiar trial in 1420 of the lord of Barbasan, who succeeded in appealing beyond Henry V to the judgment of a panel of (unspecified) officers of arms. This occurred after the surrender of Melun on 18 November 1420, and so the composition of this panel may have been similar to that of the Yuletide chapter of 1420–1, given below in note 75.

[7] J. W. Armstrong, 'Heralds in the New DNB', *The Coat of Arms*, 3rd ser., 1 (2005), pp. 167–72.

[8] Squibb, ed., *Munimenta Heraldica*, pp. 14–19; T. Rymer, ed., *Foedera, Conventiones, Litterae etc.*, 10 vols (Hagae Comitis, 1745, reprint, Farnborough, 1967) v, pt. iii, p. 142.

like Richard himself, did not last long. In his first parliament of 1485, Henry VII (1485–1509) passed an act of resumption, which cancelled large classes of grants made under his Yorkist predecessors.[9] Whether this led to the denial of the corporate capacity of the office is debatable,[10] but what is important is that the Ricardian incorporation was the formal recognition of a process, clearly under way during the reign of Henry V, by which the office of arms became increasingly professional and organised. Historians concerned with heraldry have often seen Richard's patent as the culminating point in the early growth of the armorial office in England. It is the purpose of this essay to address the question of why the office of arms developed in late medieval England, and to explain the growth of the office in the fifteenth century by placing it in its social and political context.

Almost up to the present day in England, it is the heralds themselves who have told the history of their office and of the orders of chivalry which they serve. Seventeenth and eighteenth-century heralds with an antiquarian interest, like Bysshe, Ashmole and Anstis, published medieval treatises on heraldry, wrote on the Order of the Garter, and in their annotation published much relevant primary material relating to the heralds. In the early twentieth century a lively debate ensued over heraldry and the history of the right to bear arms, led in the pages of *The Ancestor* and elsewhere by Sitwell, Baildon, Fox-Davies and Phillimore; a debate that was, as will be seen below, also very much alive in the later Middle Ages. While one side emphasised the authority of the heralds in granting arms, the other played down this authority, and argued for the legality of the assumption of arms by individual aspirants. Professional historians began to address the topic of heraldry in the 1930s and 1940s, when Evan Jones and Francis Barnard turned their attention to heraldic treatises. Anthony Wagner, a twentieth-century Garter King of Arms and distinguished historian, and Hugh London, Norfolk Herald, were the first authors to look exclusively at the history of the office of arms in England. Building on the work of Anstis, both highlight the organisation of the office in the fifteenth century. Wagner in particular was aware that, as an aspect of chivalric culture, heraldry had major implications for both landowners and the king in this period.

To begin, the question of the origin of the right to bear arms had an important bearing on attitudes to title and gentility. Late medieval England, of course, stood apart from Scotland and the Continent in coming to define its nobility very narrowly as those who received a personal summons from

---

[9]   See C. Given-Wilson *et al.*, eds, *The Parliament Rolls of Medieval England* (London, 2005), 1485 November, item 6.

[10]   Anstis believes that the revocation did not deny the officers of arms their previously granted 'corporate capacity' (*Register*, i, pp. 362–3, 362 n. 's'). Wagner, *Heralds of England*, pp. 134, 135, 137–8, is more doubtful.

the king to parliament. Thus divided off from a parliamentary peerage was that group of lesser landowners who have come to be known as the gentry, and whose counterparts in other realms constituted a lesser nobility.[11] As the use of heraldry became widespread in the thirteenth and fourteenth centuries, and increasingly became an essential means by which those of gentle or noble status were to be identified, a need arose to establish internationally recognised standards for its evolving rules and conventions. Appearing in the fourteenth century, heraldic treatises, mostly written by jurists, reflect a growing desire to clarify entitlement to arms within a legal framework.[12] The first major work of this sort was composed in the 1350s and entitled *De Insigniis et Armis Tractatus* by the Italian doctor of civil law, Bartolo di Sassoferrato (Bartolus de Saxoferrato).[13] The 'Bartolan view' emphasised honour as the reward of virtue, and played down the idea that lineage was the essence of nobility (though he conceded that lineage predisposed a man to virtuous deeds).[14] From this stance he derived his assertion that a man could lawfully assume arms on his own authority (as one might assume a surname). His proviso was that, since arms became personal property by use, one man could not adopt arms already in use by another.[15] Honoré Bouvet (wrongly Bonet) and Christine de Pisan, in their respective compositions on chivalry, built on the Bartolan view of arms, and de Pisan was later translated into English and published by William Caxton for Henry VII about the year 1489.[16] That publication underlines the point that the ideas of di Sassoferrato remained relevant throughout the fifteenth century.

[11] M. C. E. Jones, ed., *Gentry and Lesser Nobility in Late Medieval Europe* (Gloucester, 1986); M. H. Keen, *Origins of the English Gentleman: Heraldry, Chivalry and Gentility in Medieval England, c. 1300 – c. 1500* (Stroud, 2002); P. R. Coss, 'The Formation of the English Gentry', *Past and Present* 147 (1995), pp. 38–64; P. R. Coss, *The Origins of the English Gentry* (Cambridge, 2003); R. Radulescu and A. Truelove, eds, *Gentry Culture in Late Medieval England* (Manchester, 2005).

[12] See also M. H. Keen's argument that the development of blazon promoted the discussion of heraldry in the form of written treatises: 'Introduction', in *Heraldry, Pageantry and Social Display in Medieval England*, ed. P. R. Coss and M. H. Keen (Woodbridge, 2002), pp. 1–16, at 10.

[13] Bartolo di Sassoferrato, *De Insigniis et Armis Tractatus*, in E. J. Jones, ed., *Medieval Heraldry: Some Fourteenth-Century Heraldic Works* (Cardiff, 1943), pp. 221–52. See also Wagner, *Heralds and Heraldry*, ch. 8; M. H. Keen, 'The Debate over Nobility: Dante, Nicholas Upton and Bartolus', in *The Culture of Christendom: Essays in Medieval History in Commemoration of Denis L. T. Bethell*, ed. M. A. Meyer (London, 1993), pp. 257–68.

[14] James, 'English Politics', pp. 318, 321, 376.

[15] Di Sassoferrato, *De Insigniis et Armis Tractatus*, at 224, 228–3 (fourth and fifth headings). See also Sir G. Sitwell, 'The English Gentleman', *The Ancestor* 1 (1902), pp. 58–103, at 84–5.

[16] G. W. Coopland, ed., *The Tree of Battles of Honoré Bonet* (Liverpool, 1949), pp. 203–6; James, 'English Politics', pp. 319–20; A. T. P. Byles, ed., *The Book of Faytes of Armes and of Chyualrye Translated and Printed by William Caxton From the French Original by Christine de Pisan* (EETS, os 189, London, 1932, corrected reissue, 1937), pp. xi–xiii, 285–92.

The next author to deal with armorial entitlement was Johannes de Bado Aureo. His *Tractatus de Armis* (*c.* 1394) is comparable to the *Llyfr Arfau*, an anonymous work in Welsh attributed to the courtier and prelate, John Trevor (Siôn Trefor). The *Llyfr Arfau* was probably composed while Trevor held the bishopric of St Asaph (*c.* 1394/5–1410/12). Evan Jones has argued persuasively (though not conclusively) that these works are so similar that they are essentially one and the same, and that the author of both was Trevor who used de Bado Aureo as a pen name.[17] The author in question claimed that a cleric desiring arms, but without armigerous ancestors, must have arms assigned to him by a king of heralds. He also asserted that the heirs of laymen might augment or diminish their arms according to their wealth with the advice of a king of heralds, and that to avoid confusion kings of heralds should be acquainted with royal and noble ancestry. In the author's view (for which he erroneously credits di Sassoferrato), only a king, prince, king of arms or a herald could grant arms.[18]

Another gloss on this from England came about the year 1440. Nicolas Upton, a herald trained in both civil and canon law, wrote *De Studio Militari*.[19] The passage in that text dealing with the assumption of arms reads:

> in these days we openly see how many poor men, labouring in the French wars, are become noble; one by prudence, another by valour, a third by endurance, a fourth by other virtues which [. . .] ennoble mankind; of whom many of their own authority have assumed arms to be borne by themselves and their heirs [. . .] I say, however, that arms so assumed, though they are borne freely and lawfully, yet cannot be of such dignity or authority as those which are daily bestowed by the authority of princes or lords. Yet arms taken by a man's own authority, if another have not borne them before, are valid enough [. . .] Nor dare I approve of the opinion of certain men who say that heralds can give arms; but I say, if such arms are borne by any herald given, that these arms are not of greater authority than those which are taken by a man's own authority.[20]

---

[17] See E. J. Jones, *Medieval Heraldry: Tractatus de Armis by Iohannes de Bado Aureo: An Enquiry into the Authorship of a Fourteenth Century Latin Treatise* (Cardiff, 1932); Jones, ed., *Medieval Heraldry*, pp. xvii–xlv; H. S. London, 'Some Medieval Treatises on English Heraldry', *Antiquaries Journal* 33 (1953), pp. 169–83, at 170, 182. See also J. Tait, 'John Trevor (d. 1410/1412)', in *Oxford Dictionary of National Biography*, rev. R. R. Davies, xxx, pp. 204–5.

[18] *Llyfr Arfau* and *Tractatus de Armis* in Jones, ed., *Medieval Heraldry*, pp. 65, 93, 130, 181–2, and 142 (the latter for armorial grants by a king, prince, and a 'rex armorum, vel haraldus'). At p. 64 n. 1 Jones suggests that the title 'king of heralds' (*rex heraldorum*) is a contraction of 'king of heralds of arms'. See also Squibb, *High Court of Chivalry*, p. 179.

[19] Born in Devonshire about 1400, Upton served as a private herald in the retinue of Thomas Montacute, earl of Salisbury. He obtained a number of benefices, and died in 1457. See Jones, *Medieval Heraldry*, p. 5; A. Brown and C. Walker, 'Upton, Nicholas (*c.* 1400–1457)', in *Oxford Dictionary of National Biography*, lv, pp. 932–3.

[20] Translation taken from Sitwell, 'The English Gentleman', p. 86; Latin text printed in E. Bysshe, ed., *Nicolai Vptoni de Studio Militari* (London, 1654), pp. 257–8. See also Blount's

Thus Upton confirmed the established Bartolan view that men could law-fully assume their own arms without recourse to a higher authority, even though he preferred that they be bestowed. Moreover, he denied the special authority of heralds in granting arms.[21] In the year 1468, an anonymous author translated Upton's ideas on heraldry and recycled them in the first printed book to deal with the subject, entitled *The Boke of St Albans*.[22]

It was not long after Upton made his contribution that Richard Strangways, a member of the Inner Temple, compiled *Tractatus Nobilis de Lege et Exposicione Armorum*. In this collection of heraldic memoranda, jotted down and brought together about 1454, Strangways asserts that gentility depended on the possession of arms.[23] This common lawyer expressed a very different view on armorial authority from that of Upton. His argument was that the right to arms was acquired in one of four ways: by inheritance from an armigerous forebear, by marriage to an armigerous woman, by grant from a prince or herald, or by conquest (especially in trials for treason). Strangways was adamant that the assumption of arms upon a man's own authority was invalid, though marks 'such as merchants use' could be taken without the intervention of a competent authority such as a prince, herald or pursuivant.[24]

Thus, it seems that by the mid-fifteenth century, there existed two schools of thought on heralds and heraldry. Richard Strangways, and to a lesser extent de Bado Aureo (perhaps John Trevor), were the only late medieval heraldic authors to express a strong view that ran against the Bartolan school of thought to which Upton, Bouvet and de Pisan so eagerly subscribed. Strangways especially emphasised the competence of heralds in armorial matters, bolstering the idea that heralds were established and important figures in fifteenth-century chivalric society. However, the greater part of English society which participated in chivalric culture was undergoing a subtle shift in this period, the nature of which merits its own examination.

In addition to the nobility of parliamentary peers and the king himself, the English gentry – the lesser nobility of that realm in the European sense

partial translation in F. P. Barnard, ed., *The Essential Portions of Nicholas Upton's De Studio Militari, before 1446, Translated by John Blount, Fellow of All Souls (c. 1500)* (Oxford, 1931), p. 48 n. 42.

[21] Bysshe, ed., *Nicolai Vptoni de Studio Militari*, p. 258.

[22] *The Boke of St Albans* (third part), printed as appendix 5 in J. Dallaway, *Inquiries in to the Progress of the Science of Heraldry in England* (London, 1793), pp. cxi–cxii. Cf. James, 'English Politics', p. 310. See also W. P. Baildon, 'Heralds' College and Prescription', *The Ancestor* 9 (1904), pp. 214–24, at 214–15.

[23] London, 'Medieval Treatises', p. 181 n. 1.

[24] Strangway's book (BL, MS Harley 2259) is as yet unpublished. See London, 'Medieval Treatises', pp. 174, 180, 181 n. 1; See also Squibb, *High Court of Chivalry*, pp. 179–81.

– were by far the most numerous group of chivalric culture 'consumers'. The understanding of chivalry and status current among the gentry might differ from that of the king, and the dimensions of this difference had a direct bearing upon the heralds and the office of arms. The penetration of royal administration into the localities from the reigns of Henry III (1216–72) and Edward I (1272–1307) accelerated in the fourteenth century, and by the fifteenth century large numbers of lesser landowners were drawn into political society as agents of local government for the king.[25] When combined with the threat to the social hierarchy from an aggressive peasantry perceived in the aftermath of the Black Death, which was addressed through an extension of royal involvement in peace-keeping and social regulation at the village level, this phenomenon contributed to an awareness among the landed elite in the localities of their growing importance to the crown as conduits of royal authority. They served the king as JPs, as commissioners of numerous types, in the shrievalty or in other local offices, some of a very minor sort. Even simply to exercise lordship through a manorial court over the peasant tenantry was to participate in political society and to serve the crown in the governance of the realm.[26]

Those who served the king were aware of their own importance to him. As a consequence, it has been argued that a tension grew between the crown and lesser landowners in attitudes to gentility. In managing the day-to-day realities of governing their own localities, especially as officials in royal service, the gentry had a shrewder grasp of their own worth than did the crown. From the perspective of a fifteenth-century monarch, the hierarchy of lesser landowners (from the knightly elite to the emergent gentleman) was primarily defined by military service. These same landowners, on the other hand, recognised 'gentle' status as a sign of respect due to those who, by holding office and land, effectively served the king as local administrators, even if their involvement was no more than the authority of lordship that accompanied possession of a manor.[27] As a mark of their perceived status conferred by royal service, members of the sub-knightly gentry began to

---

[25]   Coss, *Origins of the English Gentry*, chs 50–7; M. C. Carpenter, *Locality and Polity: A Study in Warwickshire Landed Society, 1401–1499* (Cambridge, 1992), ch. 3; D. A. L. Morgan, 'The Individual Style of the English Gentleman', in *Gentry and Lesser Nobility*, ed. Jones, pp. 15–35, at 25; N. Denholm-Young, *The Country Gentry in the Fourteenth Century with Special References to Heraldic Rolls of Arms* (Oxford, 1969), pp. xii, 1–6, 54; G. L. Harriss, 'Political Society and the Growth of Government in Late Medieval England', *Past and Present* 138 (1993), pp. 28–57.

[26]   Coss, *Origins of the English Gentry*, ch. 10; Carpenter, *Locality and Polity*, pp. 41–7; Morgan, 'Individual Style', pp. 18–19.

[27]   Carpenter, *Locality and Polity*, pp. 41–9, 73–9, 616; Morgan, 'Individual Style', pp. 16, 18. A formal threshold of £10 in landed income for recognition as a gentleman (that is, to be 'ennobled') was not imposed by Garter until 1530: Wagner, *Heralds and Heraldry*, p. 79.

assume titles like esquire (from the mid-fourteenth century) and gentleman (from the early fifteenth century). Unlike noble dignities and the knight-hood, these terms were not clearly defined, and their use was by no means consistent, but they reflected an attempt by the gentry to delineate subtle gradations of status among themselves.[28]

However, even though the gentry increasingly saw their own importance in terms of administrative (instead of purely military) service, culture within this group maintained a military and chivalric tone throughout the century. The content of Sir John Paston's *Grete Boke* (commissioned in 1468) illustrates the point. The book was largely a compilation of chivalric, martial and judicial content, including a thirteenth-century statute of arms, and proclamations of tourneys that included details on the prize-winners and the fees paid to attendant heralds. Even if the gentry no longer demanded recognition of status exclusively in exchange for martial service, martial prowess and feats of arms remained close to the spiritual core of the identity of landed society.[29] The underlying military tone of status was reflected in the gentry's desire to bear arms – if not in the field, then in the heraldic sense – and, just as they assumed titles like gentleman and esquire, so too did they assume armorial bearings.

Indeed, practice analogous to 'prescription' (the right, on proving continuous undisturbed possession, to become the absolute owner of a piece of property) is evident in relation to coat-armour in the fifteenth century.[30] Grants and confirmations of arms in this period often made reference to the grantee's ancestors having borne them previously. In 1456, for example, Guyen King of Arms made a grant to John Bangor, and referred to the arms

---

[28] These terms were especially confused in royal records, excepting those of the law where, after the Statute of Additions (1413), they were obligatory: N. Saul, *Knights and Esquires: The Gloucestershire Gentry in the Fourteenth Century* (Oxford, 1981), pp. 26–9, 256; N. Saul, 'The Social Status of Chaucer's Franklin: A Reconsideration', *Medium Ævum* 52 (1983), pp. 10–26; Carpenter, *Locality and Polity*, pp. 41–9, 79; P. R. Coss, 'Knights, Esquires and the Origins of Social Gradation in England', *Transactions of the Royal Historical Society* 6:5 (1995), pp. 155–78; P. Maddern, 'Gentility', in *Gentry Culture*, ed. Radulescu and Truelove, pp. 18–34.

[29] Carpenter, *Locality and Polity*, pp. 49, 85–6; M. H. Keen, 'Chivalry', in *Gentry Culture*, ed. Radulescu and Truelove, pp. 35–49, at 46–7; 'Private Indentures for Life Service in Peace and War 1278–1476', in *Camden Miscellany XXXII*, ed. M. C. E. Jones and S. Walker, Camden Society, 5th ser., 3 (London, 1994), pp. 1–190, at 22. On the continuation of active military service in the far northern marches see J. W. Armstrong, 'Local Conflict in the Anglo-Scottish Borderlands, c. 1399–1488' (Ph.D. thesis, University of Cambridge, 2007), pp. 202–3. G. Lester, *Sir John Paston's 'Grete Boke': A Descriptive Catalogue, with an Introduction, of British Library MS Lansdowne 285* (Cambridge, 1984); N. Davis, ed., *Paston Letters and Papers of the Fifteenth Century*, 2 vols (Oxford, 1971–6), ii, no. 751, pp. 386–7.

[30] This term of property law is explained in W. P. W. Phillimore, *Heralds' College and Coats of Arms, Regarded from a Legal Aspect*, 3rd edn (London, 1904), pp. 26–30.

which 'ye s[ai]d John and his progenitors time out of mind hath borne'.[31] In 1470, Norroy King of Arms certified to the prior of Bridlington coat armour that his ancestors had borne for such length of time that 'neither can tongue express or the memory of man recollect'.[32] The implication in these grants (and others like them) is that prescription of arms was a practice that the heralds accepted and actively endorsed. However, it has been pointed out that, while people may have been free to assume arms, they still made the decision to seek official confirmations from armorial officers.[33] Confirmations such as those just cited suggest that the office of arms was becoming an increasingly recognised chivalric authority in the fifteenth century, through which claims to gentility and arms could be officially endorsed.

That there was a contrasting royal view on such matters (which reflected a contrasting view of gentility more generally) can be seen first of all in 1417, when Henry V issued a writ in an attempt to assert royal control over heraldic affairs. He cited that 'diverse men ... [had] arrogated to themselves arms' on previous military expeditions abroad. Henry declared that arms were not to be assumed unless the man in question had arms 'by right of his ancestors or by the gift of some person having sufficient power for this purpose'. He went on to require that all who claimed to hold arms must show 'by whose gift he holds those arms ... except for those who bore arms with us at the Battle of Agincourt'. The phrase 'by right of his ancestors' ('jure antecessorio') could be taken as an endorsement of prescription, but the requirement to show proof of the gift of arms from a person 'having sufficient power' ('ad hoc sufficientem potestatem habentis') rather indicates an attempt to halt the practice and stamp out further instances of the casual assumption of arms.[34] The king appears to have wished to impose some restraint on the status-conscious gentry who were seeking arms as proof of their gentility and as a complement to their assumed titles of gentleman and esquire. The writ's reference to those of 'sufficient authority' to grant arms is almost certainly a reference to the heralds, which bolstered the authority of the office of arms as part of the king's evident desire to regulate this aspect of the behaviour of his gentle subjects. But for once King Henry missed the point. The exception for those who served with him at Agincourt is a sign that, as sovereign, he saw

---

[31]   J. J. Howard, ed., *Miscellanea Genealogica et Heraldica*, 4 vols (London, 1868), i, p. 54.
[32]   W. H. D. Longstaffe, ed., *Heraldic Visitation of the Northern Counties in 1530, by Thomas Tonge, Norroy King of Arms*, Surtees Society, 41 (Durham, 1863), p. xxxviii; Squibb, *High Court of Chivalry*, pp. 181–3; and Baildon, 'Heralds' College', p. 125.
[33]   Phillimore, *Heralds' College*, pp. 28–9.
[34]   This writ was sent to the sheriffs of Southampton, Wiltshire, Sussex and Dorset. For the Latin see Squibb, *High Court of Chivalry*, p. 182. For an English translation see D. C. Douglas et al., eds, *English Historical Documents*, 10 vols (London, 1996), iv (1327–1485, ed. A. R. Myers), p. 1117.

military service as directly linked with the right to bear arms.[35] For a king like Henry V, who was keen to emphasise war as a 'field of aristocratic action', this point is of particular relevance.[36] Henry emphasised the role of his gentry as warriors. He did not, as some of the gentry would have preferred, also see fit to give distinguished recognition to their role as local administrators, or in wider sense, as members of the ruling elite.

Well into the fifteenth century the crown saw rolls of arms as of primarily military significance, but gradually the gentry's view that status could be identified in broader terms than just military service gained increasing currency. In this process, the heralds became less 'registrars of deeds of prowess' than validators of claims to bear arms in the heraldic sense. Indeed, towards the end of the century, the heralds' lists of armigerous families provided the crown with information on its potential public servants in the civil administration of the realm.[37] By the reign of Henry VII, the establishment of the office of arms as an official registry of gentility was well developed. Listings of 'gentlemen of the shire' existed in the reign of Edward IV (1461–70, 1471–83: a king who was credited with an elephantine memory of the lowest gentlemen throughout his kingdom), and Henry VII kept a book cataloguing 'all the lords knights and gentlemen of this realme'. These documents emphasised the income levels of their subjects and served as 'gazetteers of the gentry's armorial bearings', and they were probably the work of heralds.[38] By the first Tudor reign, Henry V's assumptions about the gentry and military service were far more obsolete than they were beginning to be when he acted on them in 1417.[39]

Given that a tension between the crown and lesser landowners over chivalry and status emerged and moved towards resolution in the course of the century, the nature of the king's engagement with chivalric culture calls for

---

[35]   The Agincourt exception has been interpreted variously as a type of 'battle honour' (which I think is essentially right), and as a technical simplification that did nothing more than eliminate, for those who had proved before Agincourt their right to bear arms, the need to duplicate this proof. See A. C. Fox-Davies, alias 'X', *The Right to Bear Arms* (London, 1900), p. 47; Sitwell, 'The English Gentleman', pp. 81–2; I. de Minvielle-Deveaux, *Law of Arms* (London, 1988), pp. 65–6; Squibb, *High Court of Chivalry*, pp. 181–2.

[36]   Morgan, 'Individual Style', p. 22.

[37]   Keen, *Chivalry*, pp. 138–9; Carpenter, *Locality and Polity*, ch. 3; Keen, 'Chivalry', in *Gentry Culture*, ed. Radulescu and Truelove.

[38]   Certainly the heralds took great interest in making their own copies of these works in the next century: Morgan, 'Individual Style', pp. 18–19; Carpenter, *Locality and Polity*, pp. 91–2. On Edward IV's memory see C. Ross, *Edward IV* (London, 1974), p. 306.

[39]   Cf. Keen's helpful view of an increasing emphasis on patrimony and pedigree, over martial service, as the essential requirements for gentility and the use of coat armour among the fifteenth-century gentry: M. H. Keen, 'Heraldry and Hierarchy: Esquires and Gentlemen', in *Orders and Hierarchies in Late Medieval and Renaissance Europe*, ed. H. Jeffrey (Basingstoke, 1999), pp. 94–108.

examination. Did he in fact exert control over the office of arms and, if so, what were his motivations? Looking ahead at the sixteenth century, Mervyn James has argued that under the initiative of Henry VIII (1509–47) the English honour system became 'nationalised' and focused on the king, who actively sought to establish himself as the 'fount of honour', the source of dignity and gentility. James contrasts these developments with what he sees as the 'self-authenticating' character of the 'honour community' in the pre-Tudor period. He argues that before the first Tudor reign 'no disciplined organisation of the heraldic office under any royal minister existed' and observes that evidence is scanty 'for any effective system of provincial heraldic jurisdiction and visitation'.[40] This interpretation is attractive in its apparent confirmation of other work which stresses the centralising of government and politics on the king from the later-fifteenth century, and the incorporation of the office of arms under Richard III could be seen as an early manifestation of the changes James outlines.[41] However, in making such claims for Tudor novelty, James overlooks very important evidence showing that Lancastrian and Yorkist kings, and indeed their Plantagenet forebears, were already founts of honour. They acted as magnets for the chivalric impulses of their subjects, and as the ultimate dispensers of honour in the realm.[42]

Although English kings had certainly long relied on heralds to serve as chivalric administrators, and despite the contemporary idea that heralds could not make armorial grants on their own authority, in many instances throughout the fifteenth century heralds granted arms without making reference to the crown.[43] For instance, Garter King of Arms' grant in 1439 to the drapers of London made no mention of 'granting' or 'authority'.[44] A grant by Clarenceux King of Arms to the company of barbers and surgeons of London, dated 1452, simply stated that this king of arms devised 'a conysauns and syne infourme of arms vnder my seall of myn armes'. The only reference

---

[40] James, 'English Politics', p. 328.

[41] For example: S. J. Gunn, *Early Tudor Government, 1485–1558* (Basingstoke, 1995), esp. pp. 6–7.

[42] For example: H. E. L. Collins, *The Order of the Garter, 1348–1461: Chivalry and Politics in Late Medieval England* (Oxford, 2000); J. Vale, *Edward III and Chivalry: Chivalric Society and its Context 1270–1350* (Woodbridge, 1982). On Edward I's Feast of the Swans in 1306, see C. Bullock-Davies, *Menestrellorum Multitudino: Minstrels at a Royal Feast* (Cardiff, 1978).

[43] Numerous fifteenth-century grants of arms are to be found in: Howard, ed., *Miscellanea Genealogica et Heraldica*, i, pp. 11, 54; W. G. D. Fletcher, 'Grant of Arms to John Kendall . . . 22 August, 21 Henry VI (1443)', *The Genealogist*, n.s. 22 (1906), pp. 61–2; Longstaff, ed., *Heraldic Visitation*, pp. xxxviii–xxxix; Baildon, 'Heralds' College', p. 125; W. A. Littledale, ed., *A Collection of Miscellaneous Grants, Crests, Confirmations, Augmentations and Exemplifications of Arms*, 2 vols, Harleian Society, old ser., 76 (London, 1925–6), i, pp. 2, 3, 41, 92; ibid., ii, pp. 149, 165, 192, 194.

[44] H. S. London, *The Life of William Bruges: The First Garter King of Arms*, Harleian Society, old ser., 111–12 (London, 1970), p. 19.

to the sovereign is in the dating of the grant by regnal year.[45] By 1480 Norroy could justify his grant of arms and crest to Christopher Brown with the phrase 'by virtue of the authority and power granted and attributed to my office of king of arms.'[46] James has argued that these grants were made 'virtute officii' – under the authority derived from the heraldic office, rather than by any specific royal empowerment of the heralds.[47] However, it was ultimately upon royal authority that the officers of arms acted; the oath of office placed royal service as the heralds' prime responsibility.[48] Despite the evidence for grants made without reference to the crown, it seems that heralds already operated on the assumption that royal authority was *implied* in their grants of arms. After all, it was obvious that, as members of the royal household, the heralds depended on the crown for their pension, food, and daily occupation. It was the king who created new officers of arms and issued them letters patent; the office itself did not make these creations as an autonomous body. Even 'private' heralds in the service of the nobility beyond the royal household were also focused on the crown. Wagner and London suggest that heralds' frequent exchanges of employment between royal and private service illustrate the point that all heralds were part of one large fraternity.[49] Although this heraldic fraternity was also international,[50] just like the law of arms, within each sovereign realm it took on a 'national' character – just as the law of arms was administered according to different 'national' usages by the fifteenth century.[51] Thus as members of a professional fraternity of arms within the English kingdom, even private heralds were ultimately subject to royal authority. The nomenclature of the heraldic hierarchy further reinforced the ideal: it was to 'kings' of arms that heralds and pursuivants were subordinate. In such a way the royal fount of honour was the model on which the armorial office functioned.[52]

[45] Howard, ed., *Miscellanea Genealogica et Heraldica*, i, p. 11.

[46] (Original in French:) Littledale, ed., *Collection of Miscellaneous Grants*, i, p. 41.

[47] James also points out that only sixty grants made by kings of arms survive from the period before 1484 ('English Politics', p. 333).

[48] F. Pilbrow, 'Chivalry and Kingship in Lancastrian and Yorkist England' (M.Phil. thesis, University of Cambridge, 1999), pp. 72–3.

[49] Wagner and London, 'Heralds of the Nobility', pp. 44–5.

[50] Keen, *Laws of War*, pp. 50, 195. For the international background of some English heralds, see A. Ailes, 'Machado, Roger (d. 1510)', in *Oxford Dictionary of National Biography*, xxxv, pp. 455–6. See also the example of the assembly of heralds at the jousting during the celebration of the marriage of Margaret of York to Charles the Bold of Burgundy, at Bruges in 1468: A. Brown and G. Small, *Court and Civic Society in the Burgundian Low Countries, c.1420–1530* (Manchester, 2007), p. 69.

[51] Wagner, *Heralds and Heraldry*, p. 24, citing the proceedings of the court of chivalry, 3 August 1408 (London, College of Arms MS Processus in Curia Marescalli), ii, p. 491.

[52] See items 7 and 10 of the English Yuletide chapter of 1420–1. For more on this chapter see below.

also in the growing professionalisation of the heralds themselves. This is in keeping with the wider growth of the lay professions and the frequent incorporation of city companies in the later Middle Ages. The heralds themselves made several armorial grants to various guilds throughout the century and, as Wagner puts it, this 'must have seemed to point a desirable path of progress'.[68] The heralds may also have aspired to follow the lead of another well-established group, the common lawyers. The latter had been developing as a professional body serving the king and his law since the thirteenth century. By the early fifteenth century, they took responsibility for their own education, admission, professional advancement and regulation, largely organised through the Inns of Court.[69] The common lawyers were hardly insulated from the concerns of heralds: not only were claims to gentility often tied up in litigation over manorial tenure, but also lawyers like Richard Strangways waded directly into the debate over the right to bear arms.[70] It would be stranger if the heralds could be shown *not* to have looked to the common lawyers as a model for professional growth.

It was mainly for two related reasons that the heralds sought to incorporate their office. First, as a corporate body, they would be entitled to partition fees paid to the office as a whole, to regulate their own professional conduct and to have their books preserved on record. Secondly, while unincorporated, the office could not hold real property. Indeed, Squibb has suggested that the grant of incorporation was merely a formality to achieve the acquisition of the Coldharbour property (Upper Thames Street, London) as a permanent home for the documents and library of the office, which had been accumulating over the decades. In 1484 all these materials were in the personal possession of individual officers of arms.[71] These two very practical sets of motivations for incorporation resulted in a patent from Richard III that was a clear statement of the professional organisation of the office.

Equally, while kings like Henry V were experimenting with the office of arms, the heralds were making their own attempts to establish their professional identity.[72] Soon after his appointment as Garter, Bruges recognised the need for a clear declaration of his rights and duties. To this end

---

[68]   Quotation from Wagner, *Heralds of England*, p. 123; cf. Phillimore, *Heralds' College*, p. 4. Grants of arms were made to twenty-four guilds before 1490. In the same period, about forty patents of arms were granted to individual recipients: Wagner, *Heralds of England*, pp. 125–6; see also S. Thrupp, *The Merchant Class of Medieval London* (Chicago, 1948).

[69]   See note 6. E. W. Ives, *The Common Lawyers of Pre-Reformation England* (Cambridge, 1983).

[70]   See also the accusations against John Paston in 1466, shortly after which he saw fit to commission his *Grete Boke*: Davis, ed., *Paston Letters*, ii, nos 896–7, pp. 549–52, esp. p. 552 for the bearing of arms.

[71]   Wagner, *Heralds of England*, p. 123; Squibb, ed., *Munimenta Heraldica*, pp. 1–2.

[72]   Cf. Wagner and London, 'Heralds of the Nobility', pp. 45–7.

he petitioned Henry V to issue to him letters patent stating, among much else, his primacy in the office of arms, and that all kings of arms, heralds and pursuivants in the king's obedience (by which he may have explicitly meant to include private heralds as well) were to recognise Garter as their 'premier et souverain' king of arms, and obey his direction. He also asked for the patent to state that no herald should be created without specific royal licence, and that Garter should be expressly commanded to report any officer of arms who disobeyed his orders to the constable (of England).[73] Bruges was clearly seeking an element of professional regulation for the office. Moreover, his reference to the privileges 'atribue en France a Montjoie roy d'armes des Francois' (who was doyen of the recently incorporated French office of arms) as precedent for some his requests further demonstrates that he was seeking to establish himself and his colleagues as a body with the features of a corporate authority.[74] The petition went unanswered by letters patent, but Garter's requests and the work he put in to them were a determined vision for the future operation of the office.

The discipline and organisation of the heralds emerge into full view when, during Yuletide 1420–1, the first recorded chapter of the office of arms met at Rouen. The resolutions of the seven officers present were mainly concerned with instituting a common seal for the office, a benevolent fund for members in hard times, and with requiring an oath of office to be sworn before new members should share in any common largess. They also suggest that private heralds were to be counted as brethren within the obedience of the office of arms, and permitted a seat in the chapter according to the dignity of their master. The officers of arms recognised Garter's primacy, and in the resolutions referred to him as 'le premier roy darmes'.[75] The resolutions of this meeting amount to a clear assertion of the organisation of the office, sixty-four years before its incorporation. Subsequent chapters are documented in 1474 and 1487, the only meetings for which evidence survives. It

---

[73] The petition is printed in London, *Bruges*, appendix 9, pp. 88–92, and Anstis, *Register*, i, p. 329 n. 'a'. For discussion see London, *Bruges*, pp. 15–18; Wagner, *Heralds of England*, pp. 48–9, 62.

[74] The French heralds were incorporated in January 1407 (Wagner, *Heralds and Heraldry*, p. 41). Montjoye was soon after recognised as *ex officio* doyen. Specifically, Bruges asked for the privilege of wearing certain garments of the peerage, as Montjoye was permitted to do. See London, *Bruges*, pp. 15, 90, 94.

[75] See note 6. Present at the chapter, which met on 25 December and 5 January, were Garter, Clarenceux and Ireland Kings of Arms, and Leopard, Clarence, Exeter and Mowbray Heralds. The chapter's resolutions (items 7 and 10 are those which seem to relate to private heralds) survive in the College of Arms in London, and are printed in London, *Bruges*, appendix 12, pp. 98–107 (and see p. 16 for comment). See also Wagner, *Heralds and Heraldry*, p. 64 n. 1; Wagner, *Heralds of England*, pp. 68–9; Wagner and London, 'Heralds of the Nobility', pp. 45–6.

stands to reason that chapters were held in the intervening periods as well, for nothing suggests that the recorded gatherings were exceptional events in and of themselves.[76] Even if the three recorded chapters were truly the only ones convened, this alone would indicate a significant level of organisation among the heralds. While they organised themselves, the heralds' position under the authority of the king should not be viewed as any detraction from their professional character. Complete independence they may not have had, but this was not what they sought. Indeed, if lawyers could in a sense serve the king who was the fount of justice, and at the same time develop as a professional body to practise the common law, then the heralds too could develop as a professional body (which practised the law of arms) and, at the same time, if more directly, serve the king who was also the fount of honour.

To return to this essay's original question of why the office of arms developed in late medieval England, certain conclusions can be drawn. Two different schools of thought on the role of heralds existed in the fifteenth century. One, the generally accepted Bartolan view, was that heralds had no greater authority to grant arms than a man had to assume arms on his own. The other argued for the more comprehensive authority of heralds, but it seems this latter opinion was far from universally accepted around the year 1400. The heralds, who spent much of the century trying to establish their professional integrity, needed to work against the limited Bartolan view of their role. Their vested interest in challenging Bartolan ideas helps to explain why they were so keen to organise professionally in the early fifteenth century. At the same time, shifting concepts of status among the gentry, with a growing emphasis on the importance of arms and titles among all lesser landowners, and the crown's eventual recognition of this shift, paralleled the professional development of the office of arms over the course of the century. The office of arms, without a doubt by *c.* 1480 a body of chivalric administrator-professionals, provided the crown with genealogical and armorial catalogues of its lesser landed subjects. These subjects the crown had come to appreciate no longer simply in military terms, but in terms of public service in the mechanisms of governance. At the same time the office of arms acted as a validating body for the coat armour which was now widely used by the gentry as the defining mark of membership in the governing elite.

Meanwhile, the king asserted increasingly firm control over the office of arms and heraldic matters just as it became more organised.[77] These were important symbolic tools of the sovereign's real power. From at least the reign

---

[76] See Wagner, *Heralds of England*, pp. 68–70, 123.

[77] The idea that the office of arms was a household department that went 'out of court' (like the office of the privy seal or the signet office), in the later Middle Ages is useful: Denholm-Young, *History and Heraldry*, pp. 56–7.

of Henry V, the office of arms was a body securely under royal control and, as an increasingly recognised chivalric authority, it served as an important agency of the king's authority as the fount of honour and chivalric leader of his realm. Some kings used the armorial office with greater efficacy than others. The later-fifteenth-century English monarchs, Edward IV, Richard III and Henry VII, each recognised the potential of the office of arms as an agency which could be harnessed to symbolise and enhance royal power. This is especially true in their attention to the minor gentry which the heralds catalogued. Of directly related importance is the use, particularly by Edward IV in the 1460s, of the civil law court of chivalry under the Constable of England.[78] Further work is needed to learn how many heralds, like Nicholas Upton, had civil law training. This would have positioned such men not only to offer armorial and genealogical evidence, but also specific counsel in the finer points of civil law to the court and those who came before it.

The heralds' response to the issues outlined above was to become an increasingly professional and organised group of royal servants. Faced with written challenges to their authority and changing ideas of status, the officers of arms chose to maintain and enhance their position in English society by the professionalisation and incorporation that were by no means unique to them. Professionalisation was a process that was not only in the heralds' interest, but also in the interest of the king who sought control over chivalric matters in his realm. Thus, the development of the English office of arms in the fifteenth century can be attributed to several different social and political changes emerging out of important debates occurring within the culture of chivalry about status, the role of the gentry and the authority of the king. It fits very neatly into the 'big picture' of the age. The bigger picture for the herald in late medieval Europe is one of a loose international collection of armorial specialists who became increasingly disciplined and organised both in participation with, and under the authority of, sovereign rulers. In England, the process was shaped by the king's changing relations with his gentry and their service to the crown in the governance of the realm. Among the pressing questions for future research is how, and how far, the heralds continued to participate in an international fraternity – conversing in an international code of custom and law (for example, through their diplomatic roles), and in a chivalric culture evolving under the influence of renaissance humanism – even as they became more focused on their particular national offices of arms.

---

[78] Cf. M. H. Keen, 'The Jurisdiction and Origins of the Constable's Court', in *War and Government in the Middle Ages*, ed. J. Gillingham and J. C. Holt (Cambridge, 1984), pp. 159–69; M. H. Keen, 'Treason Trials under the Law of Arms', Transactions of the Royal Historical Society, 5th ser., 12 (1962), pp. 85–103, at p. 85, 90, 100; Keen, *Chivalry*, pp. 175–6.

of the heralds in England. In November 1437 Henry VI had come into his majority and from 1439 the kings of arms, as agents of the crown, had been regularly granting and confirming arms under their own seals of office.[17] This necessitated the need for a common set of records (to avoid armorial duplication), agreement on who was eligible to receive arms and who could grant arms, a common diplomatic formula for the letters patent granting and confirming arms, and a shared knowledge and understanding of the laws of arms. Increasingly, too, the heralds were working together on great ceremonial occasions, such as the twenty-four officers of arms present at the churching of Edward IV's queen, Elizabeth, following the birth of Elizabeth of York in February 1466,[18] those heralds accompanying the king on his French expedition of 1475,[19] those officiating at grand spectacles, such as the famous joust between the Bastard of Burgundy and Lord Scales in 1467,[20] and the reburials of Richard Neville, earl of Salisbury, in 1463,[21] and of Richard, duke of York, in July 1476.[22] In addition the heralds were increasingly being used on diplomatic missions undertaken on behalf of their sovereign.[23] Edward's Black Book and the ordinance of 1478 defined the duties of the officers of arms at court and fifteen officers of arms took part in his funeral five years later.[24] The 1470s and 1480s also witnessed the English heralds meeting together in chapters and undertaking the first visitations (albeit primitive) in this country.[25] All this required a high degree of professionalism, discipline and, above all, close cooperation.

[17] Adrian Ailes, 'Medieval Grants of Arms: 1300–1461' (MA dissertation, University of London, 1997), p. 40.
[18] A. R. Myers, ed., *English Historical Documents IV 1327–1485* (London, 1969), p. 1168.
[19] Francis Pierrepont Barnard, ed., *Edward IV's French Expedition of 1475: The Leaders and their Badges* (Oxford, 1925, reprinted 1975), pp. 128–31, 135–8; Wagner, *Catalogue of English Medieval Rolls of Arms*, p. 107; Wagner, *Heralds of England*, pp. 70–1.
[20] CA, MS L 5, fols 87–102; Samuel Bentley, ed., *Excerpta Historica* (London, 1831), pp. 171–212; Myers, ed., *English Historical Documents IV 1327–1485*, pp. 1170–4; Campbell and Steer, eds, *Catalogue*, p. 26 and references cited there.
[21] Ann Payne, 'The Salisbury Roll of Arms *c*.1463', in *England in the Fifteenth Century: Proceedings of the 1986 Harlaxton Symposium*, ed. Daniel Williams (Woodbridge, 1987), pp. 187–98; Wagner, *Heralds of England*, pp. 106–7.
[22] Anne F. Sutton and Livia Visser-Fuchs, with P. W. Hammond, *The Reburial of Richard Duke of York 21–30 July 1476* (London, 1996), pp. 14, 17, 33.
[23] See especially John Ferguson, *English Diplomacy 1422–61* (Oxford, 1972), and London, *Life of William Bruges*, pp. 20–2.
[24] A. R. Myers, ed., *The Household of Edward IV: The Black Book and the Ordinance of 1478* (Manchester, 1959), pp. 130–1; J. Gairdner, ed., *Letters and Papers Illustrative of the Reigns of Richard III and Henry VII*, 2 vols, Rolls Series (London, 1861–3), i, p. 9.
[25] Rodney Dennys, *Heraldry and the Heralds* (London, 1982), pp. 110–11; Bodl., MS Ashmole 857, pp. 50–1; Wagner, *Heralds of England*, p. 69; Adrian Ailes, 'Le développement des "visitations" de hérauts en Angleterre et au Pays de Galles 1450–1600', *Revue du Nord* 88 (2006), pp. 659–79.

Richard of Gloucester, as Constable, sought to codify these good practices, but his ordinances did not appear *ex nihilo*. For example, the very first of the ten clauses as found in what is possibly the earliest surviving copy is clearly based on the mid-fifteenth-century oath of a king of arms taken at his creation.[26] It required a king of arms to know and register the names, arms and issue of those nobles and gentlemen in his heraldic province or 'march'. Such knowledge was vital for the maintenance of heraldic records if arms were to be protected and the correct 'differences' made to the arms of members of the same family to distinguish them heraldically from one another whilst at the same time maintaining the all-important family likeness. Again, both the creation oaths of the officers of arms and Richard's ordinances refer to the kings of arms instructing heralds and pursuivants, the holding of chapters, and the heralds having to avoid slanderous talk, unsuitable places and discredited persons.[27]

In 1504 John Wrythe, Garter King of Arms to both Richard III (1483–85) and Henry VII, died and was formally succeeded the following year by his second son, Thomas, Wallingford Pursuivant, an ambitious young man who quickly changed his surname to the more grand-sounding Wriothesley. In 1498 Henry VII had issued a writ of aid (effectively a royal commission) to Wrythe and the then Clarenceux King of Arms, Roger Machado, to go on joint visitation, though no such visit appears to have taken place.[28] Wriothesley, Garter King of Arms, was equally keen to share the privileges and profits as exercised by the two provincial kings of arms, Clarenceux and Norroy. Agreements for him to grant arms and conduct funerals in the south were made with Machado and Thomas Benolt, who had become Clarenceux in January 1511, and similar indentures were agreed with succeeding Norroys for the north.[29] In 1512 the new king, Henry VIII, issued another writ of aid permitting Wriothesley and Benolt to go on joint visitation, though again there is no evidence that this took place.[30]

It was very probably at about this time that Wriothesley decided to appeal to ancient precedent to bolster his office of Garter. A revised English version of Richard's ordinances in Wriothesley's hand exists in the

---

[26] BL, MS Cotton Faustina E 1, fols 36–7 (an almost identical copy in BL, MS Add. 6297, fols 60–1); oath in TNA, HCA 12/1, fol. 118, and see Travers Twiss, ed., *The Black Book of the Admiralty*, 4 vols (Rolls Series, 1871–6), i, pp. 295–9.
[27] TNA, HCA 12/1, fol.118; BL, MS Cotton Faustina E 1, fols 36–7.
[28] G. D. Squibb, ed., *Munimenta Heraldica 1484–1984*, Harleian Society, n.s. 4 (London, 1985), pp. 128–9.
[29] Wagner, *Heralds of England*, pp. 147, 160–1. Visitations were not specifically mentioned in the indentures as claimed in 1530 (TNA, SP 1/73, fol. 196).
[30] Squibb, ed., *Munimenta Heraldica*, p. 129.

College of Arms, London.[31] Still attributed to Richard, it begins with an entirely new clause setting out in no uncertain terms the 'sovereignty' of Garter King of Arms, who had not been mentioned by name in the previous version produced some time between 1469 and 1483. Further on it requires arms to be registered in the book of the principal king of arms, Garter, as well as those of the relevant king of arms in whose province the arms are granted. There are also new references forbidding heralds to set up funeral achievements without Garter's licence or those of the relevant provincial king; funerals were fast becoming a lucrative part of the duties of a king of arms. The new version also makes reference to the Constable, a post that went into abeyance in 1521.[32] The probability, therefore, is that this new version was produced by Wriothesley some time between 1511 and 1521 to further his position as Garter King of Arms. The fact that his brother heralds at no time made reference to this revision or, indeed, to the original version by Richard, suggests that they had not seen either and may not even have been aware that either existed; their common library and records had been dispersed in 1485 after Henry VII regranted to his mother their property at Coldharbour (Upper Thames Street, London), which they had been granted the previous year with a view to having a centralised repository.

In 1522 Garter's powers and dignity were further enhanced by new statutes of the Order of the Garter. These included reaffirming his sovereignty over the other officers of arms and granting him power and authority to correct arms wrongly used and to grant arms to those worthy and sufficient to bear them.[33] The following year, on 23 May 1523, the chapter of the College, meeting at Greenwich, agreed to yet another revision of the ordinances, though the strong probability is that (apart from Wriothesley) this was the first time the other officers of arms present had seen a copy of the ordinances.[34] Presumably these new ordinances were

[31] CA, L 8a, fols 52v–54; Campbell and Steer, eds, *Catalogue*, p. 35. Another revised English version of the Ordinances ascribed to Richard does not include the clauses giving Garter primacy (BL, MS Cotton Tiberius E VIII, fols 158–9v; CA, Heralds II, fols 701–4v). This might, therefore, have been made by a provincial king of arms after 1521 (as it does not make reference to the Constable) keen to protect his rights of visitation, heraldic funerals and the granting of arms.
[32] CA, L 8a, fol. 53v. For the office of Constable left vacant after the execution of Edward duke of Buckingham on 17 May 1521 see G. D. Squibb, *The High Court of Chivalry: A Study of the Civil Law in England* (Oxford, 1959), pp. 30–1.
[33] Wagner, *Heralds of England*, pp. 148–9.
[34] CA, A 9, fols 18v–19; Campbell and Steer, eds, *Catalogue*, p. 184. According to Anstis, the ordinances were agreed by three kings of arms and three heralds on 23 May 1523 (*Register of the Most Noble Order of the Garter*, ii p.324; A. R. Wagner, *Heralds and Heraldry in the Middle Ages*, 2nd edn (Oxford, 1956), p.62; see also Bodl., MS Ashmole

put forward by Wriothesley, since once again the document bears all the hallmarks of someone wishing to strengthen the office of Garter King of Arms. The principal difference between the 1523 ordinances and both those of Richard (produced between 1469 and 1483) and Wriothesley's first revision (probably produced between 1511 and 1521) was that these ordinances were now attributed to Thomas, duke of Clarence. There are probably several reasons for this change in authorship. Richard's involvement would have hardly gone down well with Wriothesley's Tudor master, Henry VIII. Moreover, by attributing the ordinances to Clarence, Wriothesley gave them even more ancient authority and directly linked them to a man responsible for other important pronouncements concerning the heralds in those formative years of the fifteenth century. Above all, Clarence was the brother of Henry V, a king who had created the office of Garter King of Arms, and whose war aims, in terms of his personal rights in France, were shared by Henry VIII. The reputation of the victor of Agincourt was then riding high.[35] It was, as Wriothesley later pointed out, no less than 'the right high and right victorious prince of famous memory, King Henry V' who commanded his brother to issue the ordinances; they could hardly have come from a better authority.[36]

The version agreed in 1523 carefully omits the reference, included in Wriothesley's earlier revision, to Garter King of Arms' predecessors.[37] As Wriothesley well knew, when Clarence was Constable of the Army, William Bruges, Garter King of Arms, did not have any predecessors in this office. Also absent are references to the Constable of England, an office redundant from 1521. However, for the first time visitations appear. Garter believed he could visit and grant arms wherever he pleased. In support of his primacy over the other heralds he repeatedly quoted 'Clarence's' ordinances. Benolt, Clarenceux King of Arms, was clearly unhappy with their authenticity and demanded to see the original signed and sealed version. It was not forthcoming. He accused Wriothesley of holding on to the College books and records and not letting his brother heralds consult

---

763, fol. 181v). This version is in English and a near translation of the French, for which see Wagner, *Heralds and Heraldry*, Appendix C, pp. 136–8 and references cited there. For other versions see BL, MSS Add. 6297, fols. 84v–87, and Harley 5798; CA, Vincent 151 (Vincent's Precedents), pp. 64–8 (Campbell and Steer, eds, *Catalogue*, p. 378), and Heralds II, fol. 820; see also Bodl., MSS Rawlinson B 120, fols 90–2v and Ashmole 857, p. 31.

[35] For early-sixteenth-century attitudes to Henry V see Clifford S. L. Davies, 'Henry VIII and Henry V: The Wars in France at the End of the Middle Ages', in *The End of the Middle Ages? England in the Fifteenth and Sixteenth Centuries*, ed. John L. Watts (Stroud, 1998), pp. 235–62.

[36] The quotation is taken from Garter's dispute with Clarenceux in 1530: TNA, SP 1/73, fols 178–8v.

[37] The line is in CA, L 8a, fol. 52v.

them.[38] He concluded that Wriothesley had deliberately inserted his own fraudulent statements into the originals and claimed that such additions had never been granted by Clarence; this, he emphasised, was much to Garter's shame.[39] He was right. And he was not the last to question their authenticity.[40] What we now know is that 'Clarence's' ordinances owe more to the reigns of Edward IV (1461–70, 1471–83) and Henry VIII than they do to that of Henry V.

Finally, it is worth examining another document heavily drawn upon by Wriothesley in his 1530 dispute with Benolt and which is likewise dated to the reign of Henry V. Again, it is only known from much later copies. It records the resolutions agreed upon at a chapter of the English royal kings of arms and heralds then with the king at Rouen on 5 January 1420 or 1421.[41] The city had surrendered to the English in January 1419 after a siege of twenty-four weeks, as compared with less than three weeks at Caen in 1417. The meeting was significant for two reasons. It is the first recorded chapter of the English royal officers of arms and was very probably the first time they had formally met together to discuss their office. And secondly, again for the first time in England, it drew up constitutions and ordinances for the good government of, and admission into, the office of arms. Moreover, a common seal authorising decisions was proposed. In effect the resolutions amounted to an act of voluntary self-incorporation which was very probably part of Bruges's plan and now possible with a permanent head to the body.

Once again, however, the document is not straightforward. To begin with, the dating of the document is problematic. This is given as 'Le vendredy v^m Jour de Janvier Lan Mil CCCC et xx en lannee du Regne de nostre souverain seigneur le Roy de France et Dangleterre Henry quint apres la conqueste dangleterre dedens sa noble cite de Rouen en sa duchie de normendye Et en la feste dela nativite nostre seigneur';[42] the absence of a regnal year in this instance is particularly frustrating. The 5 January was

---

[38] Benolt believed that Wriothesley's father, Garter Writhe, had taken the College library and records to his own home when the heralds had to hand back their house to Henry VII; this accusation was vehemently denied by Wriothesley. TNA, SP 1/73, fols 188v–189v, 202–2v.

[39] TNA, SP 1/73, fols 189v–190v.

[40] Wagner, *Heralds and Heraldry*, p. 62; Anstis, *Register of the Order of the Garter*, ii, pp. 323–4; Wagner, *Heralds of England*, p. 68; Bodl., MS Ashmole 857, fol. 31.

[41] The French and an English translation (from BL, MS Add. [not Harley] 4101, fols 56v–61 and 71–5) is printed in London, *Life of William Bruges*, pp. 98–107; see also Bodl., MS Ashmole 857, pp. 11–19 and 58ff. Wagner, *Heralds of England*, p. 68 n. 6, lists the following additional references: CA, MSS L 6, fols 131–5, L 14, fol. 211v–214, and Vincent 151 (Precedents) pp. 69–76; see also Campbell and Steer, eds, *Catalogue*, pp. 31, 68, 378–9.

[42] BL, MS Add. 4101, fol. 57.

indeed a Friday in 1420 but, being before 25 March, modern style dating would normally place this in the following year (1421) when 5 January was not a Friday. Henry was at Rouen on that day in both January 1420 and 1421.[43] One might have expected the latter year to be correct since Henry's new queen had just arrived in the city on her way to England for her coronation and the heralds would have needed to meet together to discuss arrangements for the occasion.[44] Also, we know that at least four of the seven officers of arms present at the chapter took part in her coronation on 23 February.[45] Unfortunately the minutes refer to Henry as 'king' of France, and following the Treaty of Troyes ratified in May 1420 he was known as 'regent and heir'. The precise year of the chapter meeting is thus difficult to pinpoint, but the probability remains that some form of January meeting did take place in 1420 or 1421 under William Bruges, Garter King of Arms, and that certain resolutions were settled.

The deference to Garter King of Arms, Wriothesley's use of the chapter minutes to support his case in 1530, and the fact that the earliest known copy (London, British Library, Additional MS 4101) is in his hand might well cast suspicion over their authenticity. However, the five kings of arms mentioned in the text: Garter, Clarenceux, Norroy, Guyenne and Ireland, are correct for the 1420s. Moreover, the heralds present are, somewhat unusually for this date, listed by both title and name, and, as far as we know, appear to be the correct individuals.[46] For example, William Boys, Exeter Herald, appears in this list, and there is reference to him as Exeter in a feet of fines concerning lands in Burnham and Dorney, Buckinghamshire, dated April 1418.[47] Indeed, Wriothesley's adversary, Benolt, did not question the validity of the minutes in themselves, and he even used them

[43] Allmand, *Henry V*, pp. 141–2, 155; James Hamilton Wylie and William Templeton Waugh, *The Reign of Henry the Fifth*, iii (Cambridge, 1929), pp. 194, 261–4.

[44] Allmand, *Henry V*, p. 155.

[45] The following 'heralds of the king' were given the customary livery of scarlet for attending the coronation of Queen Katherine: Garter, 'Clarence' (probably here Clarenceux King of Arms, rather than Clarence Herald, since he is listed between two kings of arms), Ireland, Exeter, Nottingham, Leopard, and Richmond (TNA, E 101/407/74, fol. 37; Anstis, *Register of the Most Noble Order of the Garter*, ii, pp. 324, 328); see the following note for the heralds present at Rouen. For the coronation see Allmand, *Henry V*, p. 157.

[46] They are given as William Bruges, Garter King of Arms 'of the English', William Horsley, Clarenceux King of Arms, John Kirby (Kirkby or Kiteby), Ireland King of Arms, Nicholas Serby, Leopard Herald, John Haswell (Ashwell), Clarence Herald, William Boys, Exeter Herald and Marshal to Norroy King of Arms, and Giles Waster, Mowbray Herald (Godfrey, *College of Arms Monograph*, pp. 104, 269, 271–2, 280–1; London, *Life of William Bruges*, pp. 78, 99, 103).

[47] TNA, CP 25/1/22/117, no. 6; Anstis, *Register of the Most Noble Order of the Garter*, ii, p. 380; 'Heralds of the Nobility', p. 57.

a product of these developments, and these titles were often closely tied to the emerging royal (and, perhaps, one might argue 'national') iconography.[7] For the Scottish crown, the most important of the titles it might confer from the fourteenth century was Lyon.

The title of Lyon was derived from the association of the Scottish crown with the symbol of the lion, considered by contemporary medieval commentators to be the 'king of bestes'.[8] The royal arms of Scotland were charged with a lion rampant, and during the late Middle Ages there were numerous other instances where the lion was explicitly linked with royal authority.[9] For example, the chronicler Abbot Walter Bower reported that James I of Scotland (1406–37, cr. 1424) had a huge brass bombard cast in Flanders in 1430, inscribed around its girth in gold lettering with the lines: 'For the illustrious James, worthy prince of the Scots. / Magnificent king, when I sound off, I reduce castles. / I was made at his order; therefore I am called "Lion"'.[10] Reflecting their service to the Scottish crown, all heralds acting on royal authority bore the lion rampant on their tabards.[11]

century which demonstrate a renewed interest in chivalric culture, including the first appearance of the Nine Worthies and the first foundations of orders of chivalry. Very little has been written on the Nine Worthies, but for more see Maurice Keen, *Chivalry* (New Haven and London, 1984), pp. 121–4; Katie Stevenson, *Chivalry and Knighthood in Scotland, 1424–1513* (Woodbridge, 2006), pp. 134–5, 161. For orders of chivalry see D'Arcy Jonathan Dacre Boulton, *The Knights of the Crown: The Monarchical Orders of Knighthood in Later Medieval Europe, 1325–1520* (Woodbridge, 1987); Hugh E. L. Collins, *The Order of the Garter, 1348–1461* (Oxford, 2000); Katie Stevenson, 'The Unicorn, St Andrew and the Thistle: Was there an Order of Chivalry in Late Medieval Scotland?', *Scottish Historical Review* 83 (2004), pp. 3–22.

[7] It could be argued that the use of heralds by the names of Wallace Herald and Bruce Herald in communications with England may link to the ideas of developing 'national' sentiment. *CDS*, iv, no. 466; Charles Burnett, 'Early Officers of Arms in Scotland', *Review of Scottish Culture* 9 (1995/6), p. 3. See also more recent discussion of this by Steve Boardman: 'Robert II (1371–1390)', in *Scottish Kingship, 1306–1542: Essays in Honour of Norman Macdougall*, ed. Michael Brown and Roland Tanner (Edinburgh, 2008), pp. 88–9. On emerging 'national' chivalry see Carol Edington, 'Paragons and Patriots: National Identity and the Chivalric Ideal in Late Medieval Scotland', in *Image and Identity: The Making and Re-making of Scotland through the Ages*, ed. Dauvit Broun, R. J. Finlay and Michael Lynch (Edinburgh, 1998); Roger Mason, 'Chivalry and Citizenship: Aspects of National Identity in Renaissance Scotland', in *People and Power in Scotland: Essays in Honour of T. C. Smout*, ed. Roger Mason and Norman Macdougall (Edinburgh, 1992). Of course, not all heralds received titles and unnamed heralds continued to operate: note for example the payment to unnamed heralds for their services at a tournament in 1364, *ER*, ii, p. 129, and the records of unnamed heralds sent to England in 1379, 1389, 1391, 1392 and 1398, *ER*, iii, pp. 3, 205, 275, 292, 455.

[8] Houwen, ed., *The Deidis of Armorie*, i, p. 20.

[9] For a late medieval example of the Scottish royal arms bearing the lion rampant see BL, MS Add. 45133, fol. 46v.

[10] D. E. R. Watt, ed., *Scotichronicon by Walter Bower* (Aberdeen, 1993–8), viii, pp. 263–5.

[11] J. H. Stevenson wrote that Lyon 'certainly wore the king's own armorial coat, which no

Lyon Herald first emerged in the historical record in 1377.[12] He was called Lyon King of Heralds by 1388 and Lyon King of Arms by 1412, although the office was not consistently styled king of arms until the latter part of the sixteenth century.[13] While heraldic scholars have always assumed that Lyon was the pre-eminent herald of Scotland from 1377, in the early history of the officers of arms Lyon was *not* always the first amongst the heralds. J. H. Stevenson argues in *Heraldry in Scotland* that 'if there was ever any Scots King-of-Arms other than Lyon we are unacquainted with his title', but the sources reveal that this assertion is unfounded.[14] Prior to Lyon's first appearance as king of arms in 1412, a different king of arms was operating for the Scottish crown: Rothesay King of Arms.

In 1398 Rothesay Herald was created by Robert III (1390–1406) for his son David at his investiture as duke of Rothesay.[15] After David's death in mysterious circumstances in 1402,[16] his herald passed into the service of Robert III. In early 1406 Rothesay appeared in England as Rothesay King of Arms, clearly having been co-opted into the small band of king's heralds and given some kind of authority over them. It is perhaps not co-incidental that Robert III was at that time stationed at Rothesay Castle on the Isle of Bute and, indeed, the raising of Rothesay to the status of king of arms may have reflected Robert III's attachment to the castle as a centre of Stewart power during this period.[17] On 30 March 1406 Henry IV of England (1399–1413) ordered that the bailiffs of Scarborough restore to Rothesay King of Arms the goods of Scottish merchants from Dundee and Perth that had been captured at sea by John Joly of Clay. The order clearly recognised that Rothesay had some authority over the Scottish heraldic collective as it also gave permission for some of these goods to be returned to the 'deputies' of

other subject, not even the king's son and heir might do', but this is incorrect: all heralds wore the royal arms. Stevenson, *Heraldry in Scotland*, i, p 38. For examples see *TA*, i, p. cxciii, ii, p. 188; *ER*, xvii, p. 170, 283; *RPS*, 1587/7/40, and NLS, Acc. 9309 fol. 23(a), Seton Armorial 1591 'The Habit of a Herald'. See also BL, MS Harley 6149, fols 134–9v, which may have Scottish provenance and implies the right of a herald to wear his lord's arms all over his person.

[12]   *ER*, ii, p. 553; *TA*, i, p. cxciv.

[13]   *ER*, iii, pp. 170, 191, 692.

[14]   Stevenson, *Heraldry in Scotland*, i, p. 38.

[15]   Stephen I. Boardman, *The Early Stewart Kings. Robert II and Robert III, 1371–1406* (East Linton, 1996), pp. 206–9; *TA*, i, p. cxciv. The earliest reference to Rothesay Herald dates to c. 1401, *ER*, iii, p. 552, where he received the Queen's pension.

[16]   For more on this see Stephen Boardman, 'The Man who would be King: The Lieutenancy and Death of David, Duke of Rothesay, 1378–1402', in *People and Power in Scotland: Essays in Honour of T. C. Smout*, ed. Roger Mason and Norman Macdougall (Edinburgh, 1992), pp. 1–21.

[17]   For more on the death of Robert III see Boardman, *The Early Stewart Kings*, pp. 296–7.

Plate 2. The Habit of a Scottish Herald, *c.* 1500, from the Seton Armorial of 1591. Edinburgh, National Library of Scotland, Acc. 9309 fol. 23(a). By permission of Sir Francis Ogilvy and the Trustees of the National Library of Scotland.

Rothesay King of Arms.[18] Later that year, on 3 September, Rothesay King of Arms again appeared in England in relation to this matter. Here, Henry IV ordered John Joly's four attorneys to make an agreement regarding the captured Scottish goods with Rothesay 'King of Arms of Scotland, Commissary General for the king and kingdom of Scotland'.[19] These are early examples of both the range of duties Scottish heralds might undertake and of the power vested in the king of arms to act on behalf of the crown. We hear nothing further of Rothesay King of Arms after 1406 and by the reign of James II (1437–60) the office had reverted to that of Rothesay, herald of the duke of Rothesay.[20] It would seem, then, that from the early fifteenth century, Lyon was the principal herald of the Scottish royal household.[21]

As the fifteenth century progressed, an increasing number of Scottish officers of arms were created and received meaningful titles. More often than not, the royal heralds and pursuivants were granted titles which associated them with lands in the possession of the crown (or that the crown wished to possess), and the 'private' heralds of the Scottish nobility often had names associated with the surnames, mottos or achievements of those families. Royal heralds were operating with titles including Islay, Marchmont (Roxburgh), Ross, Angus[22] and Snowdon (Stirling).[23] Royal pursuivants had titles including Bute, Carrick, Dingwall, Kintyre, Ormonde and Montrose.[24] Of course, the exceptions to this were Lyon Herald and King of Arms and Unicorn Pursuivant, offices which both received titles associated with the iconography of the crown. Private officers of arms included Endure Pursuivant of the earl of Crawford, later promoted to Lindsay Herald,[25] Hailes Pursuivant of the earl of Bothwell,[26] Slains Pursuivant of the earl of Errol[27] and Douglas

---

[18]   *CDS*, iv, no. 720.

[19]   Ibid., no. 724.

[20]   *ER*, vi, pp. 496, 498.

[21]   Katie Stevenson, 'The Scottish King of Arms: Lyon's Place in the Hierarchy of the Late Medieval Scottish Elite', in *Die 'anderen' Könige: Königtum als Hierarchiebegriff in der spätmittelalterlichen Gesellschaft*, ed. Torsten Hiltman (Paris, 2009).

[22]   Angus Herald is not mentioned in Grant's *Court of the Lord Lyon*, but there is evidence he was operating as a procurator around 1500. *ADC*, ii, pp. 382, 448–9, 463–4.

[23]   Katie Stevenson, 'Royal Propaganda: Snowdon Herald and the Cult of Chivalry in Late Medieval Scotland', in *Genealogica et Heraldica Sancta Andreae MMVI: Myth and Propaganda in Heraldry and Genealogy*, ed. James D. Floyd and Charles J. Burnett (Edinburgh, 2008).

[24]   For some examples of this see Grant, *Court of the Lord Lyon*, pp. 3–8. Many of the dates Grant puts forward can now be substantially extended and corrected.

[25]   As Endure Pursuivant, *ER*, v, pp. 630, 639, vi, pp. 23, 42, 129, 135, 304, 320, 397, 404, 501, 510, 593, 602, vii, pp. 31, 142, 214. As Lindsay Herald, *ER*, vii, pp. 295, 305, 371, 377, 425.

[26]   *ER*, xi, p. 213; *TA*, i, pp. 312, 357, ii, pp. 39, 108, 112, 158, 398.

[27]   *ER*, vi, p. 155; *Reports of the Royal Commission on Historical Manuscripts* (London, 1870–), 5th Report, Muniments of Sir John Bethune, Baronet, at Kilconquhar in the

Herald of the earl of Douglas.[28] Although these private heralds operated principally for their lords, it was not uncommon for them also to be found in royal service. This was particularly the case with heralds created for members of the extended royal family, such as Albany Herald, who emerged as the personal heraldic officer of Robert Stewart, duke of Albany, on the establishment of the dukedom in 1398.[29] After the forfeiture of the Albany-Stewarts in 1425, Albany Herald was soon elevated into the ranks of the royal officers of arms.[30] The use of politically meaningful titles for officers of arms was one way in which the crown might express its authority, from the creation of Marchmont Herald in 1436, when James I had ambitions to recapture Roxburgh Castle,[31] to the creation of Islay Herald in 1493, on the forfeiture of the lordship of the Isles. The officers of arms could thus communicate a powerful message of royal ambitions.[32]

With the expansion of the ranks of the heraldic collective, the issue of who had the right to make officers of arms emerged in late medieval Scotland. Some argued that the king could create as a herald whomever he chose; others argued that it should be done in consultation with the king of arms. Sicily Herald, a herald of Alfonso V of Aragon (d. 1458), and mid-fifteenth century commentator on matters relating to heraldry, argued that only a king, prince, count or baron was able to make a herald and the latter only with the consent of the sovereign. These ideas were picked up in Kintyre Pursuivant Adam Loutfut's *Deidis of Armorie* (1494), a free translation into Scots from French. The *Deidis* stated: 'as the auld histories sais, nan of quhat estait he be suld mak herauld bot he be king, duk or erll, prince, baroun, and of sa gret antiquitie that scantly is thar memour of the lignie quhar-of he descendit.'[33] Loutfut circulated amongst the heralds of the late fifteenth century the idea that

> princis, lordis and barounys, knychtis and squyeris, and ilkane be thaimselff wald mak officiaris of armes at thar will and pleasance, nocht knawand giff thai war men of gud fame and honour and haffand in thaim wit, prudens, discrecioun, lawte, and wisdom to keip and excers weil the said office to the honour of all

County of Fife, p. 624.

[28]   *ER*, iii, pp. 248, 355–6, 382, 410, 454–5, iv, p. 117.

[29]   *CDS*, iv, no. 569; Boardman, 'Robert III', p. 119. Another example includes Ormonde Pursuivant, created for James III's son James Stewart, gifted to him on being made duke of Ross and marquess of Ormonde in 1476. Grant, *Court of the Lord Lyon*, pp. 7, 8.

[30]   *ER*, v, pp. 310, 344, 382, 437. Albany Herald was briefly Albany Pursuivant around 1448–9.

[31]   Michael Brown, *James I* (Edinburgh, 1994), p. 163.

[32]   Snowdon Herald was also a powerful political message from the crown, connecting Scotland's royal dynasty with Arthurian traditions. For more on this see Stevenson, 'Royal Propaganda'.

[33]   Houwen, ed., *The Deidis of Armorie*, i, p. 7.

gentilmen, als weil the ta party as the tothir, quhatsumeuer rycht, wsage, stilles, or priuileges pertenand parto, sua that thai transfer nocht the richtis forsaid, and als becaus they call nocht the auld kingis of armes and herauldis that knawis thaim tharin and aucht to be present at the makyn of thaim, both now it is nocht sua, ffor now thai mak at thar awn singler pleisser and will of folkis of litil valour, mak sic as flatteraris, ianglaris, rebauldis, gormandise, mequerreaulx, murderaris, pagis and folkis without clergy, memour or wndirstanding.[34]

The good moral character and quality of the officers of arms was obviously of paramount importance. Indeed, the implication was that only the chief herald could determine the suitability of men to hold the office of herald.

The Scottish practice in the late Middle Ages was that the king created heralds; whether this was done in consultation with the existing heralds or not is too difficult to determine from the sparse surviving records. However, by 1527 this practice was beginning to change. At this time the lords of council demanded that in order that

our soverane lord and his trew lieges may be weile and trewlie servit in tyme tocum in the said office, ordains the said Lyoun to cheir xii honest vertuus trew men in the said office that he will ansuer for apoun his honour to execut thar offices justlie, and to present thame to the lordis that thair may be admittit, and thar names to be gevin to the clerkis of the signet, sa that thai insert nane in our soverane lordis letters in tyme tocum bot the xii chosin be the said Lyoun.[35]

Forty years later, parliament felt that too much freedom had been given to the king of arms in dealing with abuses amongst the heralds, and declared that provision should be made for the reform of the officers of arms under Lyon, and sought to determine 'quhat dewitie the lyon herauld suld haue at the creatioun of euery officiar', thereby reducing Lyon's power over the officers of arms.[36] A clear shift in Lyon's duties is evident between the late fifteenth and the mid-sixteenth century, when he assumed increasing responsibility for the moral character of the officers of arms.

There is little surviving evidence to reveal how a man was selected for a position as officer of arms. There is a general assumption that the status of pursuivant was required before being admitted to the office of herald, although whether this was strictly adhered to cannot be determined. Certainly, some pursuivants were promoted to herald, such as in *c.*1468 when Unicorn Pursuivant was raised to Snowdon Herald.[37] Likewise, the status

---

[34] Ibid., p. 5.
[35] *ADCP*, pp. 260–1. Stevenson, in *Heraldry in Scotland*, i, p. 46, suggests that this change did not take place until 1630. However, this is inaccurate in light of the 1527 Lords of Council ordinance.
[36] *RPS*, 1567/12/91.
[37] *ER*, vii, p. 537.

of herald is thought normally to have been held by an individual prior to his being admitted to the office of king of arms. Although there were many exceptions to this in Scotland, in general it is clear that Lyon Kings of Arms had experience in a heraldic office prior to their promotion. For example, Henry Thomson of Keillour had been Islay Herald before becoming Lyon King of Arms in 1496, Sir William Cumming of Inverallochy had been Marchmont Herald before his investiture as Lyon in 1512, Thomas Pettigrew had been Angus Herald prior to 1519, Sir David Lindsay of the Mount was Snowdon Herald before 1542 and Sir Robert Forman of Luthrie was Ross Herald prior to 1555.[38]

Having been selected for an office, formal admittance then took place. Almost nothing can be determined of the ceremony by which Scottish heralds were granted their offices. The spurious suggestion, put forward by Francis Grant, that Robert I (the Bruce) created Lyon King of Arms in 1318 by 'girding him with the belt of knighthood and assigning a salary of £100', after which Lyon 'took the oath of fidelity before the High Altar of Arbroath', is devoid of any supporting evidence.[39] Indeed, Lyon's annual salary never peaked above £30.[40] In 1527 the records of the lords of council reveal a little more. They demonstrate that the investiture ceremony for a herald or pursuivant included the swearing of an oath to Lyon King of Arms, whereupon Lyon gave him arms and presented the new officer to the king and the lords.[41] At this point he also registered the officer's name with the clerks of the signet, so that the new officer's titles might be inserted into the king's correspondence as appropriate.[42] We can assume that the investiture of Lyon King of Arms was similar to that of the heralds, with one key difference: Lyon was ritually crowned, with a crown that mirrored the king's own.[43]

The hierarchy or order of precedence of the officers of arms has never been firmly ascertained by writers on Scottish heraldry. Some difficulty arises from the medieval officers of arms not being a formally incorporated body. There were thus no rules to which they rigidly adhered. However, this was

---

[38] Ibid., xii, p. 508; Grant, *Court of the Lord Lyon*, p. 1; Stevenson, 'The Scottish King of Arms'.
[39] Grant, *Court of the Lord Lyon*, p. i.
[40] *TA*, i, p. cxcvii.
[41] The Loutfut manuscript contains other advice on the creation and investiture of pursuivants and heralds. BL, MS Harley 6149, fols 134–9v. This treatise deals first with the history of the office of arms, followed by sections on the creation and office of a pursuivant, the pursuivant's oath, the creation and office of a herald, the punishment of heralds and pursuivants in cases of misbehaviour, the colours in arms and some common charges. The treatise ends rather abruptly with an explanation of the difference between officers of arms and minstrels.
[42] *ADCP*, pp. 260–1.
[43] Lyall, 'Medieval Scottish Coronation Service', pp. 7–10; Paul, *Heraldry in Relation to Scottish History and Art*, p. 91.

a status-conscious society and there is no question that the rank and order of these officers would have been well known and readily identifiable by indicators such as standard of dress.[44] The apogee of the heraldic order was the king of arms, followed by the heralds, pursuivants, macers, messengers and trumpeters. Both Innes of Learny and Grant offered different assessments of this hierarchy, and placed the rank of macer immediately under that of herald.[45] However, dozens of lists of officers place macers below pursuivants or fail to mention them at all; hence it would seem extremely unlikely that macers held a higher status than pursuivants. Furthermore, pursuivants themselves saw their place in the heraldic hierarchy as directly subordinate to heralds. Adam Loutfut, Kintyre Pursuivant, wrote around 1494 that he was the 'obedient sone in the office of armes' to Marchmont Herald.[46] A poem at folios 151–5 of the same manuscript ends with an explanation of the three orders of heralds: pursuivants, heralds and kings of arms.[47] Moreover, in terms of titular officers, it was only the king of arms, heralds and pursuivants who were granted official names. This was the case throughout Europe and it is unlikely that practice differed in Scotland.

The key difference between Scotland's officers of arms and those of some (though not all) of her closer European neighbours is that the Scottish officers were not incorporated until, at the earliest, the end of the sixteenth century. In France incorporation had occurred in 1407 and in England in 1484 with the foundation of the College of Arms, although this was revoked the following year by Henry VII (1485–1509). During the fifteenth century English heralds were becoming increasingly professionalised and the English incorporation of 1484 was very much desired by the officers of arms. In Scotland, there is no indication that there was a desire on the part of the king or the officers of arms to incorporate, and the issue was not brought before parliament until the end of the sixteenth century as part of a wider discussion of the formalisation of heraldic duties.[48] Although there was a desire by the Stewart kings to centralise government and assert authority over chivalric culture,

---

[44] For example, on 6 May 1471 parliament decreed that given the cost of importing silk into the realm 'na man sal veir silkis in tyme cummyng in gwne, doublate and clokis except knychtis, menstrallis [and] herraldis'. *RPS*, 1471/5/7.

[45] Innes of Learny, 'Sir William Cumming of Inverallochy', p. 25; Grant, *Court of the Lord Lyon*, p. ii. Innes cites a 1587 act of parliament which lists Lyon King of Arms followed by 'the ordainer herauldis, massirs and pursevantis'. However, recent work by the team of the Scottish Parliament Project at the University of St Andrews has shown that the original manuscript does not present this order. See *RPS*, 1587/7/26. Parliamentary legislation of 1571 does use this order. See *RPS*, 1571/8/11.

[46] BL, MS Harley 6149, fol. 78. See also fol. 44.

[47] Ibid., fols 151–5. For the text of the poem see F. J. Furnivall, ed., *Queene Elizabethes Achademy* (London, 1869), pp. 93–104.

[48] *RPS*, 1587/7/40.

especially from the second half of the fifteenth century, this did not extend to a formal foundation.[49] Foundations of professional bodies during the sixteenth century, such as the College of Surgeons in 1505–6 and the College of Justice in 1532, indicated a shift towards increasing bureaucratisation and professionalisation of government and administration,[50] but it took some time for a Scottish college of heralds to be instituted.[51]

It is easier to trace the development of the jurisdiction of Lyon King of Arms over the other officers of arms. Here again heraldic scholars have mis-judged the surviving evidence. J. H. Stevenson makes the erroneous claim that 'formerly Scotland, like England, was divided into two provinces, the one on the north and the other on the south side of the Forth, and these provinces were under the management of two Deputies, appointed by the Lord Lyon for the execution of all the business of his office.'[52] There is no evidence that this was ever the case and, in fact, it seems that Lyon King of Arms managed both Scotland and the king's heralds in their entirety. By 1517 there is a clear indication that Lyon King of Arms was formally in charge of the officers of arms. In a case before the lords of council, a messenger, John Adamson, stated that he was assigned with the task of delivering important letters to Patrick Hepburn, sheriff of Berwick. How-ever, Adamson was found not to have carried out this task and the lords thus ordered that he be deprived of his arms by Lyon King of Arms and punished in whichever way Lyon felt expedient.[53] This is the earliest refer-ence we have to an expectation that Lyon was responsible for the discipline of the officers of arms. This was reiterated in 1527 by the lords of council who ordained that when couriers and messengers were not executing their duties appropriately Lyon King of Arms should discharge them from their office. Further reiteration of Lyon's authority over messengers was provided by the decree that if, in future, the messengers should fail in the execution of their duties the 'Lyoun tak thar armies fra thame and punys thar persons according to thar faultis.'[54]

By 1541 the authority of Lyon was viewed by the officers of arms them-selves as being the sole jurisdictional authority under which they operated, with the exception of the lords of council as an extension of sovereign power. However, when this idea was raised before the lords of council, the council

[49] For more on the desire of the Stewarts to control chivalric culture, see Stevenson, *Chivalry and Knighthood in Scotland*.
[50] For more on these ideas see Julian Goodare, *The Government of Scotland, 1560–1625* (Oxford, 2004).
[51] *RPS*, 1587/7/40; Stevenson, *Heraldry in Scotland*, i, pp. 57–60.
[52] Ibid., i, p. 45.
[53] *ADCP*, p. 73.
[54] *ADCP*, pp. 260–1.

did not agree: 'The lords do not accept the contention of John Meldrum, Marchmont Herald, that "be privilege of his office na schereffis nor officiaris hes jurisdiction of him in his actionis bot alanerlie Lyon king of armes and the lordis of consale".'[55] The key argument here was whether or not the officers of arms were answerable only to the king, or if other officers might have jurisdiction over them. This, then, was an issue concerning not only royal authority over the officers of arms, but also the jurisdiction of sheriffs and other officers of the royal household. The lords of council believed that the Scottish officers of arms could not act outside the authority of the king's representatives, including, we can assume, the likes of the constable and the marischal. By this argument officers of arms were not answerable *only* to the king. Nevertheless, the quasi-royal status of Lyon King of Arms made for difficult lines of demarcation of jurisdiction and authority.

By 1555, evidence suggests that chapters of heralds were held to consider cases concerning acts of misconduct by officers of arms, a precursor to Lyon's modern precedence over the Lyon Court. These chapters were called under the authority of the constable and convened by Lyon King of Arms and all of the officers of arms.[56] This was a clear move in the direction of incorporation, and certainly indicates the level of independent jurisdiction that Lyon had over the heraldic collective (although the presence of the constable was significant). In 1567 parliament made provision for the reform of the organisation of the officers of arms, which at that time was under a corrupt and exploitative Lyon. Parliament's reform legislation principally dealt with capping the Lyon's fees when new officers were created.[57] In 1587 his supremacy over the other heralds was formalised by a further act of parliament. This set rules for the organisation of what was, in effect, a college of heralds and insisted that Lyon King of Arms held a court in Edinburgh bi-annually where he should be available to hear complaints against the officers of arms.[58] This was followed in the 1590s by further reiteration of the earlier reforms. In 1592 parliament gave Lyon the task of ensuring that the numbers of officers and messengers of arms was kept within strictly prescribed limits.[59] Two years later, having become aware of the potential for Lyon to falsely declare or siphon off fines levied by his bi-annual court, parliament demanded to see the accounts of the Lyon and Lyon Clerk to ensure that the king was not being deprived of his due income from the penalties placed upon deprived officers of arms.[60]

[55] Ibid., p. 509.
[56] NLS, Adv. MS 34.6.24, fol. 139v, pp. 277–8.
[57] *RPS*, 1567/12/91.
[58] Ibid., 1587/7/40.
[59] Ibid., 1592/4/47.
[60] Ibid., 1594/4/29. This appears to be one of the earliest references to the office of Lyon

In order to bring about order amongst the officers of arms and ensure that Lyon could effectively monitor their activities, parliament in the late sixteenth century legislated for a reduction in the officers of arms operating in the kingdom to a constant number. During the fourteenth and fifteenth centuries, the numbers of heralds and pursuivants in Scotland had fluctuated considerably and was entirely dependent upon the needs and whims of the crown. A 1587 parliamentary act restricted the total number of officers of arms permitted in the kingdom. There would be seventeen named officers of arms, including Lyon, the heralds and pursuivants (making eight of each), and it allowed for another 183 officers of arms (macers, messengers-at-arms and trumpeters) to be divided between the different sheriffdoms.[61] The Scottish officers of arms were further reduced to six (three heralds and three pursuivants) in 1867 by an act of parliament. This legislation was in response to complaints of corruption amongst the ranks of the officers of arms and particularly in relation to the purchasing of offices. It declared that Lyon (himself appointed by the queen) would appoint all officers of arms, fixed Lyon's salary at £600 per annum and removed the privilege from heralds and pursuivants of charging fees for their services.[62] This was in line with an oppositional critique originating in the late eighteenth century that sought to reduce offices, pensions and sinecures which were vilified under the umbrella term 'old corruption'.[63]

There remains one further issue of late medieval hierarchy and jurisdiction which needs clarification, and that is whether the constable and marischal had authority over Lyon King of Arms and his officers. This was certainly the case in England.[64] J. H. Stevenson has argued that although it has been supposed (on an assumed analogy with the case of England) that Lyon was

---

Clerk, which arose in the sixteenth century in light of the increasing demand for records of the business of Lyon King of Arms. For an (incomplete) list of Lyon Clerks see Grant, *Court of the Lord Lyon*, p. 2.

[61] *RPS*, 1587/7/40. The division of officers of arms amongst the sheriffdoms was Orkney and Shetland, 4; Inverness and Cromarty, 10; Nairn, 2; Elgin and Forres, 5; Banff, 4; Aberdeen, 12; Kincardine, 4; Forfar, 10; Fife, 10; Kinross, 2; Clackmannan, 2; Perth, 12; Stirling, 5; Dumbarton, 4; Linlithgow, 4; Edinburgh, 24; Haddington, 4; Berwick, 4; Roxburgh, 8; Selkirk, 2; Peebles, 3; Lanark, 10; Renfrew, 4; Argyll and Tarbert, 4; Bute, 2; Ayr, 12; Wigtown, 4; and Dumfries, 12.

[62] *Public General Statutes*, 30 Victoria, c. 17 [3 May 1867], 'An Act to regulate the Court and Office of the Lyon King of Arms in Scotland, and the Emoluments of the Officers of the same'.

[63] For this see Philip Harling, *The Waning of Old Corruption: The Politics of Economical Reform in Britain, 1779–1846* (Oxford, 1996); W. D. Rubenstein, 'The End of "Old Corruption" in Britain, 1780–1860', *Past and Present* 101 (1983), pp. 55–86.

[64] Anthony Wagner, *Heralds of England: A History of the Office and College of Arms* (London, 1967), p. 39; Anthony Wagner, *Heralds and Heraldry in the Middle Ages: An Inquiry into the Growth of the Armorial Function of Heralds* (Oxford, 1956), pp. 12–24; Paul, *Heraldry in Relation to Scottish History and Art*, p 79; Stevenson, *Heraldry in Scotland*, i, p. 41.

53

at one time subordinate to the marischal and constable of Scotland, 'all evidence points to the contrary'.[65] W. Croft Dickinson modified this view and suggested that while in theory final authority over the officers of arms rested with the constable, in practice Lyon King of Arms seems to have been the key figure.[66] It is unclear why writers on Scottish heralds have come to the conclusion that the marischal and constable had little or no authority over the officers of arms in Scotland, when the evidence actually points to the exact opposite. The surviving description of a mid-fifteenth-century coronation service (possibly James II's at Holyrood) sees in the early stage of the ceremony the marischal calling upon Lyon King of Arms and the heralds to sit down before the king. After this, the marischal swore in the Lyon and crowned him 'with his auen Croune wich he is to wear at that Solenitie.'[67] Throughout the ceremony, the status of the marischal and the constable was clearly superior to that of Lyon. The marischal made demands upon the Lyon, such as having him cry out oaths, but also during the anointing Lyon carried two 'pigges of oyle', one of which he then gave to the constable, and the other to the marischal.[68] They, in turn, handed these to the bishops who 'poured it one the kinges head and vpoune vpoune one syde and the vther'.[69] The hierarchical implications of this ritual are clear. Likewise, in a surviving manuscript (albeit a problematic one) concerning the organisation of fifteenth-century judicial duels, it is equally clear that the constable and the marischal had authority over the heralds. For example, in the instance of a defendant not appearing to duel at the appointed time, the king passed orders to the constable, who in turn ordered the marischal to order a herald to call the defendant to appear.[70] Similarly, before the first joust began,

> the Constable assignd a place convenient within the lists wher the King of Arms, Heraulds, and other officers should sitt or stand, and be ready if they were call'd; ffor afterwards all things wer committed to their charge, als weill on the behalf of the Defender as Challenger; as if any thing were forgotten in ther confessions,

[65]   He goes on to argue that Burnett, in an unpublished paper of George Burnett, held in the Lyon Office, 'was of the opinion that the Lyon was never subject to either'. Stevenson, *Heraldry in Scotland*, i, p. 41.

[66]   W. Croft Dickinson, 'Courts of Special Jurisdiction', in *Introduction to Scottish Legal History* (Edinburgh, 1958), p. 397; Carol Edington, *Court and Culture in Renaissance Scotland: Sir David Lindsay of the Mount (1486–1555)* (East Linton, 1994), p. 27.

[67]   Lyall, 'Medieval Scottish Coronation Service', p. 7.

[68]   Ibid., p. 9.

[69]   Ibid., p. 8.

[70]   'The Order of Combats for Life in Scotland as they are anciently recorded in ane old Manuscript of the Law Arms and Offices of Scotland pertaining to James I King of Scots', in *The Miscellany of the Spalding Club*, ii (Aberdeen, 1842), p. 385. The surviving manuscript dates to the seventeenth century, but purports to be a copy of a manuscript dating to the reign of James I.

either toutching ther lands or consciences, or that any of them desired to eat or drink: All these wants were supplied by the Heraulds, and none other.[71]

A hierarchical subordination of Lyon to these great officers of state was thus clearly implied in the ritual aspects of these events.

Kintyre Pursuivant, in the *Deidis of Armorie*, also laid out ideas of precedence and hierarchy. Perhaps taking its cue in part from the treatise of Sicily Herald, the opening passages dealt with how the various offices of arms were first founded in Julius Caesar's time.[72] Here the constable was given precedence, followed by the admiral, the marischal, the captains and then the heralds.[73]

> Bot of al thir offices the constable had the prerogatiue for to iuge and wndirstand the debates, discordis, and querellis that mycht be movit in al dedis of armes; and war ordanit and maid cotis of armes and takinnis of princes and lordis and the difference of thaim, that mycht be kend, the tane be the tothir, and for the richt and iustice of the said craft off armes to be the mair nobly governyt.[74]

The marischal's role, according to the *Deidis of Armorie* was very much restricted to the military: 'the marschaillis ar ane office quhilk pertenis til haue the knawlege of batalyes be land and the governance of the sammyn, for thai represent the counstable'.[75] The heralds should be responsible for 'gangand and cumand betuix princis' and to'mak gud and leil message of al thingis thai salbe chargit with and tharwithall leill and trew report'.[76] In January 1555, Sir David Linsday of the Mount, Lyon King of Arms, under the authority of the constable, convened a chapter of heralds to consider the case against William Crawford, a messenger accused of various acts of extortion and oppression. Crawford was found guilty and the chapter stripped him of his office and punished him.[77] In combination, this seems to provide some intriguing evidence of a court of chivalry operating in Scotland, similar to that which had operated in England since 1348 under the constable and the marshal, although further research needs to be undertaken on this subject.[78]

Evidence for late medieval treason trials suggests that heralds were involved in these cases and that they can be linked to the probable existence

---

[71] 'Order of Combats', p. 388.
[72] Houwen, ed., *Deidis of Armorie*, i, p. xiii.
[73] Ibid., i, p. 1.
[74] Ibid., i, p. 1.
[75] Ibid., i, p. 2.
[76] Ibid., i, p. 4.
[77] NLS, Adv. MS 34.6.24, fol. 139v, pp. 277–8; Edington, *Court and Culture in Renaissance Scotland*, p. 27.
[78] G. D. Squibb, *The High Court of Chivalry: A Study of the Civil Law in England* (Oxford, 1959), pp. 1–28; Wagner, *Heralds of England*, pp. 125, 130.

of a Scottish court of chivalry. Judicial duels were often fought over matters of treason in the late Middle Ages,[79] and Scottish heralds had relevant information on their practice in their private collections.[80] Treason was a crime with which Lyon King of Arms, in particular, was intricately involved from the middle of the fifteenth century. In 1453 Sir Alexander Nairn of Sandford, Lyon King of Arms, fought a judicial duel with Sir James Logan and it would seem that this may have been prompted by a charge of treason, possibly in connection with the Black Douglases.[81] Prior to being forfeited in 1455, the ninth earl of Douglas was summoned by Lyon to appear personally before the king and the three estates under the charge of treason.[82] In 1479 Marchmont Herald, Ross Herald, Unicorn Pursuivant, Dingwall Pursuivant and two macers were commissioned by parliament to apprehend Alexander Stewart, duke of Albany, to appear on charges of treason.[83] The full complement of the officers of arms who served summons of treason on Lord Bothwell on 2 August 1488 was led by Lyon King of Arms.[84] Likewise, in 1488 Lyon was integral to the issuing of the apprehension and summons of treason of the advocate of James III (1460–88), John Ross of Montgrennan, who was charged with traitorously pursuing Prince James to beyond the Bridge of Stirling on the day preceding the Battle of Sauchieburn.[85] The powers of arrest also seem to have belonged to heralds. For example, in 1515 the Chamberlain refused to arrest George Douglas, brother of the earl of Angus, as parliament had not requested it and he argued that the arrest should be carried out by a herald.[86] By 1592 parliament formally insisted upon charges of treason being executed by officers of arms, and gave the civil magistrates explicit instruction to assist Lyon King of Arms in enforcing the acts connected with his office.[87] The Scottish court of chivalry was probably a precursor to the modern Court of the Lord Lyon, which developed once

[79] For more see George Neilson, *Trial by Combat from Before the Middle Ages to 1819 A.D.* (Boston, 1909).
[80] BL, MS Harley 6149, fols 109–15v.
[81] W. Barclay and D. D. Turnbull, eds, *Extracta e Variis Cronicis Scocie: From the Ancient Manuscript in the Advocates Library at Edinburgh* (Edinburgh, 1842), p. 243; Stevenson, *Chivalry and Knighthood in Scotland*, pp. 64–5.
[82] *RPS*, 1455/6/6; William Fraser, *The Douglas Book* (Edinburgh, 1885), i, p. 490.
[83] *RPS*, 1479/10/7.
[84] Ibid., 1488/10/14; *TA*, i, p. cxcv; Robert Pitcairn, *Ancient Criminal Trials in Scotland from 1488 to 1624* (Edinburgh, 1833), i, p. 5.
[85] Ibid., i, p. 9. Other examples of Lyon and the heralds' involvement in treason proliferate during the sixteenth century. See for example William Fraser, *The Melvilles Earls of Melville and Leslies Earls of Leven* (Edinburgh, 1890), iii, no. 86.
[86] R. H. Brodie, ed., *Letters and Papers, Foreign and Domestic of the Reign of Henry VIII, Preserved in the Public Record Office, the British Museum and Elsewhere* (London, 1920), ii, no. 779, p. 206; Fraser, *Douglas Book*, ii, p. 141.
[87] *RPS*, 1592/4/47.

Lyon took on principal responsibility for the administration of its cases.

The modern Court of the Lord Lyon is responsible principally for the laws of armorial bearings and has an associated record office in Edinburgh that holds manuscripts and books on the subject of heraldry. There has long been an assumption that because this is the contemporary sphere of expertise of the modern Scottish officers of arms, it must also have occupied the majority of the medieval heralds' time. In fact, their other activities were equally if not more important during the fifteenth century. Officers of arms' responsibilities were diverse and included the carrying of royal letters and, more importantly, associated diplomatic briefs; organising and participating in royal ceremonies, such as coronations, weddings, funerals and tournaments; acting in matters as advocate for the king and as procurators for private clients; and collecting the heraldic information of the kingdom.[88] In line with the dominance Lyon King of Arms had over the officers of arms, it was also during the sixteenth century that Lyon acquired increasing control over Scottish armoury. These powers were mostly confined to the denying of the arms of men forfeited for treason, connected to his involvement with treason trials, which thus raises the question of precisely when Lyon became responsible for the granting of arms in Scotland.

Francis Grant in the *Court of the Lord Lyon* made the rather bold claim that 'since 1542 no grant has been made by the king but by Lyon alone'.[89] He thus attributes the armorial roll of 1542 by Sir David Lindsay as being the first register of arms in Scotland and that this implied control by the king of arms (see Plate I). Indeed, this is a view that is now widely held.[90] However, as we will see, the picture is far from clear.

---

[88] In *Heraldry in Scotland*, Stevenson gives only three classes of duty 'past and present' of the officers of arms of Scotland: the first, the carrying and delivering royal messages; second, the directing and marshalling of royal and public ceremonies; and third, attending to the enforcement of the law of arms and making grants of arms. He does not identify the fourth duty of procurator and royal advocate. Stevenson, *Heraldry in Scotland*, i, p. 52.

[89] Grant, *Court of the Lord Lyon*, p. i.

[90] NLS, Adv MSS 31.4.3. Stevenson, *Heraldry in Scotland*, i, p. 62; Edington, *Court and Culture in Renaissance Scotland*, p. 37. This manuscript is not in its original form: some folios are out of logical sequence and there are many seventeenth-century additions, including the royal arms on fol. 2 and Lindsay's arms on fol. 57. Edington suggests this armorial may have had a connection to a 1540 act of parliament which ordered that all sentences for treason passed in parliament or the justice courts should be authentically copied and gathered together in one book, in part because they may be destroyed, and in part because the memory of the traitors should remain to the shame and slander of their descendants. *RPS*, 1540/12/27. David Lindsay included in his armorial the arms of the majority of traitors named in that statute, an unorthodox move given that forfeiture also meant forfeiture of arms. Lindsay justified his inclusion of these arms on the grounds that it honoured their noble predecessors, shamed the guilty and set an example which may deter others from such heinous crimes. NLS, Adv MSS 31.4.3, fol. 53. Edington, *Court and Culture in Renaissance Scotland*, p. 39.

The late medieval treatises that circulated throughout Europe on the matter of arms were primarily concerned with defining an individual's right to bear arms. The purpose of heraldry was clear: 'the principale caus of armes taking js for to knawe the personagis of noble men jn bataill or jn armes or jn tournaymentis Or to knaw a lord jn felde be ane other with his men'.[91] The *Buke of the Law of Armys*, a Scots translation (*c.*1456) by Sir Gilbert Hay of Honoré Bouvet's *L'Arbre des batailles*, stated that men should understand that some arms were given by the power of authority of emperors, kings and princes to lords and barons.[92] The real crux of the issue was when men assumed arms without royal authority. Here all sorts of problems might arise, such as 'quhethir a man yat js nocht of thair lygnie may bere leuefully thair armes at his plesaunce'.[93] Indeed, this resolved the issues raised from the 1350s, especially in Bartolus of Saxoferrato's *Tractatus de Insigniis et Armis*, where it was argued that men could assume arms by their own authority.[94] By the fifteenth century, commentators argued for regulation to avoid the types of conflicts which had arisen over two families bearing the same arms. In extreme cases in England these might be brought before the court of chivalry, such as the well-documented case of Scrope *v.* Grosvenor.[95] The 1394 *Tractatus de Armis* of Johannes de Bado Aureo argued that arms should be assigned by a king of arms, but this suggestion does not seem to have had significant impact in Scotland.[96] Indeed, it was a controversial idea in England, where in 1440 the English cleric and lawyer Nicholas Upton retorted: 'Nor dare I approve of the opinion of certain men who say that Heralds can give Arms; but I say, if such Arms are borne by any Herald given, that these Arms are not of greater authority than those which are taken by a man's own authority'.[97] Gilbert Hay's *Buke of the Law of Armys* was clear with whom final authority should rest in decisions on the granting of arms: the king. The heralds' involvement in these matters

---

[91]   Jonathan A. Glenn, ed., *The Prose Works of Sir Gilbert Hay Volume II: The Buke of the Law of Armys* (Edinburgh, 2005), part iv, ch. cxxxviii, p. 262.

[92]   Ibid., part iv, ch. cxxxvii, p. 260.

[93]   Ibid., part iv, ch. cxxxvii, pp. 259–60.

[94]   Evan John Jones, ed., *Medieval Heraldry: Some Fourteenth Century Heraldic Works, Edited with Introduction, English Translation of the Welsh Text, Arms in Colour, and Notes* (Cardiff, 1943), Appendix i, pp. 221–52.

[95]   N. Harris Nicolas, *The Controversy between Sir Richard Scrope and Sir Robert Grosvenor in the Court of Chivalry, 1385–90* (London, 1832).

[96]   Jones, ed., *Medieval Heraldry*, pp. 95–212.

[97]   Translated by George R. Sitwell in 'The English Gentleman', *The Ancestor* i (1902), p. 86. Upton's ideas were recycled in the first printed book to deal with the subject of heraldry, *The Boke of St Albans* of 1486. Bartolus's *Tractatus*, Upton's work and a copy of the *Book of St Albans* were known in Scotland and were included in the Loutfut manuscript of 1494. BL, MS Harley 6149, fols 52–61v, 62–77, 155–64v. John Meldrum, Marchmont Herald also had a copy of Bartolus of Saxoferrato's *Tractatus de Insigniis et Armis*, NLS, Adv. MS 31.6.5.

should be to inform the king of the good or bad qualities of a man desiring arms.[98] In England, the issue was not settled by Upton, and in a collection of heraldic memorabilia of the 1450s, Richard Strangways asserted that the right to bear arms was acquired in one of four ways: by inheritance, by marriage, by conquest or by grant from a prince or a herald.[99] Thus it is clear that by the mid-fifteenth century there were two schools of thought: one which emphasised the competence of heralds in armorial matters; the other, more dominant, view that grants of arms should be by the authority of the king. From the surviving evidence, it would seem that only the latter was practised in Scotland.

This raises the question of when the king of arms assumed the power to regulate the granting, denial and recording of arms in Scotland. We know in England that kings of arms did make grants during the fifteenth century, but there seems to be no evidence of this in Scotland. Stevenson argued in *Heraldry in Scotland* that

> if we may judge by the analogy of other countries, the recognition of the author-ity of these officers to regulate the assumption of arms, and the theory that the right to bear any particular ensign flowed only from the king, were growths of the fifteenth century, fully established only in the sixteenth.[100]

It is possible to give a more precise assessment than this. In 1324 it was par-liament which granted the name and arms of Keith to the heirs of the lands of Keith-Marischal and the office of marischal of the kingdom.[101] Around 1449, James II granted arms to Albany Pursuivant and around 1459 he gave arms to the earl of Angus.[102] Even confirming genealogy, a function the her-alds later controlled, was carried out independently of heraldic authority in the fifteenth century, such as the inquest (*c.* 1456) into the bastardy of David Jardine.[103] In 1471, when the king's own arms were modified, it was parlia-ment which took this decision and the king who ordained it, suggesting that the officers of arms had little, if anything, to do with this type of grant.[104] This continued throughout the sixteenth century and, in 1581, parliament passed an act empowering William Maxwell to assume the name and arms of Baillie of Lamington.[105] Thus, it can be suggested that the Scottish king

---

[98] Glenn, ed., *Buke of the Law of Armys*, part iv, ch. cxxxviii, p. 263.
[99] BL, MS Harley 2259; see especially fol. 109b. For further discussion on these debates see Squibb, *High Court of Chivalry*, pp. 178–81.
[100] Stevenson, *Heraldry in Scotland*, i, p. 61.
[101] *RPS*, 1324/1.
[102] *ER*, v, p. 344, vi, p. 580.
[103] Ibid., vi, p. 264.
[104] *RPS*, 1472/13.
[105] Ibid., 1581/10/65.

and parliament were responsible for the issuing of armorial bearings in the fifteenth and sixteenth centuries, with heralds perhaps acting on occasion as the record keepers of these decisions.

The recording of armorial bearings by heralds, a quite distinct task from the authority to grant arms, seems to have occurred as early as the fourteenth century. We have little evidence of visitations being carried out in Scotland in order to collect armorial information, although these were executed in England.[106] However, the inclusion of substantial numbers of Scottish coats in foreign armorials, such as the *Gelre Armorial*, the *Bellenville Armorial*, the *Armorial de Berry* and the *Scots Roll*, indicates that there was collection of heraldic information in late medieval Scotland.[107] Charles Burnett has argued that the recording of the arms took place in Scotland, but at the hands of visiting heralds. He also suggests that foreign heralds may have met Scottish heralds in this course of their duties, with whom they exchanged blazons.[108] Foreign heralds might also have acquired heraldic information about Scotland from native armorials, almost all of which have now been lost. Indeed, there are indications that many of the surviving armorials, most of which date from the second half of the sixteenth century, may be in part compilations from earlier armorials.[109] By 1567 there was a formal 'book of arms' or armorial register into which arms might be inserted or deleted, such as in cases of forfeiture for treason.[110] So, although Lindsay's armorial of 1542 may have been the first attempt at a comprehensive Scottish armorial, it was far from being a working register of the arms of the kingdom.

It was, moreover, not until as late as 1592 that the role of heralds as monitors of the arms of the Scottish nobility became formalised. In an act of parliament it was laid out that Lyon King of Arms and his brother heralds

[106] Paul, *Heraldry in Relation to Scottish History and Art*, p. 89.
[107] Robert Riddle Stodart, *Scottish Arms, Being a Collection of Armorial Bearings, A.D. 1370–1678: Reproduced in Facsimile from Contemporary Manuscripts with Heraldic and Genealogical Notes* (Edinburgh, 1881). On the *Armorial de Berry* see J. Storer Clouston, 'The Armorial de Berry (Scottish Section)', *Proceedings of the Society of Antiquaries of Scotland* 72 (1937–8), pp. 84–114. On the *Bellenville Roll* see BnF, MS Français 5230; Colin Campbell, 'Scottish Arms in the Bellenville Roll', *The Scottish Genealogist* 25:2 (1978), pp. 33–52. On the *Scots Roll* see BL, MS Add. 45133, fols 46b–50b; Colin Campbell, ed., *The Scots Roll: A Study of a Fifteenth Century Roll of Arms* (Kinross, 1995); Rae Redfern Brown, 'The Scots Roll' (M.Litt. dissertation, University of St Andrews, 2007).
[108] Burnett, 'Early Officers of Arms', p. 11.
[109] See for example the *Scots Roll*, BL, MS Add. 45133, fols 46b–50b, which is derived from at least two earlier armorial rolls, one dating to the mid-fifteenth century, and one to the 1490s.
[110] *RPS*, 1567/4/27, 1567/4/33. The 1567 act was followed in the parliament of 1584, when the name and arms of the deceased James Ross of Pettheveles were ordered to be deleted from the 'book of arms and nobility' on his forefeiture. Ibid., 1584/5/72.

should visit the armigerous of Scotland and matriculate their arms in heraldic registers. They were also instructed to inhibit unauthorised persons from bearing arms, under pain of escheat of the goods and gear whereon the arms were graven or painted, in addition to a £100 fine paid to Lyon and his heralds.[111] There is no mention by parliament of an exclusive right to grant arms, but as the keeper of the kingdom's armorial information, the granting of arms by the officers of arms would naturally follow in the seventeenth century. Full jurisdiction was only comprehensively granted in an act passed in 1622, by which Lyon was declared to be the only competent judge in all questions of arms.[112] Although this was repealed the following year, legislation was reissued on this matter in 1672.[113]

It is clear that officers of arms were not in control of the law of arms in medieval Scotland, but they did have a role to play in the execution of the civil law more generally. Indeed, Scottish heralds developed a prominent space for themselves in the legal administration of the kingdom.[114] While the records prior to James IV's reign (1488–1513) prohibit us from knowing if this was a function they undertook in earlier decades, from the late fifteenth and early sixteenth century we certainly find heralds acting as notaries, procurators and advocates for the king on a wide variety of matters.[115] John Finlay has pointed out that in this period the Scottish king did not enjoy a monopoly on his advocates' services, and there are many instances of the clerk register, the justice-clerk and the king's advocate all representing private clients.[116] This was also true for the heralds who acted as notaries and procurators on the behalf of a range of private clients.[117] Both Snowdon Herald and Unicorn Pursuivant were appointed in August 1478 as procurators for Robert Blackadder, archbishop of St Andrews.[118] Sir William Cumming of Inverallochy, as both Marchmont Herald and later Lyon King of Arms, acted on behalf of several clients including the earl of Errol, Burnett of Leys, Ross of Kilravock and Fraser of Stonywood.[119] Angus Herald, too, was appointed to act as a procurator for John, bishop of Ross, on 20 March 1501, in Ross's action against Sir James Dunbar for the

---

[111] Ibid., 1592/4/47.
[112] Stevenson, *Heraldry in Scotland*, i, p. 63.
[113] *RPS*, 1672/6/57; Stevenson, *Heraldry in Scotland*, i, p. 64.
[114] Burnett, 'Early Officers of Arms', p. 6.
[115] *ADCP*, pp. 42–3, 49; *ADC*, ii, pp. 40, 42–3.
[116] John Finlay, *Men of Law in Pre-Reformation Scotland* (East Linton, 2000), p. 171.
[117] For an example of Islay Herald acting as a notary see *ADCP*, p. 113.
[118] J. Dennistoun, ed., *Cartularium Comitatus de Levenax ab Initio Seculi Decimi Tertii usque ad Annum MCCCXCVIII* (Edinburgh, 1833), ii, no 78, p. 117.
[119] *ADC*, ii, pp. 295, 313; Innes of Learny, 'Sir William Cumming of Inverallochy', p. 30; *ADCP*, pp. 15, 38, 50, 56.

sum of £200.[120] It is evident that the execution of legal duties for a range of clients was a frequent task of the Scottish officers of arms and thus that many had received formal education in the law.

So, if Scottish medieval officers of arms did not spend the majority of time occupied in matters only relating to heraldry, how else might they earn their annual pensions? The most commonly performed duty of any herald was acting as a representative of the crown in matters of royal communication and diplomacy. Indeed, parliament made it clear that only a 'king of armys or a heralde of wisdome and knaulage' should be entrusted with royal communications.[121] In the domestic context, this might involve meeting foreign dignitaries at their point of entry into the kingdom and escorting them safely to the king. At Candlemas in 1477, for example, Lyon King of Arms was sent to meet and escort several English envoys to Edinburgh.[122] Similarly, in July 1489 Snowdon Herald was sent to Berwick to escort Spanish ambassadors to Edinburgh from the border.[123] Heraldic escorts were also provided for those summonsed before justice ayres and parliament.[124] By James V's reign (1513–42) it was common for officers of arms to make royal proclamations at the mercat crosses of the royal burghs, a duty which increased exponentially over the course of the sixteenth and seventeenth centuries.[125] Tax collection was also part of the remit of a herald, and in 1545 parliament directed officers of arms to assist the sheriffs and steward in distraining persons who resisted paying their tax.[126]

Officers of arms were regularly sent from the kingdom of Scotland to act on behalf of the crown.[127] On these trips, heralds might carry a variety of messages including letters from the king, or specific items, such as the collar and accoutrements of the Order of the Garter that Lyon King of Arms returned to Henry VIII of England (1509–47) on James V's death

---

120 ADC, ii, p. 464.

121 RPS, 1482/12/75.

122 CDS, iv, no. 1445. For some English and Scottish evidence of contact between officers of arms of these kingdoms see Charles J. Burnett, 'Contacts between Scottish and English Officers of Arms', in *Tribute to an Armorist*, ed. John Campbell-Kease (London, 2000).

123 TA, i, p. xci, 117.

124 ER, vii, pp. 20, 226.

125 Burnett, 'Early Officers of Arms', p. 6.

126 RPS, 1545/9/28/40.

127 See for example, ER, ii, p. 117, vi, p. 308; TA, i, pp. 46, 50,127, 279, 325, 388, ii, pp. 114, 122, 132, 352, 361, 427, 478, iii, p. 278, iv, pp. 27, 417, 501; Brodie, ed., *Letters and Papers, Foreign and Domestic of the Reign of Henry VIII*, i, nos 788, 789, 795, 1826, 2239, 5641; ADC, ii, pp. 56, 77; CDS, iv, nos 1421, 1501, 1505, 1697; Rawdon Brown, ed., *Calendar of State Papers and Manuscripts Relating to English Affairs, Existing in the Archives and Collections of Venice and in Other Libraries of Northern Italy* (London, 1864), i, no. 769; D. Macpherson *et al.*, eds, *Rotuli Scotiae in Turri Londinensi et in Domo Capitulari Westmonasteriensi Asservati* (London, 1814–19), ii, pp. 63, 227.

in 1542.[128] Historians have long assumed that heralds were little more than messengers, but this appears to be far from the case: in December 1478, for example, Lyon King of Arms was described as an ambassador, an orator and a commissioner for the king of Scots.[129] Foreign diplomacy was one of the principal duties of the officers of arms, and the Scottish sources reveal a rich level of detail about this element of their work. For example, in 1484 Lyon King of Arms was sent to negotiate a marriage between James, duke of Rothesay, and Anne, the niece of Richard III of England.[130] In 1459, Marchmont Herald was sent to the earl of Northumberland in England to discuss a truce and the security of Scottish merchants and ships along the coast, as well as to attempt to recover Scottish property taken at sea.[131] Indeed, the parliament of 1471 made it clear that heralds were integral to the composition of diplomatic embassies: 'the lordis thinkis considering the estatis of ane bishop, ane erle, ane lord of parliament, a knycht, and ane clerk, ane herald'.[132] Heralds also seem to have acted as royal representatives at foreign coronations, including at Henry IV of England's coronation in 1399.[133] Heralds were far more than simple messengers in late medieval Scotland and were invested with powers to represent the crown and to act on its behalf.

Officers of arms did enjoy diplomatic immunity, at least in principle, and were able to move reasonably freely in other kingdoms, provided that safe-conducts had been issued where these were required.[134] Across late medieval Europe, including Scotland, heralds carried white wands as a sign of this diplomatic immunity.[135] In 1432 the parliament of Scotland ordered that officers of law must each have a horn and a wand of at least three-quarters of a yard of either red or white, depending on their status.[136] Sir David Lindsay of the Mount in his poem of 1537, the *Deploration of the Deith of Quene Magdalene*, refered to the 'burneist siluer wandis' borne by

---

[128] See for example the letter of Margaret Tudor to Henry VII in 1514. Brodie, ed., *Letters and Papers, Foreign and Domestic of the Reign of Henry VIII*, no. 5614, p. 933. On the Garter accoutrements see BL, MS Royal 18 B.VI, 315 Holyrood 21 March 1543.
[129] Macpherson *et al.*, eds, *Rotuli Scotiae*, ii, p. 456.
[130] *CDS*, iv, nos 1501, 1505.
[131] *ER*, vi, p. 498.
[132] *RPS*, 1471/5/2.
[133] *CDS*, iv, no. 540.
[134] Maurice H. Keen, *The Laws of War in the Late Middle Ages* (Aldershot, 1965), pp. 196–6; Pierre Chaplais, *English Diplomatic Practice in the Middle Ages* (London, 2003), p. 139; John Ferguson, *English Diplomacy 1422–1461* (Oxford, 1972), pp. 165–6. Keen argues that a herald's coat of arms and white wand were adequate for safe-conduct, but Chaplais claims they needed a more formal safe-conduct.
[135] Keen, *Laws of War*, pp. 109–110; Chaplais, *English Diplomatic Practice in the Middle Ages*, p. 16.
[136] *RPS*, 1432/3/12.

the heralds.[137] These visual symbols of their status gave heralds authority in their actions, but also a neutrality that enabled them to observe the events of late medieval Europe.

Frequent travel and missions of diplomacy meant that Scottish heralds required certain skills, including knowledge of foreign languages.[138] They also had the need to be well acquainted with the customs and topography of the kingdoms and principalities into which they journeyed.[139] The royal library provided Scottish officers of arms with resources to assist in their preparation, and we know, for instance, that James III's collection contained a copy of the *Travels of Sir John Mandeville*, which the king had copied in 1467.[140] James III also received a copy of the travel diary of Anselm Adornes, whom the king had encouraged to visit the Holy Land around 1470.[141] Private libraries may also have been available to heralds to borrow or consult books. For example, James Douglas, lord of Dalkeith, in his will of 1390, indicated that he regularly lent his books and that his collection contained material of relevance to the officers of arms of the kingdom.[142] Likewise, Sir William Sinclair, earl of Orkney and Chancellor of Scotland, had several works of significance in his collection of the mid-1450s, including the *Buke of the Ordre of Knychthede* and the *Buke of the Law of Armys*.[143]

The heralds themselves were avid collectors of books and manuscripts relating to their areas of interest and expertise. The glimpse we have of even a small part of their libraries attests to the resources available to them. Sir

---

[137] Douglas Hamer, ed., *The Works of Sir David Lindsay of the Mount, 1490–1555* (Edinburgh and London, 1931), i, p. 110, line 40; Edington, *Court and Culture in Renaissance Scotland*, p. 234 n. 23.

[138] For example, in a letter from Lord Dacre to the Lords of Council, he reported that Lyon King of Arms (Cumming of Inverallochy) met with Dacre at Harbottle on 7 August 1515 and showed him a letter from the duke of Albany which was in French. Dacre, who must have been unable to read French, had Lyon translate this for him on the spot. Dacre then enclosed both Albany's original letter and Lyon's translation of it in his letter to the Lords. Brodie, ed., *Letters and Papers, Foreign and Domestic of the Reign of Henry VIII*, ii, no. 788, p. 210.

[139] Chaplais, *English Diplomatic Practice in the Middle Ages*, p. 140.

[140] ER, vii, p. 500.

[141] Jacques Heers and Georgette de Groer, eds, *Itinéraire d'Anselme Adorno en Terre Sainte (1470–1471)* (Paris, 1978).

[142] *Registrum Honoris de Morton* (Edinburgh, 1853), ii, no. 193, pp. 171–2; Roger Mason, 'Laicisation and the Law: The Reception of Humanism in Early Renaissance Scotland', in *A Palace in the Wild: Essays on Vernacular Culture and Humanism in Late Medieval and Renaissance Scotland*, ed. L. A. J. R. Houwen, A. A. MacDonald and S. L. Mapstone (Leuven, 2000), p. 9; David Sellar, 'Courtesy, Battle and the Brieve of Right, 1368 – A Story Continued', in *The Stair Society Miscellany II*, ed. David Sellar (Edinburgh, 1984), p. 10.

[143] NLS, Acc. 9253; Glenn, ed., *The Buke of the Law of Armys*; Jonathan A. Glenn, ed., *The Prose Works of Sir Gilbert Hay Volume III: The Buke of the Ordre of Knychthede and The Buke of the Governaunce of Princis* (Edinburgh, 1993).

William Cumming of Inverallochy, Marchmont Herald (and later Lyon King of Arms), had a range of manuscripts concerned with chivalric and heraldic subjects. For instance, he had in his library a manuscript of 173 folios compiled around 1494 by Adam Loutfut, Kintyre Pursuivant. In it is a mid-fifteenth-century Breton description of the rights of kings of arms and heralds and where they should walk when accompanying the king on official occasions; *The Gaige of Battaill* dealing with judicial duels; Loutfut's translation from French into Scots of the *Deidis of Armorie*, a heraldic history and bestiary; a short piece for heralds on how to cry largess; a treatise on the organisation of tournaments; three short texts describing the various ceremonial duties of heralds at tournament, in war, at feasts and at funerals; a treatise on the rules of battles; a short treatise on the origin of officers of arms; a Scots version of the late Middle English *Liber Armorum*; an extract from Nicholas Upton's *De Officio Militari*; a copy of a letter from Pope Pius II dealing with the place in society of officers of arms; a Scots version of William Caxton's *Book of the Ordre of Chyualry*; a treatise on the law of arms at judicial duels; a treatise on coronation rituals; a treatise on the relationship between war and crowns; two short notes on war; a translation of Vegetius's *De Re Militari*; a tract on preparations for battle; two different treatises on officers of arms; practical examples of the art of blazoning; a poem on heraldry; and a copy of Bartolus of Saxoferrato's *Tractatus de Insigniis et Armis*.[144] This manuscript was copied several times by subsequent officers of arms.[145] Cumming also had a French version of the *Book of the Order of Chivalry*.[146] Peter Thomson, Islay Herald from 1531, also had a copy of tournament rules attributed to Philip of France and an exposé of the arrangements for jousting at the marriage of Catherine of Aragon and Arthur, Prince of Wales in 1501.[147] Many of these treatises were essential for assistance in the heralds' role as organisers and participants in public and royal ceremonies. This might be to superintend the marshalling of public processions and funerals,[148] to make royal proclamations at ceremonial

---

[144] BL, MS Harley 6149.

[145] See Oxford, Queen's College, MS 161, *c*.1500; NLS, Adv. MS 31.5.3, of the first half of the sixteenth century, copied for John Scrymgeour of Mures, Master of the King's Works; NLS, Adv MS 31.3.20, from the later-sixteenth century, for David Lindsay of Rathillet; and an incomplete version at NLS, Adv MS 31.7.22, belonging to Peter Thomson, Islay Herald, dating to the first half of the sixteenth century. Houwen, ed., *Deidis of Armorie*, i, p. xxxi; Edington, *Court and Culture in Renaissance Scotland*, pp. 28–9.

[146] Houwen, ed., *Deidis of Armorie*, i, pp. xlvi–xlvii.

[147] NLS, Adv. MS 31.7.22, fols 3–34, 65–9.

[148] BL, MS Harley 6149, fols 46v–49; Paul, *Heraldry in Relation to Scottish History and Art*, pp. 90–1, 102–3. There is limited evidence for the role of heralds in funerals in medieval Scotland, although there is quite substantial evidence for this in England. Here we can assume there were parallels between the two kingdoms.

events[149] or to embody royal power in tabards of the king's arms.[150] At royal ceremonies it was the officers of arms' duty to cry largess and the Loutfut manuscript contains several folios outlining this, in order that 'herrauldis ande pursuewantis suld knaw quhen thair ar with princes and gret lordis how thair suld cry thar largesse the quhilkis ar cryit at gret festis.'[151]

From the end of the fourteenth century, Scottish heralds became increasingly important in the kingdom of Scotland, and in the fifteenth century they developed into a coherent and co-operative body of men capable of undertaking a variety of duties on behalf of the crown. The heralds of late medieval Scotland were invested with powers and responsibilities that gave them a prominent and significant role in the administration of the kingdom. Their remit was wide, but was principally concentrated on the collection of information related to the political, social and chivalric elites. This was then usefully deployed in a range of tasks including public ceremonial, domestic legal work and international diplomacy. The key phase in the development of the office of arms was the sixteenth century when Lyon King of Arms gradually took authority over all officers and was granted certain independence from the crown in matters of heraldic conduct. It was also during this century that heralds took a more active role in the monitoring of armorial bearings of the kingdom's nobility and, from 1587, became a recognised 'professional' body. Subsequent reduction in their power and jurisdiction, particularly in the nineteenth century, has limited scholars' understanding of the importance and diversity of the early heralds. Indeed, a great deal more research might be carried out on the late medieval officers of arms and, it is hoped, this essay has demonstrated that historians can no longer rely on the few works that have treated the subject to date.

---

[149] Grant, *Court of the Lord Lyon*, p. i; Paul, *Heraldry in Relation to Scottish History and Art*, p. 103.

[150] John Younge, Somerset Herald, 'The Fyancells of Margaret, Eldest Daughter of King Henry VIIth to James King of Scotland: Together with her Departure from England, Journey into Scotland, her Reception and Marriage There, and the Great Feasts Held on that Account', in *Joannis Leland Antiquarii de Rebus Britannicis Collectanea*, ed. Thomas Hearne (London, 1770), p. 293.

[151] BL, MS Harley 6149, fol. 42. For a description by the English herald Somerset of the crying of largess at Margaret Tudor's marriage celebrations see John Younge, Somerset Herald, 'The Fyancells of Margaret', p. 295. This manuscript can be found at London, College of Arms, MS 1st MS, 13, 76.

5

The March of Brittany and its Heralds in the Later Middle Ages

Michael Jones

WITNESSES AT AN INQUIRY in October 1455 to establish the vast panoply of 'droits royaux et anciens usages du pais de Bretagne', which its late medieval dukes claimed to exercise, were unanimous that among these was the right to appoint 'officiers royaux, scavoir Mareschal, Admiral, Grand-Maistre, Chancellier, President et Roy d'armes'.[1] The origins of most of these posts can be safely pushed back into the fourteenth century and those of marshal and chancellor to the early thirteenth century. That of *Grand-Maître de l'hôtel du duc* was much more recent, having apparently been created by an *ordonnance* in 1413,[2] while the first mention of a king of arms occurs a few years later when Bretagne *Roi d'armes* (Brittany King of Arms) was sent to Henry V of England in Normandy in October 1419.[3] Six months later Bretagne was similarly sent with two esquires to discuss with the lady of Belleville at Montaigu (on the border between Brittany and Poitou) issues arising from the infringement of a truce.[4] Thereafter it is possible to trace a continuous succession of kings

---

[1] Dom Pierre-Hyacinthe Morice, *Mémoires pour servir de preuves à l'histoire ecclésiastique et civile de Bretagne*, 3 vols (Paris, 1742–6), ii, cols 1651–68 at 1655, 1662 and 1666–7, of which the original is ADLA, E 59 no. 7; see Jean Kerhervé, 'Les enquêtes sur les droits "royaux et ducaux" de Bretagne aux XIV⁶ et XV⁶ siècles', in *Information et société en Occident à la fin du Moyen Âge* (Paris, 2004), pp. 405–25.

[2] Ex-Phillipps MS 18465, p. 33, eighteenth-century extracts by Dom Gui-Alexis Lobineau from lost originals (this manuscript is currently in the possession of the author). Jean Kerhervé, *L'État breton aux 14ᵉ et 15ᵉ siècles: les ducs, les hommes et l'argent* (Paris, 1987), i, pp. 223–69, for the structure and financing of the ducal household; for the Grand Maître, pp. 232–7.

[3] Ex-Phillipps MS 18465, p. 115.

[4] BnF, MS Français 8267, fol. 76r.

of arms in the duchy until well after its incorporation into the kingdom of France by the successive marriages of Duchess Anne to Charles VIII (1491) and Louis XII (1499).[5]

Given the patchy nature of records relating to the ducal household in Brittany in the fourteenth and fifteenth centuries, it is likely that Bretagne had exercised authority as a king of arms for a considerable period before he first appears in our sources. It was probably the same man, or a previous Bretagne, who made the anticlimactic announcement suspending the wager of battle between the dukes of Norfolk and Hereford at Coventry in September 1398, though the writer of the *Traison et mort de Richard II* simply calls him 'a herald of the duke of Brittany'.[6] There are, however, other indications that around 1400 heralds were still relatively uncommon at the Breton ducal court, as they were in several other French princely households. Although implied by the existence of individual kings of arms like Bretagne or Malo in the 1420s, a heraldic march of Brittany with a full hierarchy of officers of arms remains difficult to document with any precision for much of the late Middle Ages. It is, for example, only on the nomination of Bremor du Trellay as Malo *Roi d'armes* on 1 August 1463 that we get evidence of a formal appointment, and there is nothing in Breton sources to reveal the nature of the ceremony in which he took up office, even if it is probable that like other ducal councillors he took an oath.[7]

Although not mentioned when the college of French heralds was formed in 1407, a Breton march is occasionally alluded to in literary sources by the mid-fifteenth century.[8] For instance, Antoine de la Salle states Brittany was one of the twelve marches which originated from the break-up of the former *Marche des Poyers;*[9] and Gilles Le Bouvier, Berry Herald, more convincingly, given his professional interest, lists Brittany among six *Royautés d'armes* (the others were France, Berry and Touraine, Picardy, Champagne and Guyenne) and distinguishes it from its two neighbouring *duchiés d'armes*, Anjou and Normandy.[10] The celebrated but fictional chivalric challenge and subsequent jousts between a duke of Bourbon and a duke of Brittany recounted in King René of Anjou's near-contemporary *Livre des tournois*

---

[5]   Michael Jones, '*Malo et Bretagne*, rois d'armes de Bretagne', *Revue du Nord* 88 (2006), pp. 599–615.

[6]   Benjamin Williams, ed., *Chronique de la traison et mort de Richard II* (London, 1846), pp. 17–21.

[7]   ADLA, B 3, fol. 148r, with a salary of £240 p.a.

[8]   Cf. Gert Melville, 'Le Roy d'armes des François, dit Montjoye', in *Anthropologies juridiques: Mélanges Pierre Braun*, ed. J. Hoareau-Dodinau and P. Texier (Limoges, 1998), pp. 597–608.

[9]   Cf. Paul Adam-Even, 'Les fonctions militaires des hérauts d'armes', *Archives héraldiques suisses* 71 (1957), pp. 22–3, for these marches.

[10]   Anthony R. Wagner, *Heralds and Heraldry in the Middle Ages*, 2nd edn (Oxford, 1956), p. 54, citing Berry's Armorial.

also terms Brittany a march.[11] Most explicitly, a short treatise on *les marches d'armes du royaulme de France*, also written around 1450, is categorical on its location and relationship to other marches: 'Item, la marche de Bretaigne qui s'estend tout au long de la mer depuis la fin de la duchie de Normendie jusquez au pays de Xantongne, Et crie Malo hault Riche duc.'[12] Nor is it coincidental perhaps that financial evidence from around 1450 shows that the duke then employed twelve officers of arms, a number which some early authorities deemed the necessary complement for a march.[13]

Dukes Francis I (1442–50) and Peter II (1450–7), as will be seen in more detail below, were indeed deeply influenced by chivalric fashions, and may well have had an ideal march in mind as they increased their officers of arms to enhance the prestige and ceremonious nature of their court. However, if this was the case, other more powerful considerations soon led locally to the figure being exceeded, as most French princely courts grew in size over the course of the fifteenth century, even if on solemn occasions like the funeral of Francis II (1458–88) it was twelve officers who received mourning cloth, perhaps deliberately chosen to symbolise the march of Brittany.[14] Moreover, that duke, through his council, kept a close eye on armorial disputes amongst his *noblesse* and adjudicated on heraldic issues, practical evidence of the existence of an independent Breton march. In any event, it is in the context of the ducal court that most professional heralds in Brittany functioned from the late fourteenth to the early sixteenth century, although there were a few Breton heralds who served in noble households or were occasionally employed by towns. There were still others who wrote on heraldic or wider historical matters and cannot be attached to a particular household, though they will receive passing attention in this survey.[15]

---

[11] *Le Livre des tournois du Roi René (de la Bibliothèque nationale (ms. français 2695))* (Paris, 1986).

[12] BnF, MS Français 5930, fol. 31r, of which an early-sixteenth-century copy, Nouv. acq. fr., 1075, fols 36r–38v, also includes blazons for all eleven provincial kings of arms it places under the authority of Montjoye, that of Bretagne displaying ermines *semées*; cf. Melville, 'Le Roy d'armes des François', p. 602 and n. 64. For the ducal cry, see Michael Jones, '"Malo au riche duc?": Events at St-Malo in 1384 revisited', in *La ville médiévale en deçà et au-delà de ses murs: Mélanges Jean-Pierre Leguay*, ed. Philippe Lardin and Jean-Louis Roch (Rouen, 2000), pp. 229–42.

[13] Cf. Wagner, *Heralds and Heraldry*, p. 44.

[14] Morice, *Mémoires*, iii, cols 603–7.

[15] A Breton-speaking pursuivant, Toutseal, whose master remains unknown, was at the court of the duke of Austria in 1432–3. C. Schefer, ed., *Le voyage d'Outremer de Bertrandon de la Broquière* (Paris, 1892), p. 246.

Heralds in Ducal Employment

No BRETON HERALDS are known before the mid-fourteenth century, if we can dismiss Peter Heraud (or Heraut), a charter-witness on a couple of occasions around 1200, as an extremely precocious instance of a Breton herald: his surname is in all probability a family one, rather than indicating function (in one charter he is described as seneschal of Vitré).[16] A list of those who served in the household of John II (1286–1305), for instance, mentions his barber, huntsman, surgeon and launderer, even his fiddler (*vieille*) and Robert the fool, but no herald, only 'my messenger'.[17] In the later Middle Ages a *chevaucheur* or *messager* or *trompette* might receive formal promotion to the ranks of the Breton heralds, but this remained a rare event if surviving records are representative.[18]

The outbreak of the Breton Civil War (or War of Succession) in 1341, coinciding closely with more general conflict between England and France, certainly provided local stimulus for the use of heralds as messengers or intermediaries. In 1362 Derval Herald, probably employed by Sir Robert Knolles, de facto lord of Derval (Loire-Atlantique), was paid a surprisingly generous £16 for bringing a message to Edward III.[19] Chroniclers also occasionally refer to heralds anonymously at a siege or during last minute negotiations on the eve of a battle, especially in the last few years of warfare before the decisive battle of Auray on 29 September 1364. This saw the triumph of the English-supported John IV de Montfort over his French-supported rival Charles de Blois, who was killed on the field. Within just a few days, the chronicler Froissart learnt the result at Dover from a pursuivant, the future Windsor Herald, on his way to Edward III's court with the news.[20]

During the 1340s and 1350s, John IV was largely brought up in England, when Edward III was transforming court life, founding the Order of the Garter and building on a vast scale at Windsor, as well as establishing his military reputation. Despite this, during the first period of his rule as duke (1364–73), John IV does not appear to have made much use of heralds for either ceremonial or diplomatic purposes, nor were tournaments common

---

[16] Judith Everard and Michael Jones, eds, *The Charters of the Duchess Constance of Brittany and her Family, 1171–1221* (Woodbridge, 1999), nos. C59, Gu15n.

[17] Morice, *Mémoires*, i, cols 1188–90.

[18] The best documented case is that of Germain Gentilhomme, traceable between 1462 and *c*.1492. Michael Jones, 'Vers une prosopographie des hérauts bretons médiévaux: une enquête à poursuivre', *Académie des Inscriptions et Belles Lettres, Comptes rendus des séances de l'année 2001* (Paris, 2001), pp. 1399–1426 at 1419–20.

[19] TNA, E 101/393/11, fol. 70r.

[20] Cf. Jean Froissart, *Chroniques*, ed. Siméon Luce et al., 15 vols. (Paris, 1869–1975), vi, p. 173.

in the duchy. For example, the many exchanges that John had with Charles II of Navarre, then resident on his Norman estates, over the routiers who were plaguing much of north-western France in the late 1360s and early 1370s, were facilitated by a range of messengers, none of whom appear to have been heralds.[21] However, following the duke's flight once more into exile in England in April 1373, after the collapse of his government in the face of threatened French invasion, John appears to have begun tentatively to employ officers of arms. His secretary, Guillaume de Saint-André, writing a verse-life of his master in the mid-1380s, recounts that the still-surviving letter of defiance that John sent to Charles V of France in August 1373, whilst accompanying John of Gaunt on his long march from Calais to Bordeaux, was delivered by a herald.[22] Among the duke's company at the time of the earl of Buckingham's naval expedition in the autumn of 1377 there is mention of 'Richemond', probably a herald named after John's great English honour, returned to him by Edward III in 1372.[23] This name would recur when his grandson, Arthur de Richemont, constable of France (1425–58), also briefly held the ducal throne (1457–8).

It was following his return from exile in 1379 and peace with France agreed in the second treaty of Guérande (April 1381) that John IV began more deliberately to create the household, curial and state institutions that would give expression to those princely and regal rights that the inquiry of 1455 had set out to clarify, allowing the Montfort dynasty to enjoy a remarkable degree of independence until the days of Duchess Anne (1488–1514). These included regular taxation and a reformed monetary system, a *parlement* and *états* for judicial and political dealings with his subjects, a vastly improved bureaucracy and an enlarged chancery. Amongst developments symptomatic of the burgeoning ceremonious nature of the ducal court in this second period of John's rule (he died in 1399) is the appearance of two heralds (Montfort and Bretagne) who would eventually have successors in office. There was also the creation of the duke's own chivalric Order of the Ermine (1381), for which the Order of the Garter provided a partial model; John was the first foreign princely member of the Garter.[24]

[21] Michael Jones, 'Servir le duc: remarques sur le rôle des hérauts à la cour de Bretagne à la fin du Moyen Âge', in *À l'ombre du pouvoir: les entourages princiers au Moyen Âge*, ed. Alain Marchandisse and Jean-Louis Kupper (Geneva, 2003), pp. 245–65 at 246–7.

[22] Guillaume de Saint-André, *Le bon Jehan et le jeu des échecs, XIVᵉ siècle: chronique de l'État breton*, ed. Jean-Michel Cauneau and Dominique Philippe (Rennes, 2005), p. 348 ll. 1983–8; the letters of defiance survive: Michael Jones, ed., *Recueil des actes de Jean IV, duc de Bretagne*, 3 vols (Paris-Bannalec, 1980–2001), i, no. 225 and pl. ii.

[23] TNA, E 101/42/13 (October 1377).

[24] Michael Jones, 'Les signes du pouvoir. L'Ordre de l'Hermine, les devises et les hérauts des ducs de Bretagne au XVème siècle', *Mémoires de la Société d'histoire et d'archéologie de Bretagne* 68 (1991), pp. 141–73 (reprinted in Michael Jones, *Between France and England:*

As for heralds in a Breton context in these years, there is an adequate survival of evidence. One herald announced the second treaty of Guérande, though it is not clear who his master was.[25] More certainly, Froissart informs us of the sad death of Montfort at the hands of ignorant Flemish rebels in 1383, when the duke was campaigning in Flanders in the company of Charles VI and Philip, duke of Burgundy.[26] A few other brief references indicate further visits to the Low Countries by Breton heralds in these years,[27] and in 1394 Philip also rewarded a Breton herald at negotiations at Angers.[28] Bretagne's likely presence in England in 1398, where John IV had himself spent two months in the spring of that year, has been mentioned already. But although John IV also received foreign heralds at his own court, like the Portuguese Coimbra Herald, who was present at Nantes for a feast celebrating the duke's marriage in 1386 to his third wife, Joanna of Navarre,[29] he still only seems to have made occasional use of officers of arms. The close contacts renewed with the Navarrese court as a result of his last marriage and the obvious affection in which Joanna held her brother, Charles III of Navarre (1387–1425), for example, led to a lively exchange of regular messages and gifts for the rest of the couple's married life, but, just as in the first period of John's rule, it was largely accomplished through using messengers who were not formal officers of arms.[30]

As seems to be the case of some other great principalities, most notably Burgundy,[31] there was a rapid expansion of the employment of heralds in France in the early fifteenth century for a very wide range of business. Thus, although there is a gap after 1398 of twenty years before Bretagne is met again, and one of almost fifty years before a second Montfort occurs, these then became permanently filled offices of the Breton heraldic establishment for the remainder of the ducal period. It is particularly during the middle years of the reign of John V (1399–1442) that their numbers

Politics, Power and Society in Late Medieval Brittany (Aldershot and Burlington, 2003), ch. XII), at pp. 144–59 for the Ermine.

[25]   Morice, *Mémoires*, ii, col. 356.

[26]   Froissart, *Chroniques*, xi, pp. 104–5.

[27]   Information supplied by Dr Torsten Hiltmann, drawing on materials being collected for the Heraudica Burgundica website, and to whom I am grateful for several other references used in this paper.

[28]   AD Côte-d'Or, B 1501, fol. 70r.

[29]   Froissart, *Chroniques*, xiii, pp. 34–5.

[30]   Juan Ramon Castro, ed., *Catálogo del archivo general de Navarra: catálogo de la seccion de comptos*, vols. xv–xxii (Pamplona, 1956–8), passim. For Navarrese heralds at this period see María Narbona Cárceles, 'L'origine de l'office d'armes en Navarre (fin XIVᵉ – début XVᵉ siècle): étude prosopographique', *Revue du Nord* 88 (2006), pp. 631–49.

[31]   Cf. Bertrand Schnerb, 'Rois d'armes, hérauts et poursuivants à la cour de Bourgogne sous Philippe le Hardi et Jean sans Peur (1363–1419)', *Revue du Nord* 88 (2006), pp. 529–57.

increased markedly and continuity in office became much more customary. In 1418–19, for instance, three posts appear in financial records whose holders were usually replaced until the duchy lost its independence: Brest Pursuivant, Malo Herald (later King of Arms) and Ermine Herald.[32] Although a formal connection of this latter herald with the ducal chivalric order of the same name has not been successfully documented, it may well be that John V, knowing of Henry V's revised statutes for the Order of the Garter (1417),[33] with the nomination of its own king of arms, Garter, followed suit by appointing Ermine to a similar role in his own order. A few years later several other pursuivants and heralds are found, such as A ma vie, Auray, Dinan, Nantes, Rennes and Vannes, offices of which all would be held by more than one man. There is the possibility that A ma vie also had a specific role in ceremonies relating to the Ermine, since this was the motto John IV had adopted for the collar of the Order. It also occurred as his personal device, for example on his signet.[34] Later dukes would continue to use the motto liberally to proclaim ducal patronage, especially in an architectural context,[35] or to indicate ownership.[36]

There were also other officers of arms whose careers were ephemeral, like the pursuivants Dauferais, Gabriel and Oliffant under John V, or Grivyne, Saint-Aubin and Sanglier during the three short reigns of his successors, Francis I, Peter II and Arthur III. Some of them may, of course, have been promoted on the death of other heralds to the more permanent posts; there is evidence for some movement, as in the case of Dinan 'a present nommé Rennes' (1450–7).[37] Others like Sanglier had earlier served a ducal cadet before promotion to ducal service. By the latter years of John V's reign, the numbers of officers of arms and the emerging hierarchy (whether measured by title, length of service or rates of pay) were usually six or eight heralds and pursuivants under one king of arms. In the days of his immediate successors this increased, as already noted, to around a dozen. Most of the offices in existence by 1450 then had a continuous history for the rest of the ducal period, and some of them for several decades thereafter. However,

---

[32] Cf. Jones, 'Vers une prosopographie des hérauts bretons médiévaux', pp. 1424–6, appendix, for a summary list giving first mention and length of service of individual Breton heralds; some details are amended in what follows in the light of new information.

[33] Cf. Hugh E. L. Collins, *The Order of the Garter 1348–1461: Chivalry and Politics in Late Medieval England* (Oxford, 2000), pp. 31–2.

[34] Cf. Jones, ed., *Recueil des actes de Jean IV*, i, p. 44.

[35] Among many examples, ornamental friezes depicting natural ermines wearing a cape inscribed *A ma vie* are prominent, for example, at Quimper cathedral or at Le Folgoët, Finistère.

[36] Jones, 'Les signes du pouvoir', pp. 149–50, 152.

[37] ADLA, B, parchemins [non inventoriés], of which I have produced a typescript find-list in conjunction with Mme Marie-Christine Rémy, Conservatrice, ADLA.

by the 1540s only Bretagne remained of the offices established under the Montfort dynasty. In all, more than forty such offices had at least a temporary existence in the ducal period.[38]

Among reasons for the expansion of numbers witnessed in Brittany from around 1418 – apart from princely emulation or the better survival of records – are the heightened military tension that followed Henry V's conquest of Normandy and the subsequent English campaigns to subjugate Maine, Anjou and Touraine, which may have been a significant local factor. Much of the evidence from the 1420s and 1430s for the activities of Breton officers of arms shows them playing an important role both as diplomatic envoys or in carrying messages that had a military connotation, as the duke of Brittany and his council strove desperately to avoid being sucked into the wider Anglo-French conflict and to preserve Brittany's freedom for manoeuvre. The case of A ma vie, whose career can easily be traced for most of the period 1425–35, can serve as archetypal, though the same pattern is replicated by most of his colleagues in these years.[39]

In 1425 A ma vie was sent from the town of Rennes into Normandy 'pour enquerir en laquelle partie ilz [les Anglais] vouloint comme pour ce que estoint assemblez une tres grousse compaignie'. He repeated the mission in 1426 'pour ce que l'en disoit que les Anglois veulent courir en cestz parties' and again early in 1427 when he was sent 'oïr nouvelles des Angloys', defence of the north-eastern frontier of the duchy being a prime concern.[40] Later that year he was sent to the duke of Bedford, following up this mission with an urgent journey to persuade Lord Scales to stop English pillaging of the duchy because of the failure of the ladies of Vitré and Laval to swear a truce.[41] If anything, 1428 was an even busier year for him, with three further missions to 'France' or Paris, twice specifically to the duke of Bedford, whom he again visited in Paris in April 1429, and again in September when he went to explain why John V had failed to pay an instalment to Bedford of the ransom of the duke of Alençon for which he was obliged, before going on to the Burgundian court.[42]

A gap in the evidence means that what he did in 1430 is unknown, but in 1431–2 the pattern is much the same as before. In May 1431 A ma vie was

---

[38] Jones, 'Servir le duc', pp. 252–3; Jones, 'Vers une prosopographie des hérauts bretons médiévaux', pp. 1424–6; Jones, 'Malo et Bretagne', pp. 613–14.

[39] Cf. Jones, 'Servir le duc', pp. 258–9.

[40] AM Rennes, CC 796, fol. 13, 797.2, fol. 56v and 799, fol. 44v, references I owe to the generosity of Mme Laurence Moal; cf. also BnF, MS Français 8267, fol. 136, for a reference to A ma vie being sent to Normandy *c.* 10 February 1427.

[41] Ibid., fols 137, 138 and 149; René Blanchard, ed., *Lettres et mandements de Jean V, duc de Bretagne*, 5 vols (Nantes, 1889–95), iii, no. 1797.

[42] BnF, MS Français 8267, fols 137, 138, 144, 145.

once more sent to communicate with Bedford, the earl of Warwick and the council of the king of England in both Rouen and Paris, before returning again to Rouen in October 1431 to meet Henry VI. In the previous June he went with the Chancellor of Brittany (Jean de Malestroit, bishop of Nantes), Jean Pregent and Alain Coaynon on embassy 'devers le Roy [de France] et le sire de Tremoille a Amboyze'.[43] There was also another mission to Burgundy in October 1432,[44] while in 1433–4 he made at least two journeys to England to visit Gilles, John V's youngest son, who was being educated with the adolescent Henry VI, as well as further missions to Bedford in Paris.[45] Naturally he was also present with the many others heralds, including at least five Breton colleagues (Malo King of Arms, Ermine Herald and the pursuivants Montfort, Chastelaillon and Parthenay, the two last in the service of Constable Richemont), who attended the Congress of Arras in August and September 1435, undoubtedly the greatest single congregation of European officers of arms of the century.[46]

Evidence for the activities of Breton heralds post-Arras is much more patchy. Nothing is known about Brest between 1435 and 1454; there is a single reference to Auray between 1436 and 1462; Cornouaille occurs in 1432 and not again until 1449; for Nantes the gap is between 1433 and the 1450s; the same is true for Rennes; there is a void for Dinan between 1436 and the 1450s, a single reference to Ermine and Montfort in the 1440s, and so on.[47] On the other hand, both Francis I and Peter II appointed additional pursuivants and heralds, some lasting probably only for a single lifetime such as Benon, active between 1451 and *c.* 1470,[48] and Saint-Aubin, documented between 1445 and 1457 at the latest,[49] but others destined to have successors.

Among those with longer histories was Espy, almost certainly named by Francis I when he created a second ducal order of chivalry, that of the

---

[43] BnF, MS Français 11542, fols 12 and 14; Blanchard, ed., *Lettres et mandements de Jean V*, iv, no. 1970.

[44] ADN, B 1845, fol. 147v.

[45] Ex-Phillipps MS 18465, pp. 51, 65 and 71.

[46] Philippe Contamine, 'Aperçus nouveaux sur *Toison d'or*, chroniqueur de la paix d'Arras (1435)', *Revue du Nord* 88 (2006), pp. 577–96 at pp. 591–6.

[47] Evidence drawn from fragmentary accounts, especially ADLA, B, parchemins and FL, for which see Michael Jones, *Catalogue sommaire des archives du Fonds Lebreton, Abbaye Saint-Guénolé, Landévennec* (Nottingham, 1998), pp. 77–91.

[48] Morice, *Mémoires*, ii, cols 1605 (1451–2), 1685 (1454–5); ADLA, B, parchemins (1467–70); Landévennec, FL 4A/118 no. 7 (1467–8).

[49] Morice, *Mémoires*, ii, 1395 for 'Saint-Aubin nouveau poursuivant [...] pour luy aider a faire un esmail des armes du duc' (1445); ADLA, B, parchemins (1450–7), when he received £14 18s. 10d. as wages with a note: 'Il lui est passé par ceste foiz neantmoins qu'il n'estoit es ordonnances pource que Lorens Droillart [a prominent clerk of accounts from 1454 to 1478] a juré qu'il est paié et doit il rent quittance.'

Épi (ear of corn), to rival the Ermine, *c.* 1447.[50] Its history is very opaque: Christian de Mérindol has argued most forcibly for its separate existence.[51] My own view is that whatever Francis I intended (and he certainly named at least two members of the Épi and there were indeed two separate collars), later dukes largely re-amalgamated the two orders.[52] This fusion is witnessed most visibly in the evolving form of the ducal collar under Francis II. It combined both ears of corn and ermines, not to mention florid displays of the ducal arms and the addition of yet another ducal device, *La Cordelière*. This alludes to the knotted belt of St Francis, after whom two dukes were named, and was apparently first used by Francis I but more widely adopted by Francis II around 1470. In turn Duchess Anne was to exploit this later when she became queen, possibly establishing it as the emblem of a further evanescent chivalric order.[53]

Nevertheless, most references to the ducal order after Francis I's reign are in the singular, 'order' not 'orders', and it seems likely that the various devices which were used to confer or signify membership of the ducal order (whether collars of the Épi or Ermine or Cord) were intended by the latter half of the century to distinguish different categories of membership.[54] Indeed, Breton dukes always took an eclectic attitude to this with men and women, civilians and soldiers, Bretons and non-Bretons all eligible for nomination, though it was again Francis I and Peter II who did most to replenish the ranks of members.[55] Perhaps, as in some other chivalric orders, marks of distinction were granted for notable military service or as a token of crusading activity.[56] So in the case of the Breton ducal order, visible

[50]   Unfortunately the earliest financial evidence for Espy as a pursuivant can only be dated 1442 x 1450, when he received a payment of £20 ADLA, B, parchemins.

[51]   Christian de Mérindol, 'Le Collier de l'Épi, en Bretagne d'après des documents inédits conservés à Besançon (fonds Chifflet)', *Revue française d'héraldique et de sigillographie* 66 (1996), pp. 67–81.

[52]   As first argued in Jones, 'Les signes du pouvoir', pp. 153–5; for a very rare later reference to *l'Ordre d'Espiz* in 1505 see AM Rennes, AA 20, article 7, edited in Michael Jones, 'The Rituals and Significance of Ducal Civic Entries in Late Medieval Brittany', *Journal of Medieval History* 29 (2003), p. 303.

[53]   Laurent Hablot, 'Pour en finir (ou pour commencer!) avec l'ordre de la Cordelière', in *Pour en finir avec Anne de Bretagne? Actes de la journée d'étude organisée aux Archives départementales de la Loire-Atlantique, le 25 mai 2002* (Nantes, 2003), pp. 47–70 (for discussion of l'Épi see pp. 65–6).

[54]   A position which M. Hablot cautiously reinforces.

[55]   Jones, 'Les signes du pouvoir', pp. 172–3 lists all the known members of the ducal order(s).

[56]   Peter S. Lewis, 'Une devise de chevalerie inconnue, créée par un comte de Foix?', *Annales de Midi* 66 (1964), pp. 77–84 (reprinted in his *Essays in Late Medieval French History* (London, 1985), pp. 29–36); M. G. A. Vale, 'A Fourteenth-Century Order of Chivalry: The "Tiercelet"', *English Historical Review* 82 (1967), pp. 332–41.

following his capture at Agincourt, he led, as Jean Kerhervé has aptly put it, 'une existence en perpetuel mouvement', largely in the service of the kings of France, Charles VI and Charles VII, though he advised his brother on military reforms some twenty years before he was able to execute similar ones in the kingdom and paid frequent return visits to his native duchy.[70] Unfortunately, as in the case of the ducal household, only the barest fragments of once extensive financial accounts survive to document his actions. References to his officers of arms are very fugitive, although what survives also reveals his extensive use of other messengers, issuing a constant stream of orders, and casting light on the important public and private matters that concerned him.[71]

Specifically, the earliest mention so far discovered is to an otherwise anonymous herald of Arthur who was paid 10 écus by the duke of Orléans on 23 December 1412.[72] In 1435 his pursuivant Parthenay (named after his main place of residence for much of his life) was at Arras, later taking news of the treaty to Compiègne along with Feu Grégois, a pursuivant of the duke of Bourbon.[73] Parthenay can also be traced in subsequent years, going to Montlhéry in 1436 or to the Burgundian court in 1438, though there is then a gap until he occurs in accounts of 1457–8.[74] Another pursuivant who served Arthur as constable and then as duke was Sanglier, noted at the Burgundian court in 1440, then again in the 1457–8 accounts.[75] He may well have been officer of arms to the constable's own dimly perceived chivalric order for which his councillor and chamberlain, Guillaume de Vendel, received 120 écus 'pour faire ung collier de l'ordre de mondit seigneur' in June 1444,[76] while it is known that Arthur adopted the boar as one of his personal devices.[77]

Two other pursuivants who have only left a single trace in surviving accounts are Chemillé in the constable's service in 1436 and Vouvant who went from

---

[70]   Jean Kerhervé, 'Une existence en perpetuel mouvement. Arthur de Richemont, connétable de France et duc de Bretagne (1393–1458)', in *Viajeros, peregrinos, mercaderes en el occidente medieval, XVIII semana de estudios medievales* (Estella, 1991), pp. 94–114.

[71]   Michael Jones, 'Sur les pas du Connétable de Richemont: quelques sources financières inédites', in *Le prince, l'argent, les hommes au Moyen Âge: Mélanges offerts à Jean Kerhervé*, ed. Jean-Christophe Cassard, Yves Coativy, Alain Gallicé and Dominique Le Page (Rennes, 2008), pp. 271–81.

[72]   Cosneau, *Le connétable de Richemont*, p. 481.

[73]   BnF, MS Picardie 20, fol. 167r; ADN, B 1954, fol. 88v.

[74]   Guillaume Gruel, *Chronique d'Arthur de Richemont, Connétable de France, duc de Bretagne (1393–1458)*, ed. Achille Le Vavasseur (Paris, 1890), p. 120 (1436); ADN, B 1963, fol. 189r (1438); AD Ille-et-Vilaine, 1 F 1116, no. 16 (1458).

[75]   ADN, B 1969, fol. 259r (1440); Morice, *Mémoires*, ii, col. 1726 (1457–8).

[76]   Cosneau, *Le connétable de Richemont*, p. 657.

[77]   Cf. J. B. de Vaivre, 'Une enseigne du XVᵉ siècle: l'étendard du connétable de Richemont', *Archivum Heraldicum* 1/2 (1979), 10–17.

Saumur to Parthenay and back, taking letters to Jeanne d'Albret, Arthur's second wife, in October 1443.[78] The officer who has left most evidence and can be traced over the longest period in the constable's service was his pursuivant Qui que le vueille: first encountered on a mission to the dukes of Burgundy and Bedford in 1423; noted as coming from Brittany to Parthenay in October 1431 'pour le fait de certains choses qui grandement nous touchoint'; going on another (undated) mission to Burgundy; rewarded by Peter II in July 1455; and mentioned in the accounts of 1457–8, probably towards the end of a career of more than thirty years in Arthur's service.[79]

Another younger brother of John V and Arthur, Richard de Bretagne, count of Étampes (d. 1439) employed Comme(nt) qu'il soit Pursuivant for more than a decade, since he is noted in Richard's service in 1419, attended the coronation of Charles VII at Reims in July 1429, and was sent with Montfort to Craon to fetch the royal captain, Ambroise de Loré, to serve John V at Châteaubriant during one of the many alarms about threatened invasion of the duchy in the early 1430s.[80] Ainsi le vueil, pursuivant of the future Peter II, went in August 1431 to Henry VI at Rouen 'et de la au siege de Louviers devers les seigneurs estant audit siege leur porter lectres touchant la course que les Angloys d'Avranches avoient faicte davant Saint Mallou et u pays de Poulet' with demands for reparation,[81] while Passe Oultre, pursuivant of Tanguy, bastard of Brittany, was twice despatched to Mont-Saint-Michel in 1434, probably because of similar concerns about the security of north-eastern Brittany.[82] Sans Faillir Pursuivant made at least two journeys to England in 1432 and 1433 to ascertain the well-being of his master, Gilles de Bretagne, accompanying Sir Thomas Cusac, Jean Pregent and A ma vie on the latter occasion and taking, among other things, a present of greyhounds (*levriers*) from John V to his son.[83] Gilles is also the only ducal cadet, apart from the constable, who appears to have later had a herald as opposed to a pursuivant, Châteaubriant Herald, reflecting perhaps the wealth and status that came from his betrothal to the heiress of that great lordship, Françoise de Dinan. He was sent to negotiate with the English in Normandy in March 1445 shortly before Gilles's arrest and

[78] Landévennec, FL, 4A/66 (1436), for Chemillé; BnF, MSS Duchesne 70, fol. 113v, and Français 20684, p. 219, extracts from the lost accounts of Raoul de Launay, treasurer of the Constable (cf. Cosneau, *Le connétable de Richemont*, p. 658) for Vouvant.

[79] Morice, *Mémoires*, ii, col. 1194 (1423); AD Ille-et-Vilaine, 1 F 1116 (1431); BnF, MS Français 22331, p. 19, no. 100 (undated); Morice, *Mémoires*, ii, cols 1687 (1455) and 1726 (1457–8).

[80] Ex-Phillipps MS 18465, p. 115 (1419); BnF, MSS Français 8267, fol. 142 (1429), and Français 11541, fol. 27, no. 342 (1432).

[81] BnF, MS Français 11541, fol. 12, no. 115, and fol. 14, no. 138.

[82] Ex-Phillipps MS 18465, p. 67.

[83] BnF, MS Français 11541, fol. 19, no. 214, and fol. 22, no. 271.

imprisonment for alleged treasonous activities.[84] His murder in 1450, the accession of Peter II in the same year and that of Arthur in 1457, with their pursuivants being incorporated into the ducal establishment, left no officers of arms in the employ of cadets of the Montfort family for the rest of the ducal period, if our meagre records can be trusted.

Heralds in Noble and Other Service

IT SHOULD NOT SURPRISE US that it was the constable of France, Bertrand du Guesclin (d. 1380), who provides the earliest evidence for the use of heralds by Breton nobles. Cuvelier's *Chanson de geste* on the life of Bertrand makes many allusions to his heralds in various contexts (usually military), for instance, summoning troops for the expedition to Spain in 1365, warning of the arrival of the enemy, meeting with the herald of Sir Thomas Granson before the battle of Pontvallain (December 1370) and so on.[85] Philip the Bold, duke of Burgundy, gave 10 francs to Claisquin (one of the many different forms of the constable's family name) after he had fought before him with another knight dressed as savages in February 1371, and a herald of the constable received 2 francs from Philip in August 1378.[86] These may be references to Gilles Merlot, who after the constable's death, became Champagne King of Arms and was one of the founders of the French heralds' college, by which time he was king of arms of the French.[87] Of course, the possibility exists that the constable, given his multifarious military responsibilities, constant despatch of messengers and energetically peripatetic lifestyle, required more than one officer of arms in his service.[88] A rare, enamelled copper messenger-box bearing the arms of Du Guesclin survives in the Musée Dobrée at Nantes that has been dated to the constable's lifetime.[89] Perhaps it was used for the delivery of letters such as

[84]   Morice, *Mémoires*, ii, col. 1374. Abbé A. Bourdeaut, 'Gilles de Bretagne: entre la France et l'Angleterre, les causes et les auteurs du drame', *Mémoires de la Société d'histoire et d'archéologie de Bretagne* 1 (1920), pp. 53–145, is still the fullest reliable account of his tragic life.
[85]   Cuvelier, *La chanson de Bertrand du Guesclin*, ed. Jean-Claude Faucon, 3 vols (Toulouse, 1990), i, lines 8146–7, 18032, 19344 et seq., 20969–70; and specifically for his herald Glaiequin, 19383–4.
[86]   AD Côte-d'Or, B 319, fol. 12v (1371), and B 1454, fol. 76 (1378), a reference I owe to the kindness of Dr Carol Chattaway.
[87]   Melville, 'Le Roy d'armes des François', p. 597 (although the connection with Du Guesclin is not made).
[88]   Cf. Michael Jones, ed., *Letters, Orders and Musters of Bertrand du Guesclin, 1357–1380* (Woodbridge, 2004), Subject Index, 'Heralds'.
[89]   Reproduced ibid., Frontispiece; some doubts have been raised as to its authenticity (cf. Jones, 'Vers une prosopographie des hérauts bretons médiévaux', p. 1404 n. 24) but similar small boxes of the period have been found like that bearing the arms of Jean san Peur, now in the Musée Cluny, Paris (also exhibited recently in Dijon and Cleveland: *L'art à la cour de*

those from Louis, duke of Anjou, brought to him at St-Malo by his herald on 10 August 1379.[90]

Among the constable's closest companions, and one of the leading Breton captains of his day, Olivier de Mauny also employed a herald; in October 1371 he was despatched to inform the inhabitants of Périgueux that Mauny was prepared to put himself at their disposal for mopping-up operations after the reconquest of lands from the English.[91] A few years later, in 1378, on a more peaceful note, Rohan Pursuivant carried news of the birth of a son to his master, Jean I, vicomte de Rohan and his wife, Jeanne de Navarre, to the latter's brother, Charles II of Navarre, at Pamplona.[92] One of the leading Breton noble families, the Rohans continued to employ a herald in the fifteenth century, as did some of their main rivals, the counts of Laval (whose chief Breton lordship was that of Vitré), the lords of Rieux and Rays. References to them are few and widely scattered so that it is impossible to say whether there was continuity over several generations, though this might be expected in the case of the richest and most ambitious families, especially those aspiring to be ranked among the Nine Ancient Barons of Brittany, a chivalric conceit most notably encouraged by Peter II.[93]

Brittany does not seem to have been plagued by the rash of ill-trained pursuivants employed by parvenu nobles about whom unfavourable comment was occasionally made in the mid-fifteenth century. Most were employed by masters who had important military careers and came from old noble families: a pursuivant of Marshal Pierre de Rieux, for instance, announced the capture of Fécamp at Compiègne on 4 January 1436,[94] another named Donges (after one of Jean IV de Rieux's main lordships) was rewarded 'pour

Bourgogne: le mécénat de Philippe le Hardi et de Jean sans Peur (1364–1419) (Paris, 2005), p. 84 no. 25, noting that at Nantes and two others in Clermont-Ferrand and the Musée Cluny). On 28 July 1374 Philip the Bold paid Jehan de Salins, a foot messenger, £4 10s. 'pour paier une boette de messagier armoée des armes de Mgr' (AD Côte-d'Or, B 1441, fol. 59v) and on 10 November 1374 four francs 'pour une boette armoie des armes de Mgr. qu'il a fait faire pour son office' was paid to Vion, another foot messenger (B 1444, fol. 69v). Similar Breton evidence only occurs a century later: e.g. payment of £6 to Alain Maillart, goldsmith, for 'trois bouestes d'argent pour chevaucheurs d'escurie, deux esmaulx pour poursuivans, lesquelx il a faiz et baillez pour baillez a certains messagiers'. ADLA, B, parchemins, March 1483.

[90] Jones, ed., *Letters, Orders and Musters of Bertrand du Guesclin*, no. 866.

[91] Périgueux, Archives communales, CC 66, fol. 6v; for his relations with Du Guesclin see Jones, ed., *Letters, Orders and Musters of Bertrand du Guesclin*, passim.

[92] Archivo general de Navarra, Comptos, caj. 35 no. 73, a reference I owe to the kindness of Mme Béatrice Leroy.

[93] Arthur de La Borderie, *Étude historique sur les Neuf Barons de Bretagne* (Rennes, 1895), first examined this theme, but it deserves a detailed modern treatment; the earliest archival reference appears to be in a case concerning Jean II, sire de Rieux in 1405. BnF, Collection de Bourgogne 73, fol. 44, extracts by Baluze from registers of the Parlement de Paris.

[94] Cosneau, *Le connétable de Richemont*, p. 569 n. 3.

nous avoir apporté nouvelles de la descente des Anglois et pour luy aider a avoir ung cheval' *c.* 1488–90.[95] Louys, pursuivant of Gilles, lord of La Hunaudaye is mentioned around the same date.[96]

Gilles de Rays, also a marshal of France and companion of Joan of Arc, before his sad fall from grace, employed a herald called Ray in 1430, whose name, unusually, is also known: Jean de Monteclaie.[97] In 1437 Gilles also had a pursuivant called Princzay, named after one of his castles, though he comes to notice for the 'diligences qu'il fit devers son maistre pour lesdits acquests', that is, for helping John V take advantage of Gilles's growing need for ready cash to fund his prodigal lifestyle by acquiring at very advantageous prices, large chunks of the lordship of Rays.[98] Among other seigneurial heralds performing more honourable peaceful duties, is Gavre carrying a message from the countess of Laval to her husband then at Vannes in August 1440, and Rohan Pursuivant bringing the gift of a boar to Peter II in 1454–5.[99] The Breton admiral of France, Jean de Montauban (d. 1466), seems to have had a herald called Oraille-pelue who was commissioned with Messire Guillaume de Vendel to restore arms placed in the churches of Plessis-Giffart and Boismalon that had been torn down in a dispute over pre-eminences.[100] This was the right of noble families to display their heraldic achievements and to enjoy a range of practical advantages in churches of which they were patrons, a matter which gave rise to frequent dispute and often finished with orders to appear before the ducal council.[101]

Did Breton ecclesiastics have officers of arms? The great Swiss heraldist Paul Adam-Even states unambiguously: 'Les évêques bretons avaient également leurs hérauts', with a note: 'Sûrement : l'év. de Nantes – Morice, *Hist. Bret,* I, p. XXI'.[102] This refers to prefatory remarks made by Dom Morice in 1742, when discussing the rights and privileges of the bishops of Brittany, specifically in the case of Nantes that whenever the duke summoned his

[95] Landévennec, FL, 4B/133, no. 3.

[96] Arthur de La Borderie, ed., *Le Complot breton de M.CCCC.XCII* (Nantes, 1884), p. 92.

[97] BnF, MS Clairambault 902, p. 183.

[98] Morice, *Mémoires,* ii, col. 1270 and cf. Blanchard, ed., *Lettres et mandements de Jean V,* v, no. 2273. For the downfall of Gilles de Rays and the acquisition of his lands by Jean V, see Kerhervé, *L'État breton,* i, 59–60 and more fully in Abbé A. Bourdeaut, 'Champtocé, Gilles de Rays et les ducs de Bretagne', *Mémoires de la Société d'histoire et d'archéologie de Bretagne* 5 (1924), 41–150.

[99] Landévennec, FL, 4A/74 (Gavre); Morice, *Mémoires,* ii, col. 1686 (Rohan).

[100] *Notice des archives de Monsieur le Marquis du Hallay-Coetquen* (Paris, 1851), p. 41, Pièces diverses, L 2 (undated); these archives were unfortunately lost in the First World War.

[101] Michel Nassiet, 'Signes de parenté, signes de seigneurie: un système idéologique (XVᵉ–XVIᵉ siècle)', *Mémoires de la Société d'histoire et d'archéologie de Bretagne* 68 (1991), pp. 175–232 is the best introduction; at pp. 231–2 he lists many specific disputes.

[102] Adam-Even, 'Les fonctions militaires', 22.

host,' Il envoyoit ensuite avertir l'Evêque du jour & du lieu de l'assemblée; & quand le moment étoit venu, les Héraults du Duc & ceux de l'Evêque faisoient marcher les hommes de leurs dépendances', with those of the bishop marching under their own banner.[103] Although the Breton feudal host continued to be summoned as late as the fifteenth century and there is evidence that ducal officers of arms were occasionally involved in transmitting orders for the summons, even taking musters, the placing of Morice's remarks immediately after discussing Henry II's and Duke Geoffrey Plantagenet's relations with the bishop of Nantes, suggests he was referring to an earlier period for which, as we have seen there is no specific evidence of heraldic activity in Brittany. Unfortunately, nothing seen during the preparation of this essay throws additional light on this intriguing possibility.

More certainly, although once more the limitations of the evidence must be stressed, since only two towns (Rennes and Nantes) have left anything like substantial financial records for the fifteenth century, the employment of heralds and pursuivants by town councils, alongside other messengers and, in the case of Rennes, a succession of *trompettes*, can be noted.[104] In 1425, for instance, the council despatched Jean Aubret and Jean Perrot to Avranches and Lower Normandy 'pour savoir des nouvelles des Anglais et se il estoit vroy si celle armée et assamblée se fessoit telles comme l'en avoit rapporté par un poursuivant qui estoit eschapé des Englais', while in the following year it was a pursuivant that Rennes sent to Antrain, Saint-James de Beuvron and Avranches 'pour avoir des nouvelles'.[105] In 1443 Nantes paid a shilling to an unidentified ducal pursuivant 'qui fut par deux fois de Nantes a Chasteaubrient, devers monsieur dudit lieu, pour savoir et s'enqerir des nouvelles des Anglois, estant a Pouencé et en rapporter response',[106] while the town of Fougères was happy to contribute to the expenses of 'certains poursuyvans quelx estoint venuz depar le duc et son conseill' with 'secret news' in 1488.[107] In 1487 Guingamp had sent 'Guingamp le poursuivant l'un desd. bourgeois' with letters to Francis II, and in 1488 during a French invasion of the duchy, he was playing an important part in arranging terms for his fellow townsmen when he was seized by Jacques le Moine, *Grant escuier de Bretaigne*, who removed his 'esmail' and confiscated the letters and safe-conducts he was carrying before leaving town without informing the burgesses where he was going 'dont nous suymes grandement desplaiss[e]tz'.[108]

---

[103] Morice, *Mémoires*, i, p. xxi.
[104] AM Rennes, BB 36 and 41 for many individual orders and quittances relating to the town's *trompettes* and *messagers*.
[105] AM Rennes, CC 796, fol. 7v, and 797.1, fol. 19v.
[106] AM Nantes, CC 88.
[107] AM Fougères, CC 4, no. 5, fol. 3v.
[108] AM Guingamp, AA 3, no. 43 and AA 7, Livre rouge, no. 8

Both Rennes and Nantes between 1488 and 1491 made several payments to Breton, French and even Imperial heralds and pursuivants (Duchess Anne was married by proxy to Maximilian, king of the Romans in 1489) acting as intermediaries or proclaiming peace between the duchy and kingdom.[109] This was sealed by the marriage of Anne to Charles VIII in December 1491, followed by the king's ceremonial entry into Brittany when Nantes gave 10 écus d'or, £42 10s. Breton, 'A Montjoye, roy des heraulx de France, pour son droit pour la venue du Roy notre sire'.[110] With Anne thereafter usually absent from the duchy, living mainly at Blois or Amboise, the number of Breton heralds that she regularly used declined to five or six,[111] though some of them still occur in urban records after her death in 1514,[112] maintaining contacts between the royal court and the *bonnes villes* of the duchy.

Professional Activities

BESIDES A PREPONDERANCE OF EVIDENCE relating to military and diplomatic activities, some Breton heralds during the ducal period have left traces in literary and historical remains, although the writers remain unidentified. There is, however, only one significant heraldic treatise of Breton origin, the *Argentaye Tract*, so called because its first known owner was Jean Guillemet, sire de l'Argentaye (Côtes-d'Armor) who lived in the late sixteenth century.[113] There is the possibility that it was written by one of his ancestors, a Breton gentleman or herald with a smattering of civil and canon law,[114] familiar with Ramon Lull's *Ordre de chevalerie* and Jacques de Longuyon's poem on the Nine Worthies, as well as more recent technical treatises such as Prinsault's tracts, composed *c.* 1466–7, possibly Sicily Herald's treatise *c.* 1434–7 and the *Blason des couleurs* of *c.* 1457. He also makes use of Bartolus via Honoré Bouvet's *L'Arbre des batailles* and of the *Songe du*

---

[109] AM Rennes, AA 3, 21 and 42; AM Nantes, CC 103 and 265.
[110] AM Nantes, CC 103.
[111] In 1496–8 she was using five pursuivants: Étampes, Fougères, Plaisance, Hennebont and Vannes.
[112] Manuscripts of the *Commemoracion* generally show three Breton heralds keeping watch over the queen's body; accounts of her funerals shows that these were Bretagne, Hennebont and Vannes.
[113] Alan Manning, *The Argentaye Tract, edited from Paris, BN, Fonds français 11,464* (Toronto, Buffalo and London, 1983), pp. 20–1, for discussion of the probable author; its first possessor performed homage in succession to his father, Guillaume, for L'Argentaye en Quessoy on 3 January 1586 (AD Côtes-d'Armor, E 759).
[114] In 1481–2 an earlier Jean Guillemet was keeper of Henry Tudor during his exile in the duchy (ADLA, E 212, no. 16, fol. 4).

Vergier.[115] The author put his work together *c.* 1482–92 in the dying days of the independent duchy though no reference hints at recent political events. Instead he discusses general heraldic themes like the origins of heralds and the right to bear arms, before moving on to discussion of tinctures and metals, ordinaries, sub-ordinaries, cadency and other matters in a brisk and logical fashion in less than forty folios liberally illustrated with coats of arms. Many examples are drawn from Brittany. When listing types of banners and standards, for instance, he notes many bear arms and sometimes a device, citing specifically the duke's *A ma vie*. Not particularly novel, the work is nevertheless more than plagiarism and contains some interesting remarks on, for example, the arms of bastards or on husbands in hypergamic marriages, a not infrequent occurrence in the duchy.[116] Evidence from other sources reveals that many Breton gentlemen of this period had a detailed knowledge of the heraldry of their localities, which probably not infrequently formed a topic of casual conversation amongst neighbours.[117]

The manuscript which currently contains the *Argentaye Tract* also includes other pieces which would be of interest to a herald, such as instructions on the coronation of emperors and kings, a short treatise on standards and the role of great officers such as the constable, marshal and master of the crossbowmen in battle, another on warfare and gages of battle, obligatory blazoning of the arms of the nine *preux* and nine *preuses*, the kings of France and the twelve peers, and a Breton roll of arms, which internal evidence suggests was compiled around 1450. Earlier rolls are known to have existed, dating back to the well-known muster of the feudal host at Ploërmel in 1294 as well as to the second treaty of Guérande (1381), but none has survived in the original.[118] As for other miscellanies mixing heraldic and historical materials (some of considerable contemporary importance for the defence of the duke's position vis-à-vis his sovereign, the king of France) and which might legitimately be attributed to an officer of arms, perhaps in ducal service, at least three manuscripts dating to the late fifteenth or early sixteenth century can be cited: Carpentras, Bibliothèque municipale, MSS 591 and 592 and Aix-en-Provence, Bibliothèque Mejanès MS 648. Part at least of the two Carpentras manuscripts are of Breton origin, and in that from Aix

---

[115] Manning, *The Argentaye Tract*, pp. 17–26.

[116] Ibid., pp. 21–2.

[117] This particularly emerges from testimony given at the inquiries made in pre-eminence disputes after the defacing of arms, cf. Nassiet, 'Signes de parenté'.

[118] Michel Pastoreau, 'L'héraldique bretonne des origines à la guerre de succession de Bretagne', *Bulletin de la Société archéologique du Finistère* 101 (1973), pp. 140–7; Michel Pastoreau, 'Le rôle d'armes du second traité de Guérande (1381): Une "photographie" de l'héraldique bretonne à la fin du XIVe siècle', *Bulletin de la Société nationale des antiquaires de France* 104 (1976), pp. 103–52, both reprinted in his *L'Hermine et le Sinople: études d'héraldique médiévale* (Paris, 1982), pp. 200–7 and 208–58.

the diversity of its contents parallels that in the manuscript containing the *Argentaye Tract*.[119] Three other similar compilations (Paris, Bibliothèque Sainte-Geneviève MSS 1993 and 1994; Bibliothèque nationale de France, MS français 5037) also contain elements indicating Breton interest and probable origins around 1450. If not collected by a herald, they are perhaps to be associated with the 'historical' work undertaken by clerks in the Breton chancery of which there had been an active tradition since the late fourteenth century.[120]

As noted above, tournaments were not held very frequently in Brittany before the mid-fifteenth century.[121] There seems to have been a brief flurry of enthusiasm on the eve of the Civil War, one allegedly being held at Rennes to mark the marriage of Jeanne de Penthièvre, heiress to the duchy, and Charles de Blois in 1337.[122] Accounts from the lordship of Aubigné specifically mention *tournez* at Rennes in 1340 which may be those in which the young Bertrand du Guesclin appeared and Cuvelier described at length.[123] The long weeks of waiting during some sieges in the Civil War were enlivened, if we can further trust Froissart or Cuvelier, by the occasional joust including several in which Du Guesclin is also reputed to have taken part.[124] There is then a long gap until mention of a tournament organised by Guyon de Molac and François de Tiercent in 1447.[125] In 1454 or 1455 Bretagne Herald was sent to jousts at Quimperlé,[126] though Brittany is not known to have hosted any notable *pas d'armes*.

---

[119] Carpentras, Bibliothèque municipale, MS 591 was certainly later owned by the learned Breton genealogist and historian, Guy Autret, sire de Missirien (d. *c.*1653); Aix-en-Provence, Bibliothèque Mejanès, MS 648, 164 folios, is a particularly rich collection of fourteenth to fifteenth-century Breton historical, genealogical and political texts; I hope to examine the Breton aspects of these manuscripts in greater detail on another occasion.

[120] A brief resumé of some contents of the Paris, Bibliothèque Sainte-Geneviève manuscripts can be found in Marigold Anne Norbye, 'A Popular Example of "National Literature" in the Hundred Years War: *A tous nobles qui aiment beaux faits et bonnes histoires*', *Nottingham Medieval Studies* 51 (2007), p. 126, Table 3; for the general context see Michael Jones, 'Memory, Invention and the Breton State: The First Inventory of the Ducal Archives (1395) and the Beginnings of Montfort Historiography', *Journal of Medieval History* 33 (2007), pp. 275–96.

[121] Jean-Christophe Cassard, 'Les tournois dans le Duché de Bretagne', in *Le tournoi au Moyen Âge*, ed. Nicole Gontier (Lyon: Cahiers du Centre d'histoire médiévale, no. 2, 2003), pp. 165–82, is a good recent synthesis but makes little use of unpublished archival material.

[122] Siméon Luce, *Histoire de Bertrand du Guesclin et de son époque: la jeunesse de Bertrand (1320–1364)* (Paris, 1876), p. 25, citing Cuvelier; but see next note.

[123] AD Ille-et-Vilaine, 1 F 1542 (1340); Cuvelier, *La chanson*, ed. Faucon, i, 16–21, liasses xx–xxix, allegedly at the age of 16 or 17 (he was born *c.*1323, Jones, ed., *Letters, Orders and Musters of Bertrand du Guesclin*, pp. xxii–xxiii).

[124] Luce, *Histoire de Bertrand du Guesclin*, pp. 122–3.

[125] Morice, *Mémoires*, ii, col. 1412.

[126] Ibid., col. 1687.

Like Francis I and Peter II, Francis II was a moderate enthusiast for tournaments and they occurred sporadically throughout his reign. Nantes appears to have been the main centre: one was organised there on 5 November 1459 when Bretagne had to separate contestants in danger of serious injuries.[127] The *chevaucheur* Germain Gentilhomme, promoted pursuivant and herald by 1490, was sent to Fougères in 1474 'pour recouvrer des chevaulx pour les joustes assignés tenir a Nantes au premier jour de l'an', while in 1477 the town's receiver Guillaume Géraut was paid 'pour les lices de jouxte [...] rapportant relaccion de Bretaigne herault qu'il eut la charge de veoir faire icelles lices' and 'pour la construction d'autres lices qui furent faictes oud. Bouffay ou moys de decembre derrain'.[128] However, the fullest evidence for the professional advice of Bretagne on the organisation of jousts, the construction of lists and stands from which they could be viewed, comes from the accounts of Rennes in the summer of 1505 as the town prepared to welcome Queen Anne at her *joyeuse entrée*, an event that unfortunately had to be cancelled at the last minute for fear of the plague, but not before preparations had reached an advanced stage.[129]

Finally, the question of the extent to which heralds were called upon to provide expert opinion on armorial matters during the ducal period can be raised. As noted many cases concerning the breaking or defacement of arms came before the ducal council by the time of Francis II, though there is little evidence that professional testimony or advice was given by the duke's officers of arms. The only hint of involvement with such matters that has so far been discovered is payment to Bretagne, who was sent to forbid Loup de Belouan, sire de Kergroes, and his brothers from using the arms of Avaugour on pain of a fine of 1000 silver marks in 1480.[130] Conversely evidence of the council's record in adjudicating on a genuine armorial issue is not impressive: in December 1462 it was called upon to decide whether a charter of Arthur II (1305–12) 'soeant en nostre general parlement o la solempnité de nos troes Estaz' by which he granted to his kinsman Bonabé, lord of Derval the right to include two quarters of ermine in his family arms was genuine. The letters were allegedly 'fermes et entieres en escripture, signe et seel', bearing a seal 'ou aparoissent les armes de Dreuex et ung quartier de Bretaigne en la caractere duquel est escript S[ignum] Parlamenti Britanie,

---

[127]   Le Père Augustin du Paz, *Histoire généalogique de plusieurs maisons illustres de Bretagne* (Paris, 1620), p. 276.
[128]   ADLA, B, Parchemins (chevaux); B 8, fol. 28v (lices).
[129]   AM Rennes, AA 20 pièce 7, edited in Jones, 'The Rituals and Significance of Ducal Civic entries in Late Medieval Brittany', pp. 299–305.
[130]   ADLA, B 9, fol. 173v. In 1504, the family of Kerjagu was forced to admit publicly to Queen Anne's premier herald (?Bretagne) that it had usurped the arms of the Arrel family (AD Côtes-d'Armor, E 2117, cited by Nassiet, 'Signes de parenté', p. 216).

led. seel pendent en ung laz de soye de couleur violet'.[131] It was of course a recent forgery, probably produced at the moment that the lord of Derval was being considered for promotion to the ranks of the Nine Barons in 1451, as any competent chancery clerk worth his salt could have confirmed,[132] while any herald should have testified that until very recently the branch of the Derval family to which Jean de Derval belonged had traditionally borne quarterly first and fourth, gules, a cross *patée*, argent, second and third, gules, two *fasces* argent, and that it was the current lord who had added the two quarters of ermine for which he now sought retrospective sanction.[133] In effect this was granted to him since the spurious letters were accepted as genuine, though the reasons for doing so were political, not heraldic: confrontation with Louis XI loomed and Francis II needed all the support he could muster from his great nobles.

Conclusions

THROUGHOUT THIS ESSAY there has been a continual lament about the scanty nature of the evidence relating to the march of Brittany and its heralds in the later Middle Ages; there is much we cannot know about them or can only dimly perceive. However, the existence of that march cannot be doubted and enough snippets in chronicle and documentary sources relating to the careers of individual officers of arms, material remains (manuscripts containing treatises or historical compilations of value to Breton heralds or Du Guesclin's messenger's box), and more general information on the ducal court, its structure and chivalric aspects (castles and churches decorated with ducal devices or linked with the ducal orders, interest in tournaments and so on) survive to provide a context for the activities of Breton heralds. Evolving slowly from the late fourteenth century, officers of arms played an increasingly diverse part in promoting and maintaining the interests of the Montfort dukes of Brittany until the loss of independence in 1491. The existing records privilege in particular the military and diplomatic roles of Breton heralds, less is known about their ceremonial duties, intellectual interests or social position. For some, the reign of Duchess/ Queen Anne was a golden age, their status by then firmly assured, their rewards munificent, as they represented their mistress at home and on the European stage. But it was an Indian summer. By the 1520s their numbers

---

[131]   ADLA, E 131 f. 225v, of which the 'original' still survives in ADLA, E 152 no. 1, with the date 30 April 1302 (cf. Morice, *Mémoires*, i, col. 1177).
[132]   Morice, *Mémoires*, ii, cols 1560–1 for Peter II's letters of 19 May 1451 promoting Jean, sire de Derval.
[133]   Cf. Michel Nassiet, 'Un cas de manipulation de la parenté: la maison de Derval', *Bulletin de la Société archéologique de Nantes et de la Loire-Atlantique* 131 (1996), pp. 59–68.

had dwindled, only Bretagne was listed with the other French kings of arms, and after 1547 even trace is lost of him, apart from a brief reappearance in the early eighteenth century when there was once again, for a short moment, a duke of Brittany.[134]

---

[134] Information kindly supplied by M. Michel Pastoreau.

6

City Heralds in the Burgundian Low Countries

Franck Viltart and Henri Simonneau

I N 1438, a delegation of the Damoiseaux brotherhood of the city of Valenciennes in Hainault made its entry during the annual jousts of the Épinette in the city of Lille. Savage men led the way, sounding horns and trumpets, followed by Franquevie, the herald of the city, wearing the coat of arms of Valenciennes, and also dressed up as a savage. Twenty-four gentlemen on horseback followed Franquevie in the procession and finally came a wagon with a large reproduction of Valenciennes, on which seven young ladies wore the arms of the city. This delegation was welcomed by the king of the Épinette, who stood in front of one of the town gates.[1] Here, in this civic space, heralds participated in the symbolic representation of the city, wearing the arms of the city, accompanying its representatives, observing the celebratory jousts and hosting other heralds who were in attendance.

For many years, officers of arms have been almost exclusively observed and described as a part of noble and chivalric culture. However, recent scholarly research has shown that towards the end of the Middle Ages heralds were integrated into some urban societies and civic hierarchies, particularly in the Burgundian Low Countries.[2] The economic wealth of the Burgundian Netherlandish cities and their greater territories enabled the development of a festive culture, which became increasingly sumptuous during the fourteenth and the fifteenth centuries. Jousts and gatherings organised by the urban elites of these territories, from Hainault to Holland, show that as the Burgundian state made territorial acquisitions in these areas there was a

---

[1] Valenciennes, Bibilothèque municipale, MS 806; ADN, B 7662.

[2] This work is based on the database project initiated by Werner Paravicini and Torsten Hiltmann at the German Historical Institute in Paris. This project proposes to build a multifunctional source-orientated database, in order to follow the development of the office of arms in the Burgundian sources within original texts followed by an Officers of Arms Catalogue. The project will be online in 2009 at <http://www.heraudica.org>.

Plate 4. Delegation of the Damoiseaux of Valenciennes arriving in Lille. Late fifteenth century. Bibliothèque municipale de Valenciennes, MS 806. Photograph by Franck Viltart and Henri Simonneau.

simultaneous increase in civic activities and festivals. The takeover of these regions by the dukes of Burgundy is marked by the intervention of ducal power in urban festivals, where both urban heralds and those of the nobility were in close contact. Two cities in particular illuminate some of the issues of city heralds in the Burgundian Low Countries: Lille and Valenciennes. In these two cities, archival sources are very rich and demonstrate that the city heralds had an important place in civic administration.

Recent historiography has revealed the existence of a dynamic network of cities in the Burgundian Low Countries, and the progressive forming of an urban identity, through feasts, jousts, tournaments, religious processions, sports and rhetorical competitions (where men 'jousted' using poems and plays).[3] It is through the study of these festivities that the figure of the city herald appears in a precise role with specific functions. This essay will assess the role of city heralds and ask a range of questions about them: Why did some cities use heralds? What were their functions in these urban communities? What impact did this have on their collective identity? These are crucial questions concerning a much-misunderstood office; it is vital to shed new light on this important figure in heraldry and urban administration.

City Heralds: A Phenomenological Approach

THE ORIGIN of the medieval office of arms remains a subject still requiring much investigation.[4] The herald's first appearance in literary sources can be traced back to the end of the twelfth century.[5] However, from the mid-fourteenth to the mid-sixteenth century, officers of arms carved out astonishing careers for themselves. After almost two centuries of itinerant employment as jugglers, gleemen and minstrels of doubtful reputation, making a living from occasional gifts and donations, they were now employed by kings, princes and nobleman, as well as by cities. By the beginning of the fifteenth century, heralds were employed in most European kingdoms and principalities. Heralds had the same origins as their minstrel and musical companions, that is to say they were non-nobles, who offered their services to the nobility. By the same token, as soon as officers

---

[3]   The first to identify and explain the phenomenon was Évelyne van den Neste in her study, *Tournois, joutes, pas d'armes dans les villes de Flandre à la fin du Moyen Age 1300–1486* (Paris, 1996). See also Élodie Lecuppre-Desjardins, *La ville des ceremonies: essai sur la communication politique dans les anciens Pays-Bas bourguignons 1100–1800* (Turnhout, 2004); Willem Pieter Blockmans, Walter Prevenier, Edward Peters, Elizabeth Fackelman, eds, *The Promised Lands: The Low Countries under Burgundian Rule 1369–1530* (Philadelphia, 1999). For more on competitions and chambers of rhetoric in the Burgundian Low Countries see Anne-Laure van Bruaene, *Rederijkerskamers en de stedelijke cultuur in de Zuidelijke Nederlanden (1400–1650)* (Amsterdam, 2008).
[4]   See Bertrand Schnerb, 'Le héraut, figure européenne XIVᵉ–XVᵉ siècles', *Revue du Nord* 88, no. 366–7 (2006).
[5]   For the origin of the office of arms see Richard Wagner, *Heralds and Heraldry in the Middle Ages* (Oxford, 1956), pp. 25–40; from the same author, *Heralds of England* (London, 1967).

of arms appeared in the service of noblemen, heralds could also easily have found themselves in similar positions in the service of the cities. Heralds first appear in city records in the early decades of the fourteenth century: the earliest in records of the Low Countries is that of the city of Ghent in 1324.[6] Much like noblemen's heralds, heralds in the service of cities always remained anonymous, although sometimes a title was ascribed to their office. More often than not, however, city records simply note the city of origin for their identification (see Appendix 1).[7] Records show that twelve Burgundian cities employed a herald: we also know they were similarly used within the heart of the French kingdom, with city heralds in Amiens, Laon, Meaux, Orléans and Paris.[8] It is well established that noblemen's heralds often bore the name of the territorial possessions of their master and hence sometimes of a city, but the city heralds often bore a name related to the civic identity of the city and almost never the name of the city itself. This, of course, can be seen as a deliberate desire not to utilise the name of the urban lordship: only the lords could give the name of a city to their heralds. There were many heralds who bore city names but who were not in the service of that city. For example, the regent of Hainault, Duke Albert of Bavaria, had a herald with the name of Brussels in 1371.[9] The duke of Burgundy, Philip the Good, had a herald named Salins in 1442,[10] and Charles the Bold, duke of Burgundy, had one with the name of Bethune.[11] Edward IV also had a Calais Pursuivant in 1462.[12]

Cities used heralds in their service from the early fourteenth century. The titles of these city heralds, which began to appear in the second half of the fourteenth century, are for the most part tied to aspects of urban festivity. This shows very clearly, and with certainty, that we have here a phenomenon closely linked to festal activities and to the representation of the city within a festive framework. Here we are dealing with the urban elite, regrouped through the forming of an association. They may have been manifested as a society of tourneyers like that of the 'Ours Blanc' of Bruges or the '31 kings'

[6] Wim van Anrooij, *Spiegel von ridderschap: Heraut Gelre en zijn ereredes* (Amsterdam, 1990), pp. 16–28.
[7] See the database project: <http://www.heraudica.org>.
[8] For the city of Amiens (1431) see ADN, B 1942, fol. 98r. For Laon (1400) see AM Douai, CC 205, fol. 289. For Meaux (1376) see AM Valenciennes, CC 733, fol. 14r. For Orléans, with the name of 'Coeur de Lys' (1436), see Orléans City Records cited in Régine Pernoud, Marie Véronique Clin, *Joan of Arc: Her Story* (New York,1998), p. 233. For Paris, with the name of 'Loyal Cœur' (1461), see Jean de Roye, *Chronique scandaleuse* (Paris, 1894), t. 1, 25.
[9] AM Valenciennes, CC 728, fol. 12v. We still do not know why the count of Hainault held a herald with the name of Brussels, which is located in Brabant.
[10] ADN, B 1978, fols 102r–v.
[11] ADN, B 1978, fols 102 r–v; B 2064, fol. 253r.
[12] ADN, B 2045, fol. 267r.

of Tournai, of a bourgeois guild, like 'Franquevie' in Valenciennes, or even of the annual city festival, such as that of Lille, the Épinette.[13] Indeed, the connection between the Épinette and Épinette Herald was so strong that Épinette Herald sometimes acted as the ritual inversion figure of the king of the Épinette. We find the same case in Bruges where the herald of the city, Bierkin, is often cited as the herald of the Forestier of Bruges, the winner of the city's annual jousting competition.[14]

The heads of jousting and ceremonial societies were not only elected for their sportsmanship, but also for their financial resources. They were elected on a yearly basis and were responsible for the organisation of the civic jousts for that year. We are hence faced with an economically wealthy layer of urban society that had recourse to utilising the service of heralds. The different acts of heralds (laid out in Appendix 1) reinforce the notion that their role essentially comprised the public pronouncement of the festivities and the jousts. Until the beginning of the fifteenth century, Lille, Bruges, Tournai, Valenciennes and Mons were part of a dense urban network, due in part to the jousts, tournaments and feasts at which the bourgeoisie of these cities met and confronted each other. But urban jousts progressively disappeared at the end of the century: this was the case in Valenciennes, Douai, Tournai, and Ypres. The huge cost of these events is the principal reason why they disappeared. There were only two cities which continued to run them: Lille, with its feasts of Épinette, and Bruges, with the tournament of the Forestier.

These jousting competitions were not the only type of social links between medieval cities. Other contests were also taking place. For example, there were the Puys in northern France or the chambers of rhetoric in the southern Netherlands.[15] There are some similarities in their organisation to that of civic tournaments. The president of the feast of the Puy Notre-Dame in Lille, for example, was the Prince of the Puy, in a similar model to the jousts of the Épinette. And while in Flanders, in Hainault or in Brabant urban tournaments were disappearing, literary brotherhoods (chambers of rhetoric) were growing in popularity. Rhetorical contests were organised by the local bourgeoisie and contributed to the preservation of social networks inside and outside the city. At the end of the fifteenth and during the whole sixteenth century, the Puys and the chambers of rhetoric were highly

[13] See Neste, *Tournois, joutes, pas d'armes dans les villes de Flandre*, pp.113–21, 189–99.
[14] AM Lille, CC 16226, fol. 99r (1426).
[15] Michèle Gally, *Parler d'amour au puy d'Arras* (Orléans, 2004); Anne-Laure van Bruaene, 'A wonderful tryumfe, for the wynning of a pryse: Guilds, Ritual, Theatre, and the Urban Network in the Southern Low Countries, ca. 1450–1650', *Renaissance Quarterly*, 59: 2 (2006), pp. 374–405.

successful.[16] Between 1480 and 1565, when rhetorician culture enjoyed its heyday, on average more than two competitions each year were organised between different localities.

As for the role of heralds, they also found a place in the new civic competitions that gradually replaced jousting events from the latter part of the fifteenth century. Their services, for example, were called upon to announce the rhetorical contests of the literary brotherhoods. Indeed, in the archives of the city of Mons in Hainault there are no less than thirteen references to heralds who came to the city to announce rhetorical contests between 1483 and 1519. Four of these heralds came from Tournai and nine from Valenciennes:

> Au herault de la ville de Vallenchiennes qui le XXᵉ dudit march IIIIˣˣ XIII en ce compte vint de par ceulx de Vallenchiennes a messires eschevins de Mons dire et nonchier le prince dudit Vallenchiennes faisoit et tenoit esbattemens en celle ville de Vallenchiennes au Casimodo enssuivant.[17]

Of even more significance is that heralds not only announced these rhetorical competitions, but might also be competitors in them. At the end of the fifteenth century, we find more and more officers of arms who have skills in producing written documentation, not only in descriptions of tournaments and the like, but also in poetry and rhetoric, with famous examples including Gelre Herald.[18] In this respect, one record in the archives of Valenciennes is revealing: Franquevie Herald received from the city of Valenciennes 42s. 10d. because he had won the biggest prize (a crown) during a rhetorical contest organised in Mons by the prince of Bon Vouloir, while he was in the company of the Prince de Plaisir of Valenciennes.

> A luy, pour consideracion que a ladite feste de Tornay il gaigna et obtint comme celluy qui le mieulx avoit besongné l'en ouvre de retoricque le princhipal pris et joyau a ce ordonné, a scavoir le couronne que il rapporta a son rethour d'illecq en la compaignie du prince de plaisir de ceste ville, fu encoires donnet en tant comme ce redone vie a l'honneur de ceste dicte ville XL s. bl. de XLII s. X d.[19]

---

[16] Ibid.

[17] 'To the herald of the city of Valenciennes, who came the 20th March 1493 from those of Valenciennes to the municipal magistrates of Mons, to say and announce that the prince of Valenciennes celebrates a feast in the city of Valenciennes the next Quasimodo.' Mons, Archives de l'État, MS 1580, fol. 50r.

[18] See van Anrooij, *Spiegel von ridderschap*; and from the same author 'Bayern, Herolde und Literatur im spätmittelalterlichen Reich', *650 Jahre Herzogtum Niederbayern-Straubing-Holland*, ed. Alfons Huber, Johannes Prammer (Straubing, 2005), pp. 235–75.

[19] 'To Franquevie, Herald of Valenciennes, in consideration that in the feast of Tournai he won, as someone who had made the best rhetorical speech, the principal prize and jewel, a crown, that he brought back in company with the 'Prince of Plaisir' of this city, and because he returned honour to this city (Valenciennes), XL sous blanc of XLII sous, X deniers.' AM Valenciennes, CC 747, fol. 85v.

City heralds might also be messengers or town criers, but only in special circumstances and for great events. As with the heralds in the service of lords,
the function of the city herald seems to be always related to the question of
honour and glorification. Communication between cities passed through a
network of messengers, through which the heralds took a particular place
in the announcement of festivities and tournaments. Even though city messengers sometimes performed the same type of announcement, the city
heralds were, by the end of the fourteenth century, the exclusive actors of
the announcement of the *cri public*, as we can see in Valenciennes in 1363:
'A I hiraut de Namur, liquels avoit criiet une feste de joustes le premier
jour d'avril donnet dou commande le prevost, XV s.'[20] A city, by having
its own herald, showed its importance to the other urban communities.
Genuine competition between cities was apparent on the occasion of civic
tournaments and other ritual festivals. In close comparison with heralds in
the service of noblemen and their knowledge of nobility, armoury and the
honourable and chivalric accomplishment of knighthood, the city herald's
first duty was to adapt this specialist knowledge to the needs of his urban
societies. This leads to the conclusion that the city herald's role and function was required and desired by the emerging bourgeois class, attracted to
the ideas and values of the nobility.

The studies of Jacques Heers on cities and festivities during the Middle Ages have succeeded in demonstrating that urban festivities were not
as compartmentalised as previously had been thought.[21] Urban elites,
peasants, clerks and nobles could very well interact with one another at
the festival grounds. Each one was, of course, clearly distinguished from
the other but they interacted nonetheless and created a dynamic of mutual
recognition. The jousting itself reflected this, and by the late fourteenth
century battles were no longer uniquely reserved to the nobility, but instead
a mix of combatants was possible.[22] The range of activities made possible
through the festivity allowed for the appearance of the city heralds. But how
did the governing powers perceive the creation of these heralds by the cities,
who had previously been solely the preserve of the nobility? To answer this
question, it is necessary to study the relationships between the power of
the dukes of Burgundy and the urban elites within the framework of urban
festivities.

---

[20] 'To a Herald of Namur, who had pronounced a feast of jousts the first day of April,
given by order of the provost, XV sous.' AM Valenciennes, CC 704, fol. 15r. See on this
subject, Didier Lett, Nicolas Offenstadt, *Haro ! Noël ! Oyé!: Pratiques du cri au Moyen Age*
(Paris, 2003).
[21] Jacques Heers, *Fêtes des fous et carnavals* (Paris, 1983).
[22] See Neste, *Tournois, joutes, pas d'armes dans les villes de Flandre*, pp. 141–3.

City Heralds and the Dukes of Burgundy

THE RISE OF FESTIVITIES in the Low Countries and the Burgundian Netherlandish cities at the end of the Middle Ages encouraged the formation of collective identities of different urban communities. The bourgeois tournament societies, guilds and others expressed their need for construction of identity through these festivities. In this manner, festivities increased in number and in duration and thus the cities spent accordingly, which enabled a surge of honour upon them as well as a certain 'renommée'.[23] The city heralds took on a more and more important role during urban jousts which, according to Évelyne van den Neste, imitated the model of chivalric tournaments.[24] Just as the urban jousts tended to imitate a model which had hitherto been entirely noble in its interests, so too the urban herald existed as an imitation of his noble counterpart. In origin, the city herald did not have the propagation of the honour of his lords as a principal goal, and in this way his functions were distinct from those of the heralds in the service of lords and princes. The city herald had, for example, no real military functions. It is undeniable, however, that the office of arms had become indispensable to the carrying out of civic tournaments in the middle of the fourteenth century, and therefore his presence and his role within these jousts was of growing significance. As master of ceremonies, the city herald, wearing the city's coat of arms, was placed at the head of the procession of his city as it travelled to a festivity. Here, he alone welcomed the prince.

The urban herald's role as representative of the city allowed him to enter into a complex web of relations between the city and the noble elites. Next to princely and noble heralds, the urban herald emerges as a strong figure of relative independence in the city. Indeed, city heralds wielded so much individual power that noblemen might intervene by creating city heralds for themselves. For example, two different heralds from the Flemish cities of Ypres and Bruges are named as Griffon around the year 1370, and of the heralds of nobility during the same period we also find a Griffon in the service of the count of Flanders.[25]

The arrival of the dukes of Burgundy in the Netherlands, and notably in Flanders, continued this tendency for a lord to impose his own heralds upon the cities as a strong political message. This is the case with Nevers Herald, mentioned as herald of the city of Bruges from 1400, who was almost certainly imposed upon Bruges by the count of Nevers, the future duke of Burgundy, John the Fearless.[26] This was also the case a few

---

[23] Lecuppre-Desjardins, *La ville des cérémonies*, pp. 184–5.
[24] Neste, *Tournois, joutes, pas d'armes dans les villes de Flandre*, p. 190.
[25] AM Valenciennes, CC 723, fol. 21r , CC 729, fol. 9v, CC 731, fol. 11v.
[26] *Bulletin de la société historique et littéraire de Tournai*, t. 5 (Tournai, 1878), p. 181.

years later, in 1417, with the mention of Charolais Herald as a city herald of Bruges, a herald who had originally been in the service of the count of Charolais.[27] The importance and the wealth of this Flemish city explain the duke's interference in civic business. In 1422, a jousting troop from Arras, in the company of Philip the Good, was in Artois, returning from the jousts of the Épinette of Lille. At the head of the troop was the master and treasurer of the city, Palent, who wished to be made a pursuivant. However, Duke Philip decided to elevate Palent beyond this status and made him the herald of the city of Arras.[28] This episode is revealing in other ways too, principally in its revelation of the diversity of the group coming back from the joust. Surrounding the duke of Burgundy was a variety of nobles, city notables and bourgeois. It is clear that, in Arras at least, the office of herald acted as a reward for loyalty from the city to the duke of Burgundy.

The growth of the power of the dukes of Burgundy in this area was followed by a political utilisation of urban festivals. The nomination of city heralds by the dukes confirms this. The festivals offered the dukes the means to be known by the citizens, and to assure their popularity, particularly when a duke participated directly in the spectacle. During the fifteenth century, for example, the urban jousts in the Burgundian Netherlands had become so important that Duke Philip the Good participated in them himself.[29] By these displays of power and personal commitment to civic ritual, and the use of city heralds, the dukes increased their foothold in the urban setting. We must not, then, separate the phenomenon of city heralds from the rise of officers of arms in the service of nobility, notably in the territories of Holland, Flanders, Brabant, Hainault and Artois, during the fourteenth and the fifteenth centuries. If we agree that the dukes of Burgundy tended to name their own heralds in the city, they were simply resuscitating an organisation of the office of arms already present in these territories during the fourteenth century.

During the great assemblies that were the urban jousts, the heralds came into close contact with one another. Sources survive which illuminate their organisation and there were distinctions between the status of pursuivant, heralds and 'kings of heralds', later known as kings of arms. We note the existence of a king of heralds of Brabant in 1376, in Hainault 'Barbantson den coninc vanden hyrauden wt Heneg' in 1384, and in Artois a 'rex heraldorum comitatus Arthesie' from 1388.[30] It is certain that heralds of the nobility met with city heralds during city jousts and civic tournaments. In

---

[27] AM Douai, CC 209, fol. 359r.

[28] AM Arras, BB 6, fol. 80v.

[29] Élodie Lecuppre-Desjardins, *La ville des cérémonies* (Turnhout, 2004), pp. 200–5.

[30] AM Valenciennes, CC 733, fol. 15v; La Haye, ARA, AGH, 1239, fol. 88v; Paris, Archives nationales, JJ 132, no 58.

1388, for example, the records of the city of Tournai mentioned the kings of arms of Corbie, Champagne, Artois and Flanders meeting at the Tournai festivals.[31]

Aside from these festivals, the city served as a space for encounters and hospitality for the heralds. Rare documentation of these encounters between heralds has been discovered, including one example of a receipt from a hotel caretaker of Lille, who received £9 18s. from the treasurer of the duke of Burgundy for the accommodation and feeding of the French Guyenne King of Arms and Monsigny Herald. Guyenne and Monsigny had also been hosted by the herald of the city of Lille, Épinette, and the ducal Luxembourg Herald in 1482.[32] Likewise, the Burgundian kings of arms attended different urban jousts on behalf of the duke of Burgundy, where they were hosted with equal courtesy. In 1421, we know the duke of Burgundy gave a donation to his king of arms of Flanders and Artois, and all the other officers of arms, for their participation in the jousts in Lille.[33] The sending of the duke's representatives marks the importance accorded by the duke to their participation in the festivities. And the organisation of the heralds demonstrates the desire for the integration of the different territories under Burgundian control. The duke accorded himself, through the intermediary of his kings of arms, donations and largesse to the heralds present at the jousts, whether they were city heralds or others. He also sometimes conferred upon them the right to wear a blazon with his arms. Through his control by means of donations and largesse to his officers the duke also controlled part of his city and its elites. This continued during the fifteenth century despite a decline in civic tournaments and jousts.

Épinette and Franquevie: Two City Heralds

Two urban heralds are particularly well known in the late Middle Ages: Franquevie in Valenciennes and Épinette in Lille. The city archives in both Valenciennes and Lille are well endowed with records and enable us to obtain a clear picture of the city heralds' activities.

Franquevie, sometimes written as *Franke Vie*, meaning 'free life' in reference to freedom claims by the city of Valenciennes, was not paid by the city itself, but by a brotherhood of gentlemen from Valenciennes, the Royés de Notre-Dame-du-Saint-Cordon, or the Damoiseaux brotherhood. During the fifteenth century, Franquevie was never invited to undertake any missions related to diplomatic embassies or long-distance messengering,

---

[31] *Bulletin de la société historique et littéraire de Tournai*, t. 5 (Tournai, 1878), p. 145.

[32] ADN, B 7599, 157.068.

[33] ADN, B 1923, fols 92v–97r.

Plate 5: Épinette, city herald of Lille, during urban jousting. Fifteenth century. Bibliothèque Municipale de Valenciennes, MS 806. Photograph by Franck Viltart and Henri Simonneau.

but instead he was only present at the city's feasts. Every year, he received money for the procession in the city of the Saint-Cordon, and for his trip to Lille during the feasts of the Épinette to escort Valencienne's delegation. In 1511, he received 42s. 10d. because he assisted the Prince de Plaisance, newly elected to organise his feast.[34] The same year, he received 34s. to help

---

[34] BL, MS Egerton 1644.

during the funeral of the countess of Charolais.[35] Thus, the herald of Valenciennes was a character present during urban ceremonies like processions, feasts and tournaments, both inside and outside of the city.[36] In a way he was the master of ceremonies and representative of the urban community, particularly the city's gentlemen. A manuscript preserved in Valenciennes's library describes the entry of the delegation of the Damoiseaux during the festivities of the Épinette in 1435, 1438, 1442 and 1447.[37] The people of Valenciennes wanted their city to be represented, but they wanted also to impress the other competitors. This delegation was welcomed by the king of the Épinette himself who stood in front of one of the town gates. Here, the herald acted as a symbolic representation of the town, and accompanied the jousters during the processions and the competition with his coat of arms. The role of Franquevie could thus not survive the disappearance of urban jousts from the middle of the sixteenth century: he leaves no trace after 1571.

Épinette, in Lille, was a rather different sort of herald. Aside from his missions for the city, he was the only urban herald who frequently undertook missions on behalf of the dukes of Burgundy. Lille was a very important city for the Valois dukes of Burgundy, in both financial and military terms (there was an arsenal here, for instance). During the time of Charles the Bold, between 1467 and 1477, Épinette undertook twenty-five missions of mail-coach service, the carrying of letters to various noblemen. Among these missions, seventeen concerned the duke himself. Three others were on behalf of the towns of Arras and Douai, and only one dealt with feasts of the Épinette. Of course, Épinette Herald had a role during the tournaments of Lille, but many of the duties that he undertook were not related to the feasts, but to the town itself. The very rich records of Lille offer a great deal of information concerning the role of Épinette within the city. First, he was the city's messenger. When, in 1489, the prince of Chimay wanted to speak with 'un homme bien entendant pour oyr ce qu'il voulloit déclarer et en faire rapport', that is to say, a man able to listen to what the prince wanted to declare, the town sent Épinette Herald to him.[38] Épinette also had a privileged relationship with other ambassadors. When an ambassador had to travel to a city, it was often Épinette who guided them through Flanders: like many heralds, Épinette had a great knowledge of roads and the city's hinterland. He might also organise ambassadorial receptions where he could collect important information. In 1478, for example, the city paid 24s.

[35] Ibid.
[36] See Henry D'Outreman, *Histoire de la ville de Valenciennes* (XVIIth c.) (Douai, 1975), p. 394.
[37] Valenciennes, Bibilothèque municipale, MS 806.
[38] AM Lille, 16228, fol. 97r.

to Épinette, because he received a messenger from Denmark at the Golden Head tavern in Lille.[39] The herald bought food and wine for both of them, and also read a message intended for the king of France. This information was of much interest to the magistrates of Lille. Besides his function as a messenger, Épinette was also a town crier at important occasions. In 1483 it was Épinette who announced the peace of Arras in the town square.[40] In 1477, when an officer of Maximilian was married in Lille, it was Épinette who took part in the ceremony as the representative of the city.[41]

But when we read the city's records, it seems that this herald might have another role within the city. Some of his missions exceeded his role as representative of Lille. For example, in 1435, Druet Beauregard, herald of the city, was given a charge to inspect the moats, the fortifications and all the artillery with the captain of Lille.[42] In 1477 Épinette, commanded the watch of the city gates:

A Jaspart du Bos, herault de l'Espinette de ceste dicte ville, pour son sallaire d'année au commandement desdis eschevins au long de ceste dicte année commandé le ghet chacun jour aux nobles et officiers de ladite ville qui estoient ordonnez faire ledit ghet a tour aux portes de ladite ville avecq ceulx du commun pour avoir le regard audessus d'eulx des gens allans et venans en icelle ville pour ce VI £.[43]

This was an unusual privilege for a herald. In 1478, a mention in city records clearly indicates that Épinette must be always ready to undertake any missions for the city:

A Jaspart du Bos herault de l'Espinette que par lesdis eschevins conseil et huyt hommes accordé lui a esté pour pluiseurs services par lui fais au long de ceste dicte année a icelle ville et avoir tousjours esté prest a toutes heures quant ordonné et commandé lui a esté pour aller d'un costé et d'autre pour les besongnes d'icelle ville en l'absence des serviteurs de ladite ville et autrement considere aussi la suspence de la feste de ladite Espinette a quoy il a grant dommaige et interest, VI £.[44]

---

[39] AM Lille, 16217, fol. 98r.
[40] AM Lille, 16222, fols 92v–93r.
[41] AM Lille, 16216, fol. 76v.
[42] AM Lille, 16177, fols 75v–77r.
[43] 'To Jaspart du Bos, herald of the Épinette of this city (Lille), for his salary of the year, by order of the magistrates, because he commanded all this year the watch every day to the noblemen and town officers who were ordered to make this watch at the town's gates, and also to watch the people who enter and leave the city, for this VI livres.' AM Lille, 16217, fol. 54v.
[44] 'To Jaspart du Bos, Herald of the Épinette, accorded by the magistrates and eight men, for his services to the town all this year and always standing ready any time when required to move from side to side due to the lack of servants, and also because of the suspension of the feast of the Épinette, which is a great financial loss for him, VI livres.' AM Lille, 16224, fol. 112r.

To command the watch stay was an important task. It demonstrated that in the city of Lille Épinette Herald was a highly respected person. This record also indicates that the disappearance of the feasts of the Épinette was, in fact, the beginning of the decline of the office in Lille at the end of the fifteenth century. Indeed, after 1486, when the last urban tournament took place in Lille, Épinette's salary was composed only of gifts from the city as compensation for what he had not been receiving since the festivities had ended. Finally, in 1505, Épinette formally resigned. On this occasion, he declared that he could no longer stay in the service of the city, and consequently he returned his office, despite his long service, to join Philip the Handsome on his travels to Spain.[45] The loss of Épinette Herald was a blow to the city of Lille, even though there were no festivities of the Épinette by this time. Indeed, in 1537, the town re-created the office. In Lille, as in Valenciennes, the herald was an important character for urban magistrates and had an important role in the constitution of civic identity, both inside and outside of the city. This is the principal reason why the officers were respected, as they kept with them the memory of the urban elite. Indeed, they were invited to commit this memory to paper and parchment.

Engherrant le Franc, the herald in Valenciennes at the end of the fifteenth century, is one who demonstrated the city herald's duty to record the important moments in the city's history. Engherrant le Franc was the author of the *Ditier faits et armoriés pour les noces de nobles bourgeois et pour la confrérie des Damoiseaux de cette ville*, a compendium of poems for the wedding of local bourgeoisie and members of the brotherhood of the Damoiseaux.[46] This type of literature was a domain in which heralds were particularly well regarded: each poem described the armorial achievements of the bride and groom. Engherrant le Franc thus made an urban genealogy of the more important families of the town, a sort of *memoria* of the bourgeoisie. This type of literature, of course, demonstrated the self-consciousness of a powerful social group, the urban elite. But we have to imagine that Engherrant le Franc did not only write these poems, but that he also proclaimed them during the wedding, in front of an audience. There is a link here between these Ditiers and the Puys: there was an oral function of the herald, which is not always revealed in town records or archives. This seems to be an important function of the urban herald, and one of the main reasons for his social use. The social role of the city herald tended to be the same as that of the noblemen's herald. The herald of a lord was a mirror of

---

45 AM Lille, 16242, fol. 84r.
46 *Ditiers faits et armoriés par Engherant Le Franc, héraut d'armes de Valenciennes, pour des noces de nobles bourgeois et pour la Confrérie des Damoiseaux de cette ville (XVth c.)* (Mons, 1856).

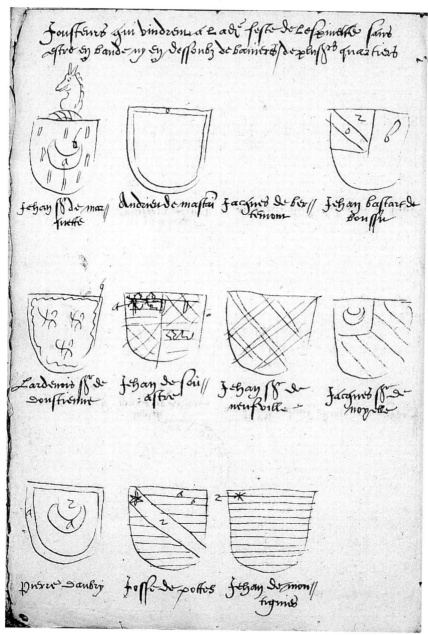

Plate 6. Armorial of the Jousts of the Épinette of Lille, 1435–1442. Lille, Archives Départementales du Nord, B 7662, fol. 21v. Photograph by Franck Viltart and Henri Simonneau.

chivalry: he had to describe his lord, to keep the memory of his chivalric exploits, to glorify the purity of his lord's blood and his nobility. With the description of urban jousts and the glorification of local family dynasties, the city herald had a similar role for the bourgeoisie.

The same happened in Lille, even though the main functions of the officer of arms here were quite different from in Valenciennes. In 1481, Jaspart Dubos received from the magistrates of the town £6 for an historical armorial of the kings of the Épinette, from the time that the jousting had first started.[47] It is recorded in the register of the town that this armorial had to be reproduced 'par le moyen dudit registre recouvrer et en faire autres nouviaulx partout'.[48] For Lille, it was a way to preserve the memory of the kings of Épinette and of glory of the jousts, at a time when it was clear that the jousting was dying out. Like the Ditier of Engherrant le Franc, this armorial is part of the self-consciousness of the bourgeoisie, through the *memoria*. It is also interesting to observe that this armorial was subsequently reproduced many times during the sixteenth century. François Boniface has shown that new insertions were introduced in later copies to include important contemporary families.[49]

The jousts in Lille and Bruges and the rhetorical contests in Valenciennes, Mons and Tournai were still prestigious for cities at the end of the fifteenth century, but they were always performed under the close control of the city's bourgeoisie. These feasts were a way to build a social network between families who were at the head of the city. The literary production of heralds (armorials and poetry) contributed to a picture of the city through the commemoration of these families. The work of the heralds does not describe the progress of the jousts, but is much more concerned with the presence of the local nobility and bourgeoisie. The urban herald was above all else the mirror of the urban bourgeoisie.

Conclusion

IT IS WORTH REMEMBERING that the herald was, in his earliest manifestation, a non-noble figure in the service of nobility. Hence the herald's position was between his original social status of commoner and the world of nobility. The case of city heralds shows us that this intermediary position was especially useful to the development of an urban identity through civic

[47] AM Lille, 16220, fol. 104v. This may be a working copy of the armorial made by the herald himself.

[48] Michel Popoff, ed., *Armorial des rois de l'Épinette de Lille, 1283–1486* (Paris, 1984).

[49] François Boniface, *Aperçu général sur les armoriaux des fêtes de l'Épinette de Lille (1283–1486): origine, falsification, essai de chronologie et de filiation, ajouts* in *Cahiers du Léopard d'Or* 8 (Paris, 1997).

rituals and city festivals, and particularly within tournaments. The herald was not always a central or essential element but he was often mentioned as an active participant or a simple onlooker, and always as a representative of the city. This context is favourable to the development of the office of arms in general, in which the city heralds clearly played a role. At the end of the fifteenth century, some cities, including Valenciennes and Tournai, again called upon their city heralds in a new role at rhetorical contests, which contributed to the construction of urban culture in the Low Countries. City heralds not only contributed to the forging of urban identity, but also played an important role in the shaping of public space through representations inside and outside of towns. The figure of the city herald gave to the urban communities an additional splendour, which the dukes of Burgundy understood very well. They recuperated these servants and transformed them into actors of the political integration of the cities in the Burgundian states. Thanks to the city herald, we can better understand the development of officers of arms in late medieval Europe, and we are also able to investigate more fully the relationships between states, cities and nobility.

Appendix 1.
City heralds in the Burgundian Low Countries in the 14th to 15th centuries

City	Herald	Years attested	Action
Arras	–	1365	Carries a letter from the jousts of the city of Arras.
	Palent	1421	Baptism as pursuivant
Bruges	Griffon	1354–92	Public announcement of a festival in the city of Bruges
	Nevers	1400	Public announcement of a joust
	Pursuivant Hanekine	1408	Accompanies a troop of combatants to the jousts of the Épinette of Lille.
	Poursuivant Ours/ Ourson/ Franchequin / Franq/ Berquin/ Bierkin	1407–45	Public announcement of jousts Receives a blazon from the duke of Burgundy
	Charolais	1417	Public announcement of jousts
Douai	Paon	1356–75	Public announcement of jousts
Ghent	–	1324	–

Lille	Épinette	1388 to 16th century	Public announcement of jousts Guides military troops. Hosts and guides heralds. Receives a gift from the duke of Burgundy. Receives a blazon. Makes an armorial of the kings of the Épinette of Lille.
Malines	4 *hérauts*	1404	Receives a gift from the duke of Burgundy.
Namur	–	1363	–
Nivelle	Winedalle	1398	Public announcement of jousts in Brabant
Termonde	–	1404–21	Receives a gift.
Tournai*	Triboul	1362	Carries a letter for the jousts of the city of Tournai
	Ghertier	1379	Public announcement of jousts
	–	1405–1539	–
Valenciennes	Franquevie	1367 to 16th century	Representation in the festivities of the Épinette in Lille. Carries letters of the jousts of the city of Valenciennes. Participates in rhetoric jousts. Evicts soldiers. Representation in the Golden Fleece festivities.
Ypres	–	1357	Carries a letter of jousts of Ypres.
	Griffon	1362–73	Public announcement of jousts

* *Tournai belonged to the French Kingdom*

7

King of Arms of the Ruwieren:
A Special Function in the German Empire[*]

Wim van Anrooij

ROM THE LAST QUARTER of the thirteenth century onwards, England, France and the Low Countries witnessed a professionalisation of the office of herald and a corresponding emerging hierarchy within the ranks of the officers. Heralds began to form part of a ranking system according to function and with opportunities for promotion, within which pursuivants, heralds (in the stricter sense of the word) and kings of arms could be distinguished.[1] Territorial rulers who attached importance to representation, and who were able to afford it, appointed one or more of such officers. In the more centrally governed England and France, this system was extended upwards in the second half of the fourteenth century, by introducing kings of arms who came directly under the competency of the crown.[2] These royal officers exerted authority over any other kings of arms and lesser heraldic officers that were active in the territories belonging to the realm. In England it was Garter, the king of arms of the order of that name, who in the long run was to hold this prominent and prestigious position. In France the name of Montjoye, identical to the French motto and already in use for heralds, was attached to this particular rank of king of arms.

---

[*] The English translation of this contribution is by Dr Wim Tigges (University of Leiden).

[1] Anthony Richard Wagner, *Heralds and Heraldry in the Middle Ages: An Inquiry into the Growth of the Armorial Function of Heralds*, 2nd edn (Oxford, 1956), pp. 25–40; Wim van Anrooij, *Spiegel van ridderschap: Heraut Gelre en zijn ereredes* (Amsterdam, 1990), pp. 16–28.

[2] Hugh Stanford London, *The Life of William Bruges: The First Garter King of Arms* (London, 1970), p. 17 and Appendix x; see also P. Adam-Even, 'Les fonctions militaires des hérauts d'armes: leur influence sur le développement de l'héraldique', *Archives héraldiques suisses* 71 (1957), p. 21; and van Anrooij, *Spiegel van ridderschap*, p. 67.

In the politically weak and fragmented German Empire such a 'super-king of arms' was lacking, but the introduction of the ranking system of pursuivants, heralds and kings of arms was also not to reach maturity until the fifteenth century.[3] Within the German Empire, the Low Countries were ahead of the times in this respect. Not until the early fifteenth century did the emperor have an Imperial herald in his service, but this Romreich (a contraction of 'Römisches Reich', Roman Empire) had no jurisdiction over the heralds who were active elsewhere in the Empire.[4] Therefore, it is all the more remarkable that from the fourteenth century the emperor appointed a special kind of king of arms, the King of Arms of the Ruwieren.[5] Such an appointment did not automatically lead to a position at the Imperial court. A herald who was appointed King of Arms of the Ruwieren usually combined that function with an extant appointment as herald in the service of a territorial ruler. No special title was attached to the office, as was the case in England and France: in principle the newly appointed officer was described by his territorial title of office, to which when occasion arose was added the appellation of 'King of Arms of the Ruwieren'.[6]

In 1938 the historian Johan Huizinga published an article in which he paid attention to the origins of this special office of king of arms in Germany.[7] Since then a number of new sources have been uncovered to supplement Huizinga's archival and literary survey. We are now acquainted with a further ten manuscripts, nearly all of them originating from the fifteenth century, written in the hands of three heralds who were also Kings of Arms of the Ruwieren. From Claes Heynenzoon (Gelre Herald and Beyeren Herald) six are extant, from Hendrik van Heessel (Österrich Herald) one and from Hermann von Brüninghausen (Juliers Herald) three.[8] This essay

---

[3] Lutz Roemheld, 'Die diplomatischen Funktionen der Herolde im späten Mittelalter' (Ph.D. thesis, Ruprecht-Karl-Universität, Heidelberg, 1964), p. 80; van Anrooij, *Spiegel van ridderschap*, pp. 16–28.

[4] Gustav A. Seyler, *Geschichte der Heraldik (Wappenwesen, Wappenkunst, Wappenwissenschaft)* (Nürnberg, 1890; repr. Neustadt an der Aisch, 1970), p. 29.

[5] Etymologically, 'Ruwieren' is to be considered as referring to the inhabitants of the banks of the Rhine.

[6] H. Kern, 'Over de taal der Batavieren en Franken', *Jaarboek van de Maatschappij der Nederlandsche Letterkunde* (1866), pp. 104–5; Johan Huizinga, 'Ruyers und Poyers', in *Wirtschaft und Kultur: Festschrift zum 70. Geburtstag von Alfons Dopsch* (Baden bei Wien and Leipzig, 1938), pp. 542–3. Cf. also Wolf-Dieter Heim, *Romanen und Germanen in Charlemagnes Reich: Untersuchung zur Benennung romanischer und germanischer Völker, Sprachen und Länder in französischen Dichtungen des Mittelalters* (Munich, 1984), pp. 330–47.

[7] Huizinga, 'Ruyers und Poyers'.

[8] Wim van Anrooij, 'The Gelre Wapenboek and its Most Important Miniatures', in *Masters and Miniatures: Proceedings of the Congress on Medieval Manuscript Illumination in the Northern Netherlands (Utrecht, 10–13 December 1989)*, ed. Koert van der Horst and Johann-Christian Klamt (Doornspijk, 1991), pp. 295–302 (Claes Heynenzoon); Wim van

---

not recorded. On 20 November 1365 a nobleman from Holland, Otto van
Arkel, declared that he had received an annuity from the town of Bois-le-
Duc 'bi hande des coninx van den Ruyren, ons knapen' (from the hands of
the King of Arms of the Ruwieren, our servant), who at that time appears
to have been in his service. A subsequent payment of the annuity 'bi hande
des coninx van den Ruwyren' (from the hands of the King of Arms of the
Ruwieren), this time lacking the addition 'ons knapen', is dated 27 January
1366. From the testament of the neighbours, Henricus van Moordrecht,
knight and citizen of Bois-le-Duc, and his spouse Katherina van der Aa,
drafted on 8 September 1367, it appears that Jan van Steensel lived close to
the 'Conincs brugge' (king's bridge), a bridge across the Dieze which had
been named after him, and on premises which were later to become part of
the court of Zevenbergen. On 8 November 1371 'Johannes de Steensel, rex
armorum' figures as a witness in Bois-le-Duc.[24] Jan van Steensel died before
17 September 1387, for on this date Jan van Brolyo already owned the house
of his father-in-law, having inherited it.[25] After Jan van Steensel, the special
office of King of Arms of the Ruwieren was to be held by at least five others.

Claes Heynenzoon, Gelre Herald and Beyeren Herald

IN THE LATE FOURTEENTH CENTURY another herald who was to hold
the special office made his appearance: Gelre (Guelders) Herald.[26] His
actual name was Claes Heynenzoon. He started his career as a messenger
in the service of Count John of Blois who resided in Schoonhoven and who
was a vassal of Albert of Bavaria, count of Holland (1358–1404). Claes Heynenzoon was attested as a messenger in 1371–3 and in 1376. In the period
1380–1401/2 he was herald in the service of William I, duke of Guelders,
and his official appellation was Gelre. From 1403 onwards we find him to be

[24] The fact that the documents of 20 November 1365 and 27 January 1366 refer to an
annuity which Otto van Arkel receives from the town of Bois-le-Duc, added to the fact that
on 8 November 1371 Jan van Steensel appears as a witness in Bois-le-Duc, allows hardly
any room for the doubt expressed by van Blokland, *Beyeren quondam Gelre Armorum
Rex de Ruyris*, p. 36, as to whether the King of Arms of the Ruwieren who appears in the
documents from 1365 and 1366 may in fact be identified with Jan van Steensel.
[25] On 17 September 1387 Jan van Brolyo sold a fee-farm on behalf of the Convent of
Poor Clares in Bois-le-Duc from the dwelling of his father-in-law, the late 'Iohannis dicti
Coninck Jan de Steensel'. De Bruijn, '"Magnus ortus"', p. 33 n. 4. In a deed of conveyance
dated 23 December 1405 the premises are described as 'the dwelling of the late Jan called
'coninc Jan Steensel', father-in-law of Jan van Brolyo, and which later belonged to the same
Jan van Brolyo'. De Bruijn, '"Magnus ortus"', p. 34. I am grateful to Prof. Dr Hans Janssen
(University of Leiden), who gave me access to the internal report by Dr M. W. J. de Bruijn
(Utrecht). Hoeben, *Brabantse heraldiek in historisch perspectief*, p. 89, wrongly assumes that
in 1404/5 Jan van Steensel was still alive.
[26] The biographical data is taken from van Anrooij, *Spiegel van ridderschap*, pp. 56–67.

in the service of Holland, from the very start amongst the retinue of Albert's son William, who was soon afterwards to succeed his father as William VI of Holland (1404–17). In Holland, Claes Heynenzoon answered to the territorial appellation of Beyeren. This appellation may be somewhat unexpected, but it can be explained as follows: in the era of Albert of Bavaria and William VI the powerful block of Holland, Zeeland and Hainaut formed a personal union with German Bavaria-Straubing, from which the counts of Holland derived their ducal title. Beyeren Herald probably died in 1414.

There are six manuscripts known to be in the hand of this herald from the late fourteenth century but primarily the early fifteenth century. They contain historiographical and literary texts as well as various collections of coats of arms.[27] One of these manuscripts is the *Gelre Armorial* (Brussels, Royal Library, 15.652–56), which has been characterised by Maurice Keen as 'with little doubt the finest of all the armorial books of the Middle Ages'.[28] The *Gelre Armorial* developed in phases.[29] Its nucleus is a general armorial – from which the codex as a whole derives its name – which is preceded by preliminary matter of a literary nature, consisting of heraldically illuminated heralds' verse and two short chronicles that are also accompanied by heraldic arms. Gelre Herald probably started the general armorial around 1395, i.e. still during his Gelre period. The miniature of a herald wearing a mantle with the lion of Guelders (fol. 122r) points to the period during which the compiler of the codex was still connected to the court at Guelders. Full-page miniatures of heralds often occur in medieval armorials, but the *Gelre Armorial* contains the earliest example in Europe.[30]

Some years after making the general armorial, Gelre Herald added the literary texts to the manuscript.[31] The general armorial thus starts at fol. 26r with an opening miniature on which is depicted an emperor enthroned (with orb, sword and imperial crown) and, standing, the seven electors. A representation with this theme is relatively rare in medieval armorials. It is very tempting to relate this opening of the general armorial to Gelre's function as King of Arms of the Ruwieren. The miniature shows the emperor who had appointed him. The armorial has a European

---

[27] Brussels, Royal Library, 17.914 and 15.652–6; The Hague, Royal Library, 71 H 39 and 131 G 37; Gotha, Landesbibliothek, Membr. II 219; the Beyeren Armorial is in private possession. Van Anrooij, 'The Gelre Wapenboek'.

[28] Keen, *Chivalry*, p. 140; Jan van Helmont, ed., *Gelre B.R. Ms. 15652–56* (Louvain, 1992) contains a facsimile of the *Gelre Armorial* in black and white.

[29] Van Anrooij, *Spiegel van ridderschap*, pp. 78–114.

[30] Egon von Berchem, 'Die Herolde und ihre Beziehungen zum Wappenwesen: eine vorläufige Materialsammlung zur Geschichte des Heroldswesens', in *Beiträge zur Geschichte der Heraldik*, ed. E. von Berchem, D. L. Galbreath, Otto Hupp *et al.* (Berlin, 1939; repr. Neustadt an der Aisch, 1972), pp. 115–219.

[31] Van Anrooij, *Spiegel van ridderschap*, pp. 78–114.

Plate 7. Gelre Herald in the *Gelre Armorial*, in the hand of Claes Heynenzoon (Gelre Herald). Brussels, Royal Library, 15.652–56, fol. 122r. By permission of the Royal Library.

outlook. It opens with the emperor's coat of arms (fol. 26v). The nobility from the heraldic provinces between Meuse and Rhine are well represented, but arms from other areas occur as well. The heraldic province of the bishop of Cologne opens with the (attributed) arms of the three Magi (fol. 28v), who were revered in Cologne.[32] These are the only attributed arms in the entire codex.

The literary preliminaries include seventeen poems, among which are twelve *Ehrenreden* or heraldic poems of praise, a genre which arose in the late thirteenth century and which was practised by heralds from the German Empire from the middle of the fourteenth century onwards.[33] For his *Ehrenreden*, Gelre Herald took his bearings from the Middle and Lower Rhenish panegyric *Minnerede* tradition, which flourished in the first half of the fourteenth century.[34] Eight poems from the literary preliminaries are written in Ripuarian, the language of the area around Cologne.[35] The literary preliminaries betray a wide geographical outlook, ranging from Holstein in the north to Nidau in the south and Holland in the west, but the emphasis lies on the territory between the Meuse and the Rhine, the area for which the author was particularly responsible as King of Arms of the Ruwieren. Against the background of his office as king of arms it can also be understood why in the literary preliminaries Gelre Herald copied two texts from Brabant: a little chronicle concerning the dukes of that territory (fols 4ra–6vb) and *Van den ever* (fols 1ra–2vb), a poem on Duke John III of Brabant, with which he opened the preliminaries.

In the manuscript The Hague, Royal Library, 131 G 37, which originates after Gelre's transfer to Holland, the Brabant chronicle appeared again. Its text, however, had been greatly expanded and forms the core text in the codex (fols 1ra–19ra).[36] Following it are five genealogies of the Trojan, Brabantine, Carolingian, Lower-Lorrainean and French rulers who reigned in Brabant (fol. 19ra–va). The Brabantine section of the manuscript originated around 1402/4 and at first it formed a single unit of employment, which

[32] Wim van Anrooij, 'Heraldische aspecten van insignes', in *Heilig en profaan 2. 1200 laatmiddeleeuwse insignes uit openbare en particuliere collecties*, ed. H. J. E. van Beuningen, A. M. Koldeweij and D. Kicken (Cothen, 2001), pp. 229–30.
[33] Stephanie Cain van D'Elden, 'Peter Suchenwirt and Heraldic Poetry' (Ph.D. thesis, University of Minnesota, 1974); Claudia Brinker, *Von manigen helden gute tat: Geschichte als Exempel bei Peter Suchenwirt* (Bern, Frankfurt am Main, New York and Paris, 1987); van Anrooij, *Spiegel van ridderschap*.
[34] Van Anrooij, *Spiegel van ridderschap*, p. 132.
[35] Ibid., p. 71.
[36] Wim van Anrooij, 'Het Haagse handschrift van heraut Beyeren: de wordingsgeschiedenis van een autograaf', *Tijdschrift voor Nederlandse taal- en letterkunde* 104 (1988), pp. 1–20. The codex has been edited in its entirety together with a colour facsimile, Verbij-Schillings, ed., *Het Haagse handschrift van heraut Beyeren*.

The fifteenth-century heraldic codex Antwerp, Hendrik Conscience Library, B. 89.420 can be considered to be Hendrik van Heessel's manuscript. It opens with a verse lament in German about the decline of chivalry (fols 2r–v4). The text cannot be dated more precisely than between 1433 and 1461. Various European rulers are addressed and summoned to turn the tide. The author identifies himself as 'Osterich eerhalld' (Österrich Herald) (fol. 4v) and refers to himself as 'ein Conig der wappen in Ruwir des Heiligh Romisch Rych' (a King of Arms of the Ruwieren of the Holy Roman Empire) (fol. 4v). The author of this text, then, is Hendrik van Heessel, who by this poem illustrated that he was able to write verse in German. Fols 84r–91r include a tract in Latin about the origins of the office of herald. The codex also contains a translation of it into German (fols 63v–70r), prepared by Johann Hartlieb, court physician in Munich. Hartlieb dedicates the translation to his 'getruwer und wolbeschaider tugenreicher wolgezogen lieber frund Heinrich von Heessel, erhallt des hauss zu Osterich, konig der wappen von Ruifir' (faithful and modest, virtuous, well-mannered dear friend Hendrik van Heessel, herald of the house of Austria, King of Arms of the Ruwieren) (fol. 63v).

The highly diversified contents of the manuscript can be related to its compiler's biography without any further problem. Thus, for instance, his overtures to the dukes of Burgundy from the early 1440s onwards are apparent from the appearance, in Latin, of the entitlement of Philip the Good (fol. 98v). They also make it clear why besides German and Latin texts the Antwerp codex contains a Middle Dutch chronicle of the county of Holland (fols 164v–185v), for Jacoba of Bavaria had been succeeded by Philip the Good as count of Holland. The historiographical text, included in the manuscript on 28 July 1456, is preceded by a series of twenty-six full-length portraits of the counts of Holland (fols 151r–162v). Preceding those are the coats of arms of the members of the Burgundian Order of the Golden Fleece (fols 115v–145r) in a composition which suggests the assembly on 2 May 1456 in The Hague. Hendrik van Heessel appears to have been present on that occasion.

The connections of Hendrik van Heessel with Philip the Good go back to an even earlier time. As a matter of fact, between 17 June 1433 and 9 December 1437, the duke of Burgundy had been involved in his appointment as king of arms. Fols 27v–28r of the Antwerp codex contain the coat of arms of Bavaria quartered with Holland, surrounded by eight related coats of arms. On fol. 28v there follows the coat of arms of Philip the Good, surrounded by those of his parents and two of his grandparents. Fol. 29r depicts the arms of Philip's son Charles the Bold (who was born on 11 November 1433) as count of Charolais. This coat of arms too is surrounded by those of his parents and two of his grandparents. The inclusion in the codex of the data concerning Philip the Good and his son may be related to the fact that on 12 April 1433 Emperor Sigismund had appointed the duke of Burgundy as count of Holland, Zeeland and Hainault.

Shortly after Hendrik van Heessel retired from the service of the Burgundian court, yet another king of arms is mentioned in the sources. On 6 July 1467 the 'coninck van den herauden of van den Royeren' (King of Arms of the heralds or of the Ruwieren) received eight postulaat-guilders from Frank van Borselen, count of Oostervant, who was in Brielle at the time.[51] It is not clear if this still refers to Hendrik van Heessel or to his successor, whether in the service of Philip the Good or not. In any case, at the capture of Venlo (1473) Charles the Bold (1467–77) had a King of Arms of the Ruwieren among his retinue.[52] In June 1476 'le roy de Royer' (the King of Arms of the Ruwieren) received a payment from the duke of Burgundy, together with the Burgundian heralds Golden Fleece King of Arms, Brabant King of Arms and Artois King of Arms.[53]

Hermann von Brüninghausen, Juliers Herald

AFTER HIS DEATH, Charles the Bold was succeeded by Mary of Burgundy, who was married to Maximilian of Habsburg on 19 August 1477. According to a notice in the account of the purveyor-general, on 5 September 1477 Maximilian sent Hermann von Brüninghausen 'dit Juilliers, roy des Royers' (entitled Juliers, King of Arms of the Ruwieren) from Bruges to Louvain in order to receive a legation from Duke William II of Juliers-Berg (1475–1511). Hermann von Brüninghausen's territorial appellation, then, was Juliers, which means that he was in the service of Duke William II of Juliers-Berg.[54] During the years 1477–79 Hermann von Brüninghausen performed various assignments on behalf of Maximilian, who in 1480 placed him on the daily pay-roll of the household ('escroes des gaiges') and retained him in his service for at least eight years.[55] His appointment as King of Arms of the Ruwieren must have taken place before

---

[51] Von Seggern, 'Hermann von Brüninghausen', pp. 110–11. Von Seggern correctly remarks (p. 115) that this cannot refer to the later King of Arms of the Ruwieren Hermann von Brüninghausen.

[52] Hoeben, *Brabantse heraldiek in historisch perspectief*, p. 91.

[53] Von Seggern, 'Hermann von Brüninghausen', p. 111.

[54] Ibid., p. 112 leaves open the possibility that it can be deduced from the notification that Hermann von Brüninghausen had formerly been in the service of Juliers. This, however, seems to be unlikely.

[55] Various assignments from October 1477 (Hiltmann and Viltart Database *Les hérauts d'armes dans les sources bourguignonnes*, source ID 12906) to November 1479 (ibid., source ID 13258); daily pay-roll of the household from 6 August 1480 (ibid., source ID 18665) to 29 January 1488 (ibid., source ID 18848).

Plate 9. Scheme of the quarterings of Philip the Good in the hand of Hendrik van Heessel (Österrich Herald). Antwerp, Stadsbibliotheek, B. 89.420, fol. 28v. By permission of the Stadsbibliotheek Antwerpen.

1477. In the period from 1461 until at least 19 February 1470 he served Duke Gerald of Juliers-Berg (1437–75) as pursuivant; in the sources he is briefly indicated by his Christian name. In that same year of 1470, Hermann von Brüninghausen was promoted to 'herault d'armes', and he was in the service of William, son of Duke Gerald of Juliers-Berg; in this capacity he was mentioned in 1471 as well.[56] Therefore, his appointment as King of Arms of the Ruwieren must have taken place between 1471 and 1477. The year 1474 seems to be the most likely: in that year Emperor Frederick III engaged the duke of Juliers-Berg's herald (who must have been Brüninghausen).[57] Hence, it is almost certain that at the capture of Venlo (1473) Charles the Bold, who had a King of Arms of the Ruwieren on the daily pay-roll of his household from 18 May 1471 up to his death,[58] was accompanied by a predecessor of Hermann von Brüninghausen.

Three manuscripts have been preserved in Hermann von Brüninghausen's hand, all of which have been poorly researched.[59] Manuscript Munich, Bayerischen Staatsbibliothek, Cod. icon. 318, can be characterised as the fraternity-book of the Order of St Hubert.[60] On fol. 1v there is a reference to the founder of the Order, Duke Gerald of Juliers-Berg (d. 1475), as if he was still alive.[61] However, the manuscript was probably compiled during the early years of the reign of William of Juliers-Berg (1475–1511).[62] It contains the coats of arms and the quartering schemes of all the members of the Order, together with notes concerning the funerals of members and the admissions of new members (fols 5r–114v). Some of the notes are by

---

[56] Ibid., source ID 10686.

[57] '. . . 1474 drückt sich das gesteigerte Interesse des Kaisers am Niederrhein darin aus, dass er den Herold des Herzogs von Jülich-Berg zu seinem Diener – wenn nicht Herold – annahm', with reference to HHStA Wien, RHR-Ant., Taxregister fol. 270v, Heinig, 'Die Türhüter und Herolde Friedrichs III', p. 372.

[58] Hiltmann and Viltart Database *Les hérauts d'armes dans les sources bourguignonnes*, source ID 91129 (18 May 1471) and source ID 91332 (9 December 1476).

[59] C. van den Bergen-Pantens, *De heraldiek in de handschriften voor 1600: tentoonstelling Brussel, Koninklijke Bibliotheek Albert I, Nassaukapel, van 8 mei tot 15 juni 1985* (Brussels, 1985), p. 57 points at the possibility that a picture in manuscript Brussels, Royal Library, IV 164, fol. 1r, may represent Hermann von Brüninghausen.

[60] The manuscript can be consulted on-line at: <http://mdzx.bib-bvb.de/codicon/Blatt_bsb00006309,00001.html?prozent=1>.

[61] Holger Kruse and Wilko Ossoba, 'St. Hubertus (1444/45)', *Ritterorden und Adelsgesellschaften im spätmittelalterlichen Deutschland: ein systematisches Verzeichnis*, ed. Holger Kruse, Werner Paravicini, Andreas Ranft (Frankfurt am Main, Bern, New York and Paris, 1991), pp. 352–76.

[62] On the basis of its contents, Reuter arrives at a date between 1473 and 1500. Marianne Reuter, 'Beschreibung der Handschrift Cod.icon. 318 Tresorhandschrift', *BSB-CodIcon Online: Elektronischer Katalog der Codices Iconographici Monacenses der Bayerischen Staatsbibliothek München* (Wed Feb 27 23:38:21 CET 2008).

Plate 10. Possible representation of Herman von Brüninghausen (Juliers Herald) in a sixteenth-century manuscript. Brussels, Royal Library, IV 164, fol. (r.) before fol. 1. By permission of the Royal Library.

a second or third hand.[63] The manuscript opens with the statutes of the Order (fols 2r–4v).

Just like the *Gelre Armorial*, manuscript Kraków, Biblioteka Jagiellońska, Germ. Quart. 1479 contains a picture of an emperor enthroned (with orb, sword and imperial crown), in this case Frederick III (fol. 7r).[64] He is surrounded by the arms of the seven electors, Austria and the Pope, as well as the Imperial coat of arms (see Plate II). The facing folio contains a corresponding note about the coronation of Emperor Frederick III in 1447. As 'tenth Worthy' Frederick III was being placed in the tradition of the Nine Worthies: fol. 5r includes the arms of the three Jews, fol. 6r those of the three Christians (the arms of the three pagans appear to have gone missing). This 'heraltz bouch' (fol. 13v) was compiled by 'Herman eyn tornyrkunde herald' (fol. 13v) by request of Duke William of Juliers-Berg. On fol. 127v the year 1481 is given as a date; Hermann von Brüninghausen mentions his name and styles himself 'cony[n]ck der vappery' (king of arms). The manuscript mainly consists of a record of the coats of arms of the members of the Order of St Hubert. Its Lower Rhenish leanings appear from elsewhere in the manuscript as well. On fols 55r–56r there is a short prose chronicle of the dukes of Cleves. Fols 64v–65v describe how people of knightly birth in Cleves were buried. Furthermore, the manuscript contains a number of page-size depictions of rulers and knights – and their spouses – from the regions between the Meuse and the Rhine.

Manuscript Vienna, Österreichischen Nationalbibliothek, Cod. 2899, fols 1r–8r, contains a written family tree (with blazons) of Philip the Upright, count palatine on the Rhine (1476–1508), and his wife Margaret.[65] At the beginning of the text the year of its origin and its authorship are worded as follows: 'In dem Jare uns Herren dusent veir hondert eyn ind eychtzycht ist dyt boiche gemacht van eyme heralt genant Herman van Bruninckusen koninck van Ruweir des Hilgen Rychs' (in the year of our Lord 1481 this book was made by one herald named Hermann von Brüninghausen, King of Arms of the Ruwieren of the Holy Roman Empire) (fol. 1r).

After Hermann von Brüninghausen hardly any information exists concerning the office of King of Arms of the Ruwieren. From the period of

---

[63]   Ibid., with examples.
[64]   Volker Schmidtchen, 'Hermann von Bruychoysen (Brunchoyften, Brüninghausen)', in *Die deutsche Literatur des Mittelalters: Verfasserlexikon* (Berlin and New York, 1981), iii, column 1053, incorrectly states that the manuscript was lost during World War II. The manuscript was originally preserved in the Royal Library in Berlin, under the same pressmark. Cf. the table of contents in *Neue Erwerbungen der Handschriftenabteilung*, ii (Berlin, 1917), pp. 77–9.
[65]   The remainder of the manuscript is a later addition dating from the first half of the sixteenth century. Hermann Menhardt, *Verzeichnis der altdeutschen literarischen Handschriften der Österreichischen Nationalbibliothek* (Berlin, 1960), p. 561.

Emperor Maximilian the formula of a charter of appointment has been preserved. The text was drawn up in view of the appointment of a herald employed by one of Maximilian's vassals. No concrete names are inserted. Maximilian knew the herald in question, who had visited many kingdoms and distant countries and who had on more than one occasion been a guest at the Imperial court. Convinced of his knowledge, ability and virtue, Maximilian decided to appoint him 'zu unserem unnd des Heil. Röm. Reichs König der Wapen von Rifor' (as our King of Arms of the Ruwieren and of the Holy Roman Empire).[66] If an appointment took place, it happened in the period when Maximilian was emperor of the German Empire (1508–19).

Conclusion

It is possible that the opening years of the Hundred Years War formed the context within which the idea arose of instituting a King of Arms of the Ruwieren. Such a functionary had as his special field of activity the territories between the Rivers Meuse and Rhine. Antoine de la Salle and Olivier de la Marche indicate who was involved in the appointment of such a functionary: in his capacity of margrave of the German Empire the duke of Brabant nominated a candidate, and the emperor appointed him. All the relevant archival documents and other handwritten data, which together cover the period of *c.* 1360 to *c.* 1500, seem to confirm this division of roles.

None of the ten manuscripts of the three Kings of Arms of the Ruwieren that have been preserved is completely devoted to this special function. Closest to this are the earliest part of the *Gelre Armorial* (the armorial portion, including the depiction of the emperor and seven electors as its opening miniature and headed by the emperor's coat of arms), the earliest part of The Hague manuscript 131 G 37 (containing a little Brabantine chronicle and a series of Brabantine genealogies), both by Claes Heynenzoon, and also the earliest section of the Vienna manuscript (with the text of Hermann von Brüninghausen concerning Philip the Upright, count palatine on the Rhine, and his spouse). The selection of knights that Gelre Herald honoured with an *Ehrenrede* (and which he included in the *Gelre Armorial*) betrays a bias towards the regions between Meuse and Rhine, but partly transcends that region as well, to the north as well as to the south and to the west. Hermann von Brüninghausen's manuscripts contain a picture of the emperor with the coats of arms of the seven electors (MS Kraków), they relate to the Juliers Order of St Hubert (MSS Kraków and Munich) and generally betray a bias towards the region between the Meuse and the Rhine. Most of the manuscripts can be understood as being authored by

---

[66] Seyler, *Geschichte der Heraldik*, p. 28.

men with a double function, that of herald (within a specific territory) and that of king of arms, the accent usually lying on the territorial function.

This picture is confirmed by the manner in which the special office is referred to in contemporary sources. The appellation of King of Arms of the Ruwieren is usually an addition following the territorial title of office. The territorial title indicates who the herald was serving in any case. Two names of Kings of Arms of the Ruwieren refer to territories between the Meuse and the Rhine (Gelre Herald, Juliers Herald), and one to Brabant (Louvain). As Österrich Herald, Hendrik van Heessel may have served successive German emperors, but to some extent concomitantly with his German tenure he was soon to be a member of the household of Philip the Good, duke of Brabant; he originated from the region between the Meuse and the Rhine. Jan van Steensel is the only one to whom this argument does not apply: no territorial title is known and being Brabantine by birth he did not originate from the area between Meuse and Rhine.

In the course of his career a herald was able to change masters and to adopt another official title, but this did not affect his function of King of Arms of the Ruwieren. We see this happen in the case of Gelre Herald, who became Beyeren Herald, and also in that of Österrich Herald, who while in Burgundian service did not adopt a territorial title but was only referred to as King of Arms of the Ruwieren. This also goes for Jan van Steensel, who was paid by three different employers during the years 1362–5, continuing all the while to live in Bois-le-Duc.

The vicissitudes of the duchy of Brabant during the fifteenth century caused the successive dukes of Burgundy, Philip the Good and Charles the Bold, to be directly involved in the nomination of a new functionary to the emperor. In the fifteenth century it became usual for the newly appointed King of Arms of the Ruwieren to enter the service of either of the two parties involved in his appointment, and under a territorial title. If so desired, the other party could employ him simultaneously as king of arms. It is also from the fifteenth century onwards – presumably by the initiative of the emperor – that the office of King of Arms of the Ruwieren was emphatically paraded as a function within the Holy Roman Empire. With the succession of Maximilian of Habsburg in the Low Countries, nomination and appointment finally came into the same hands, Maximilian being both duke of Brabant and Holy Roman Emperor. During Maximilian's reign as emperor hardly anything is heard about the office of King of Arms of the Ruwieren. From this fact it can be tentatively deduced that previous dukes of Brabant thought the appointment of a King of Arms of the Ruwieren, whom they themselves had nominated, to be an instrument to exert influence within the German Empire.

Plate 11. Detail of the façade of the Palazzo Vecchio showing (left) the arms of the Florentine *populus* and (right) the arms of the city of Florence. Photograph by Laura Cirri.

However, they did so within the framework of a recognised heraldic iconography and language. The main coats of arms of Florence and its offices were constituted by the combination of the colour gules and the metal argent: Tuscany and its cities were under Imperial jurisdiction and even if they conquered and maintained their freedom, heraldically they still made reference to the colours of the ancient Imperial *vexillum*: argent, a cross gules.[11] This combination of colours was very common among the coats of arms of the Tuscan cities, such as Lucca, Pistoia and Pisa, and other communes in north Italy.[12] Florence, too, made reference to its history of Imperial overlordship in its use of gules and argent.

Although operating as a political republic, the Florentine elite recognised and subscribed to the types of chivalric and courtly culture found in the European principalities. The Palazzo Vecchio, also known as the Palazzo della Signoria, was the space in which politics, civic power and public life

[11] Borgia, 'Gli stemmi dello Stato toscano', p. 342.
[12] V. Favini and A. Savorelli, *Segni di Toscana. Identità e territorio attraverso l'araldica dei comuni: storia e invenzione grafica (secoli XIII–XVII)* (Florence, 2007), p. 22.

Plate 12. The Palazzo Vecchio in Florence. Photograph by Laura Cirri.

intersected.[13] The priors and the standard-bearer of justice resided in the Palazzo Vecchio and when in office were restricted to leaving the building only for official events and celebrations. Inside the palace there was public space in which civic business could be conducted and a private area for the signoria. The Palazzo Vecchio was the focal point of power for Florentine citizens and acted in the same way as royal palaces did elsewhere. As a republic,

[13] N. Rubinstein, *The Palazzo Vecchio 1298–1532: Government, Architecture, and Imagery in the Civic Palace of The Florentine Republic* (Oxford, 1995).

138

Florence was a city without a court,[14] but courtly and chivalric attitudes were evident at each level of municipal society, especially during the fifteenth century. The commercial and trade relations of the city improved its position in the eyes of Europe and encouraged connections with the courts of Italy and the major western European monarchies. Florentine diaries and chronicles, written between the end of the fourteenth and the beginning of the fifteenth century, reveal a great attention to every kind of celebration and courtly ceremonial, including the official welcoming of remarkable guests and foreign ambassadors.[15] Florence, although politically distinct, styled its cultural life on the chivalric fashions influencing the rest of Europe.[16] The image the city presented of itself in its ritual and ceremonial life shaped the definition of the ruling elite and the relationship they entertained with those they governed.[17] The increased interest in romances, in heraldic fashions, and in jousts, tournaments and *armeggerie* served to reconstitute the elite into an urban nobility.[18] And in all of this, the signoria denoted their approval and patronage of these quasi-courtly pastimes through the prominent display of their own coats of arms and the arms of the commune.[19]

Alongside the increased interest in chivalric culture in the fifteenth century was the emergence of the office of herald in late medieval Florence. In 1452, the Holy Roman Emperor, Frederick III (1452–93) entered into Florence, accompanied by heralds acting as important diplomatic functionaries.[20] This had a profound influence on the Florentine chivalric community and it was not long after this that the first herald appeared in Florentine employment. Of course, the Republic had used minstrels and messengers during the fourteenth century and the emergence of an officer of arms was a natural development. Some of these fourteenth-century *sindicus et referendarius* were even dubbed to knighthood when they were appointed ambassadors by the signoria and sent to foreign courts.[21] The evolution of the office of the *sindicus et referendarius* took place at the end of the fourteenth century, at a time when there was need for both administrative functions, and skills in poetry and recital.[22] It was only during the fifteenth century

---

[14]   P. Ventrone, 'Cerimonialità e spettacolo nella festa cavalleresca fiorentina del quattrocento', in *La civiltà del torneo (sec. XII–XVII): giostre e tornei tra medioevo ed età moderna* (Rome, 1990), p. 36.

[15]   Ibid., p. 36.

[16]   Ibid., p. 40.

[17]   Cardini, 'Symbols and Rituals in Florence', p. 500.

[18]   Ibid. p. 502.

[19]   Borgia, 'L'araldica in Firenze al tempo del Duca d'Atene'.

[20]   ASFI, Carte di corredo 61, fols 2r–v.

[21]   R. C. Trexler, *The Libro Cerimoniale of the Florentine Republic* (Geneva, 1978), pp. 35–7.

[22]   *Statuta populi et communis Florentiae publica auctoritate collecta castigata et praeposita anno salutis MCCCCXV* (Freiburg, 1771–83), ii, p. 514.

that the priors understood the necessity of employing a range of officials with different remits: in 1456 Francesco Filarete became the first Florentine herald, styled 'araldo della Signoria'.[23] However, no heraldic collective emerged and Filarete was the sole Florentine herald during the fifteenth century.

Filarete was born in 1419 and during his life proved his versatility in different fields, from writing lyric odes to competing as an architect with a project for the creation of the façade of the cathedral in Florence.[24] Filarete's career as herald of the signoria proved successful and he was soon entrusted with the types of duties expected of heralds operating in some kingdoms and principalities of Europe. In 1475, the signoria ordered Filarete to write a ceremonial book, as a manual of protocol intended for use by future heralds of the signoria and civic officials. This manuscript, *Ceremonie notate in tempi di Francesco Filarethe Heraldo*, is now held in the state archive of Florence.[25] The main purpose of the book was to record and codify the conduct of the signoria during official ceremonies. But it also acts as a history of late medieval Florence, and it reports on the main events that occurred during three different periods; the entries for the first two (1452–76, 1495–9) can be attributed to Filarete, while his son-in-law, Angelo Manfidi, to whom the position of herald of the signoria passed after Filarete's death in 1504, continued recording in the *Ceremonie notate* between 1515 and 1522.

Among the main events described in the book was Frederick III's visit to Florence in 1452, en route to his coronation as Holy Roman Emperor by Pope Nicholas V. An account of this entry opened the *Ceremonie notate*.[26] The signoria welcomed him with civic celebrations and Filarete underlined the fact that the Florentine citizens chose to present themselves as a free population, not subjected to any Imperial authority. Other events which caught the attention of Filarete were the visits of Pope Pius II (1405–64) and Galeazzo Maria Sforza, duke of Milan (1444–76), in 1459.[27] Pius II was on his way to Mantua, where he had summoned the Christian princes trying to organise a crusade against the Turks between June 1459 and January 1460. Sforza and his retinue, including a Milanese herald, were met by a large number of young Florentine citizens, sent on behalf of the signoria. A

[23] ASFI, Prov., 147, fols 67v–68r.

[24] Trexler, *The Libro Cerimoniale*, p. 49.

[25] The disordered folios of the manuscript were probably first paginated during the seventeenth century by Carlo di Tommaso Strozzi. In fact, a modern folio offers an alternative manuscript description and title: 'N. 413 Cerimoniale della Repubblica fiorentina, e memoria de trattamenti, e renfreschi fatti dalla medesima, scritto per francesco filerete Araldo della Repubblica, dall'anno 1450 al 1522, e da Angelo Manfidio Araldo similmente. Originale, Del Senatore Carlo di Tommaso Strozzi. 1670'.

[26] ASFI, Carte di corredo 61, fols 2r–v.

[27] ASFI, Carte di corredo 61, fol. 3v.

Tournaments, Heraldry and Heralds in the Kingdom of Poland in the Late Middle Ages

Bogdan Wojciech Brzustowicz and Katie Stevenson

THE WAYS in which tournaments influenced the development of heraldry – and, as a consequence, the role of heralds – have long been an area of historical research.[1] However, such research has been dominated by western European scholars, and there has been little, if any, examination of the heraldic history of other European regions. This is especially disappointing as the experiences of central and eastern Europe offer different perspectives from those provided by their western European counterparts. Therefore, this essay attempts to redress some of this imbalance by concentrating on the kingdom of Poland, a kingdom that has been largely overlooked by scholars of medieval chivalric culture, yet is one which reveals much about the diffusion of chivalry and heraldry across wider Europe. For example, the tournament was well known and frequently practised in medieval Poland but Polish tournaments are wholly unfamiliar to western European scholars. Moreover, the tournament had a profound influence on the development of a distinctive Polish heraldic

---

[1] N. Drejholt, 'Heralds and Heraldry', in *Riddarlek och Tornerspel: Tournaments and the Dream of Chivalry*, ed. L. Rangström (Stockholm, 1992), pp. 321–5; L. Fenske, 'Adel und Rittertum im Spiegel im früher heraldischer Formen und deren Entwicklung', in *Das ritterliche Turnier im Mittelalter: Beiträge zu einer vergleichenden Formen und Verhaltensgeschichte des Rittertums*, ed. J. Fleckenstein (Göttingen, 1985), pp. 75–160; L. Kurras, 'Von Wappen und Herolden', in *Das grosse Buch der Turniere. Cod. Vat. Ross. 711* (Stuttgart and Zürich, 1996), pp. 107–11; R. Dennys, *Heraldry and the Heralds* (London, 1982); M. Pastoureau, *Traité d' héraldique* (Paris, 1979), pp. 39–41; W. Leonhard, *Das grosse Buch der Wappekunst: Entwicklung, Elemente, Bildmotive, Gestaltung* (Munich, 1978), pp. 18–20; O. Neubecker, *Heraldik Wappen – ihr ursprung, sinn und Wert* (Frankfurt am Main, 1977), pp. 14–18; A. R. Wagner, *Heralds and Heraldry in the Middle Ages* (London, 1939).

culture.[2] However, the practitioners of this culture, the officers of arms, had a short-term role in the history of Polish chivalry, operating only in the latter half of the fourteenth century to the mid-fifteenth century.[3]

Western European chivalric culture had started to permeate Polish elite society from the end of the eleventh century.[4] The crusades, military skirmishes, pilgrimages and diplomatic contact ensured that Polish knights had ample points of contact with western culture. Chivalry developed in Poland as it did elsewhere and from the thirteenth century onwards Polish knights took on increasing social status and standing in elite and political society. This was accompanied by patterns that are comparable with western European practices in the customs of dubbing, ideas on idealised chivalric behaviour, and the development and popularity of the tournament. Courts were pivotal in the diffusion of chivalric culture into Poland via the frontier region and cultural crossroad of Silesia (bordering with Germany and Bohemia). During the period of the break-up of Poland into dukedoms and especially from the thirteenth century, the impetus was from the ducal courts; and, after the restitution of the Polish kingdom in 1320, from the royal court. In the late Middle Ages the court of the grand master of the Order of the Teutonic Knights was also a strong stimulus to chivalrous activities.[5]

Silesia was the principal area to which tournaments were introduced and the region from which their popularity spread throughout medieval Poland.[6] The first recorded tournament held here was in 1225, when the

[2] B. W. Brzustowicz, *Turniej rycerski w Królestwie Polskim w późnym średniowieczu i renesansie na tle europejskim* (Warsaw, 2003); J. Szymczak, 'Knightly Tournaments in Medieval Poland', *Fasciculi Archaeologiae Historicae* 8 (Łódź, 1995), pp. 9–28; S. K. Kuczyński, 'Turnieje rycerskie w średniowiecznej Polsce', in *Biedni i bogaci. Studia z dziejów społeczeństwa i kultury ofiarowane Bronisławowi Geremkowi w sześćdziesiątą rocznicę urodzin* (Warsaw, 1992), pp. 295–306.

[3] Despite the many attempts made by Polish scholars, it cannot be proved that heralds were present earlier than the fourteenth century: although the first mention of a named herald in Polish employ is connected with the Jagiełłon Dynasty (in Poland from 1386), we can only conjecture that heralds were known under the Piasts at the end of the thirteenth century and earlier-fourteenth century. S. K. Kuczyński, 'Heroldowie króla polskiego', in *Venerabiles, nobiles et honesti. Studia z dziejów społeczeństwa polski średniowiecznej*, ed. A. Radzimiński, A. Supruniuk and J. Wroniszewski (Toruń, 1997), p. 333; S. K. Kuczyński, 'Les hérauts d'armes dans la Pologne médiévale', *Revue du Nord* 88, no. 366–7 (2006), p. 652.

[4] U. Świderska, *Kultura rycerska w średniowiecznej Polsce* (Zielona Góra, 2001), pp. 16–21; D. Piwowarczyk, *Obyczaj rycerski w Polsce późnośredniowiecznej XIV–XV w.* (Warsaw, 1998), pp. 8–24.

[5] Bogdan W. Brzustowicz, 'Turnieje rycerskie a zakon krzyżacki na ziemiach polskich w średniowieczu', in *Studia z dziejów polskiej historiografii wojskowej*, ed. B. Miśkiewicz (Poznań, 2002), vi, pp. 119–35.

[6] T. Jurek, *Obce rycerstwo na Śląsku do połowy XIV wieku* (Poznań, 1996), pp. 113–48; M. Cetwinski, *Rycerstwo śląskie do końca XIII wieku* (Wrocław, 1980), i, p. 146; K. Maleczyński, *Historia Śląska* (Wrocław, 1960), i:1, p. 586.

fortress at Lubusz-on-Oder (on the German–Silesian–Greater Poland border), controlled by the Piast duke of Greater Poland, Ladislaus Laskonogi (d. 1231), was lost to Louis IV, landgrave of Thuringia. A Thuringian source recorded that this tournament took place on Saturday 18 August of that year to commemorate the conquest.[7] In this we find a clear example of western and, specifically, Germanic chivalric sports being imported directly into Silesia. While the spectacle was unlikely to have included Poles, its performance in Silesia would have sent clear messages to Silesian locals and Polish elites alike, that power and control might be won through brute force and military skills. Chivalry, in its most martial form, had arrived in Poland. This was the first of many cultural exchanges on the Silesian frontier. The *Book of Henryków* records a tournament held on 24 February 1243 in Lwówek Śląski (Lower Silesia), which was organised by Duke Boleslaus the Rogatka of the Piast dynasty (d. 1278). Duke Boleslaus was fond of tournaments and under his patronage their popularity increased in medieval Poland. Among the participants in the tournament was Albert the Beard, the son of a German immigrant who had arrived in Silesia at the beginning of the thirteenth century. Albert the Beard played a leading role in the event and, according to the *Henryków* chronicler, insisted that Duke Boleslaus made an offering to the Cistercians of Henryków before any knight would joust.[8] It seems likely that the chronicler, himself of the house of the Cistercians of Henryków, provided a dramatised account of the offering. Nevertheless, it serves to illustrate not only the links between the knightly and monastic communities, but also the diversity of the 'local' participants in tournaments in Silesia. There is additional evidence that

---

[7] 'Annales Reinhardsbrunnenses', *Thüringische Geschichtsquellen*, ed. F. X. Wegele (Jena, 1854), i, pp. 181–2. See J. Fleckenstein, 'Das Turnier als höfisches Fest im hochmittelalterlichen Deutschland', in *Das ritterliche Turnier im Mittelalter: Beiträge zu einer vergleichenden Formen und Verhaltensgeschichte des Rittertums*, ed. J. Fleckenstein (Göttingen, 1985), p. 244; R. Barber and J. Barker, *Tournaments: Jousts, Chivalry and Pageants in the Middle Ages* (Woodbridge, 1989), p. 49; Szymczak, 'Knightly Tournaments', p. 11. The chronicler Jan Długosz records many tournaments which allegedly occurred at the courts of the early Piasts in the eleventh and twelfth centuries, but other records do not support that these took place and it would instead seem that they were the imagination of Długosz: J. Długosz, *Annales seu Cronicae Incliti Regni Poloniae*, lib. I–II (Warsaw, 1964), p. 234; lib. III–IV (Warsaw, 1970), pp. 95, 294; lib. V–VI (Warsaw, 1973), pp. 24, 49, 110, 200, 232. See Brzustowicz, *Turniej rycerski w Królestwie Polskim*, pp. 193–4; Szymczak, 'Knightly Tournaments', pp. 10–11.

[8] R. Grodecki, ed., *Liber Fundationis Claustri Sancte Marie Virginis in Heinrichow czyli Księga Henrykowska* (Wrocław, 1991), p. 129; W. Irgang, ed., *Schlesisches Urkundenbuch, vol. II (1231–1250)* (Vienna, Cologne and Graz, 1977), p. 145, no. 241. See Kuczyński, 'Turnieje rycerskie', p. 298; Szymczak, 'Knightly Tournaments', p. 11; J. Mularczyk, 'Bolesław II Rogatka na tle sytuacji polityczno-społecznej Śląska', in *Społeczeństwo polski średniowiecznej*, ed. S. K. Kuczyński (Warsaw, 2001), ix, pp. 113–42.

German and Czech chivalric culture was reaching Poland via the nexus of Silesia.[9] For example, linguistic borrowings into the Polish vernacular from German, including terms such as *Ritter* (knight), *Huld* (homage), *Turnier* (tournament) and *Erbe* (coat of arms), are a clear indication that it was German-speaking cultures that influenced Polish conceptions of knighthood and chivalry.

Boleslaus's grandson, Henry IV Probus (d. 1290), duke of Wrocław (Lower Silesia), and a claimant to the Polish throne, was also a keen patron of tournaments and cemented their popularity amongst the Silesian knightly class. Henry IV was heavily influenced by Czech chivalric culture, having spent his adolescence in Prague at the court of the king of Bohemia, Ottokar II (d. 1278), which was an important centre for all types of chivalric and courtly pursuits including the support of a collection of minnesingers, which included Henry himself in its ranks. Duke Henry regularly oversaw tournaments, including a four-day tournament at the bishop of Wrocław's town of Nysa in Silesia in 1284. This was the cause of some consternation for the incumbent bishop of Wrocław, Tomasz II, who complained bitterly about Henry's disregard for the law in brutally forcing his way into Nysa, which was 'indixit torneamentum (ludendo torneamentum)' (he proclaimed a tournament by playing a tournament). Even worse, in Tomasz's view, the town's provisions were commandeered for the use of the participants in the tournament.[10] Henry's passion for tournaments was identified by the jousts held in *c.* 1288 to honour his marriage to Matilda of Brandenberg,[11] and his reputation for skill in the lists was memorialised around 1320 in a miniature of Codex Manesse. This miniature shows the young duke as a tournament champion being handed a laurel wreath of red flowers by several young ladies.[12] His dress and arms are similar to those

---

[9]   In the kingdom of Bohemia the first tournaments were organised during the reign of King Wenceslaus I (1230–54): J. Macek, *Česká středověká šlechta* (Prague, 1997), p. 114; J. Macek, 'Das Turnier im mittelalterlichen Böhmen', in *Das ritterliche Turnier im Mittelalter: Beiträge zu einer vergleichenden Formen- und Verhaltensgeschichte des Rittertums*, ed. J. Fleckenstein (Göttingen, 1985), p. 372; W. Iwańczak, *Po stopách rytířských příběhů. Rytířský ideál v českém písemnictví 14 století* (Prague, 2001), p. 146; W. Iwańczak, 'Turniej rycerski w Królestwie Czeskim-próba analizy kulturowej', *Przegląd humanistyczny* 27 (1983), fasciculus 5, p. 42.

[10]   G. A. Stenzel, ed., *Urkunden zur Geschichte des Bisthums Breslau im Mittelalter* (Breslau, 1845), no. CIX. See Kuczyński, 'Turnieje rycerskie', p. 299; J. Szymczak, 'Koszty zabawy turniejowej w Polsce Piastów i Jagiełłonów', in *Kultura średniowiecznego Śląska i Czech. Zamek*, ed. K. Wachowski (Wrocław, 1996), p. 34.

[11]   J. Bumke, *Mäzene im Mittelalter: die Gönner und Auftraggeber der höfischen Literatur in Deutschland 1150–1300* (Munich, 1979), pp. 206, 637.

[12]   Heidelberg, Universitäts-Bibliothek Ruprecht-Karls-Universität, Große Heidelberger Liederhandschrift (Codex Manesse), Cod. Pal. germ. 848, fol. 11v; I. E. Walther, ed., *Codex Manesse: die Miniaturen der Großen Heidelberger Leiderhandschrift* (Frankfurt am Main,

of other Silesian dukes depicted in tombstones, plates and seals (see Plate III). Most striking in this illumination is the heraldic decoration: the rich heraldic emblems shown on Duke Henry IV Probus in the Codex Manesse are indicative of key transformations in Silesian heraldry.

The earliest coats of arms in Poland began to appear in the second half of the thirteenth century. However, these were not copies of western styles of heraldic symbolism, which by the end of the twelfth cenutry were predominantly ancestral heraldry used to identify not only the individual, but also his lineage and family community. Instead, from the end of the twelfth century in Poland, simple marks made up of a combination of straight and curved lines were used as a practical means of quick identification in battle and as a means of legitimising written documentation by attaching a personalised seal. Polish coats of arms shared similar principles to their western counterparts, but rather than being granted to individuals or discrete family units, Polish coats of arms were granted to clans. Thus, a number of unrelated families, usually with different family names, could use the same coat of arms that identified them with a particular clan grouping. Further, each coat of arms was bestowed with a proper name: for example, the earliest arms used by Polish heraldic clans included Topór, Lis, Rawa, Laska, Łabędź, Rola, Dołęga, Wczele, Cielepały and Sokola.[13] These simple symbols evolved into western styles of charges over the course of the later Middle Ages. Indeed, by the middle of the fourteenth century the older Polish line-markings lost favour amongst the Polish nobility and new, imported charges were placed upon Polish shields.[14] These charges were predominantly based upon the most common heraldic animals and emblems in western heraldry. It might be argued that this development was a direct result of the expansion of chivalric practices into Polish territories from the frontier cultural hub of Silesia. For instance, it was in Silesia that coats of arms first became functionally useful from the second half of thirteenth century, as a ready means of identifying men in skirmishes, sieges and routine border fighting, as well

---

1988), plate 5, p. 10; K. Wutke, 'Der Minnesänger Herzog Heinrich von Pressela in der bisherigen Beurteilung', *Zeitschrift des Vereins für Geschichte (und Altertum) Schlesiens* 56 (1922), pp. 1–32; Z. Wawrzonowska, *Uzbrojenie i ubiór rycerski Piastów śląskich od XII do XIV wieku* (Łódź, 1976), pp. 101–2; M. Kaganiec, *Heraldyka Piastów śląskich 1146–1707* (Katowice, 1992), pp. 32–3, 101–2; S. Mikucki, 'Heraldyka Piastów śląskich do schyłku XIV w.', in *Historia Śląska* (Kraków, 1936), iii, p. 12.

[13] J. Bieniak, *Polskie rycerstwo średniowieczne: wybór pism* (Kraków, 2002), pp. 109–10. On Polish knight clans see J. Bieniak, 'Knights' Clans in Medieval Poland', in *The Polish Nobility in the Middle Ages*, ed. A. Gąsiorowski (Wrocław, 1984).

[14] On the evolution of the coats of arms in medieval Polish heraldry see Bieniak, *Polskie rycerstwo średniowieczne*, pp. 109–15; S. K. Kuczyński, 'Le premier armorial polonais du XVe siècle l'auteur, l'oeuvre, la méthode', in *Les armoriaux: histoire héraldique, sociale et culturelle des armoriaux mediévaux*, ed. L. Holte, M. Pastoureau, H. Textex (Paris, 1997), pp. 125–7.

as in the lists. It was in Silesia that western coats of arms were popularised. Moreover, an intense period of migration by Germans of the knightly class to Silesia in the late twelfth and thirteenth centuries meant that the western style of coats of arms became more popular elsewhere in Poland as chivalric cultural practices became more widespread. However, the adoption of new styles of western heraldry were not wholesale, and amongst families of newcomers the picture is rather different. Instead of continuing to use their own arms, or acquiring arms that were fashionable amongst the Polish nobility, these foreign immigrants sometimes adopted the original Polish style of emblem (for example German families: Luchow acquired the coat of arms Rogala, Stewitz, the coat of arms Leliwa, Kottwitz, and temporarily the coat of arms Wieniawa), both in order to add authenticity to their claims to Polish noble ancestry and to achieve the consequent social position that this conferred.[15] Indeed, as heraldry increasingly told the story of lineage, then those wishing to benefit from an impression of long-standing service in Poland might well allude to this by adopting the oldest form of visual identification.

Important as Silesia was in the propagation of chivalry in Poland, there were other avenues through which elite Polish culture might be influenced. The Teutonic Order, for example, played an important role in the reception of chivalric culture in medieval Poland, drawing western European knights to Prussia with the opportunity of internationl fame and a chance to hone their military skills by fighting against the pagan Prussians and Lithuanians. Local contact between the Order and the Polish territories was also regular: until the 1380s Polish knights participated very willingly in the crusades, and Polish dukes were in close communication with the grand master.[16] Here, at the court of the grand master, were to be found the experts in chivalry: in particular, the officers of arms, who engaged in a range of messenger services, diplomacy, mashalling of court rituals and ceremonies and

---

[15] Jurek, *Obce rycerstwo*, pp. 128–9.

[16] W. Paravicini, *Die Preussenreisen des europäischen Adels* (Sigmaringen, 1989), i, pp. 138–42, also see plate ii; K. Górski and J. Pakulski, 'Udział Polaków w krzyżackich rejzach na Litwę w latach siedemdziesiątych i osiemdziesiątych XIV stulecia', *Zapiski historyczne* 52:3 (1987), pp. 39–56; L. Pudłowski, 'Udział rycerzy polskich w krzyżackich rejzach', in *Poznańskie towarzystwo przyjaciół nauk. Wydział nauk o sztuce: Sprawozdania nr 108 za rok 1991* (Poznań, 1991), pp. 5–12; L. Pudłowski, 'In Dei laudem et pro honore militari': 14th Century Heraldic Image of Polish Crusaders in Koenigsberg', in *Genealogica et Heraldica: Report of the 20th International Congress of Genealogical and Heraldic Sciences in Uppsala 9–13 August 1992*, ed. L. Wikström (Stockholm, 1996), pp. 331–7; A. Supruniuk, 'U kresu wypraw krzyżowych: udział rycerzy i stronników mazowieckich w krzyżackich rejzach na Litwę na podstawie czternastowiecznych herbarzy', *Teki historyczne* 21 (1994–5), pp. 52–83; A. Supruniuk, 'O wyprawach do Prus rycerzy polskich i wojnie domowej w Koronie w latach 1382–1385', *Zapiski historyczne* 65:2 (2000), pp. 31–55.

who utilised their knowledge of all types of marital activity. Some heralds acted on behalf of the Order or the Polish dukedoms, and many others visited from courts throughout Europe. This was a vibrant military setting in which heralds' roles in negotiation, diplomacy and chivalry were essential to the smooth operation of the Order.

The Order of Teutonic Knights had its own heralds, the chief of whom was Prussia King of Arms (Preusserland). Although Prussia Kings of Arms operated during the fourteenth century (recorded between the years 1338 and 1403), their personal names are difficult to determine. One, Berthold, is recorded in 1439 as Preusserland during the leadership of Grand Master Paul von Rusdorf (1422–41).[17] Polish and international heralds were especially prominent at the court of the grand master from the second half of the fourteenth century as a result of an intensified crusading campaign during this time.[18] There was a constant influx of foreign guests, who were richly entertained by feasts, dances, hunting and tournaments organised by the Order's officers of arms.[19] So too were foreign heralds to be found frequently at the Polish ducal and royal courts and here they were used in similar ways to the Teutonic Order's heralds. For example, it is evident that Polish heralds acquired and circulated information concerning the heraldic achievements of the Polish nobility, certainly at least as far as the Low Countries where Bellenville Herald and Gelre Herald included Polish coats of arms in their armorials.[20] At the courts of the grand master held in Toruń and Malbork, Polish knights came across the custom of the honourable table (*mensa honoris, Ehrentisch, table d'honneur*), modelled on the Arthurian Round Table, and here heralds played an important role in

---

[17] Paravicini, *Die Preussenreisen*, i, pp. 329–32, see also plate 47, ii, pp. 129–30; A. R. Chodyński, 'Styl i formy życia świeckiego na dworze wielkich mistrzów w Malborku', in *Zamek i dwór w średniowieczu od XI do XV wieku*, ed. J. Wiesiołowski (Poznań, 2001), p. 104.

[18] For visits paid by the foreign heralds to the court of the Grand Master see: E. Joachim, ed., *Das Marienburger Tresslerbuch der Jahre 1399–1409* (Königsberg, 1896), p. 24 (the French herald, Franczoser); p.160 (the herald of the Polish king, Polanlant); p. 300 (the herald of the Würtenberg prince); p. 377 (the herald of the Bohemian king, Karlstein); p. 418 (the English king of arms, Engillant); p. 429 (the pursuivant of the prince of Słupsk); p. 473 (the herald of the Hungarian king, Ungerland); p. 531 (the pursuivant of the lord of Schwartzburg); p. 559 (Johann Tiltenberg, the pursuivant of Nassau).

[19] S. Selzer, *Artushöfe im Ostseeraum: ritterlich-höfische Kultur in den Städten des Preußenlandes im 14. und 15. Jahrhundert* (Frankfurt am Main, 1996), especially p. 36–43; Paravicini, *Die Preussenreisen*, ii, pp. 122–37; Chodyński, 'Styl i formy życia świeckiego na dworze Wielkich Mistrzów', pp. 104–10.

[20] S. Mikucki, 'Rycerstwo słowiańskie w Wapenboek Gelrego', *Studia źródłoznawcze* 3 (1958), pp. 103–21; A. Heymowski, 'Herby polskie w paryskim Armorial Bellenville', *Studia źródłoznawcze* 32/33 (1990), pp.113–27.

the jousting custom.[21] As elsewhere, these highly literate and well-informed officers of arms played a crucial role in the promotion of the history and fame of their patrons, such as Wigand of Marburg, the renowned German chronicler and herald of the Teutonic Knights, who was commissioned by Grand Master Winrych von Kniprode (1351–82) to write a chivalric ballad on the fights between the Teutonic Knights and Lithuanians.[22] The court of the grand master in the fourteenth and fifteenth centuries was evidently a hotbed of cultural exchange and further research should offer excellent insights into what might be seen as a microcosm of a cosmopolitan court.

However, the principal place at which a thriving heraldic community can be located was at the Polish royal court. Contemporary sources are, of course, sparse and it is difficult to determine how many heralds there were, the dates of their service, their names and networks, their duties or how they were remunerated. We can determine virtually nothing of their interactions with one another: whether or not there was a domestic heraldic community or a college eludes us, although further work in this field may illuminate these problems. However, there is sufficient evidence in Polish records to achieve a basic handle on their principal activities. As we would expect, there are passing references to heralds in chronicle accounts, but the only Polish chronicler to mention heralds with any frequency was the fifteenth-century chronicler Jan Długosz.[23] Their activities are better recorded in official administrative and financial records. Here we find they acted as representatives, spokesmen and envoys (*orator*, *nuntius*, *legatus*) and as heraldic officials, who checked coats of arms during tournaments and were consulted on matters of chivalry. Alongside this work, Polish officers of arms were consulted for advice on raising men to the ranks of the nobility ('praeco, deinde officialis, minister, cuius erant cura insignium nobilium, morum militarium iurisdictio, quin etiam dignitatum equestrium imposito', 'a herald, then an official, a minister in charge of the nobles' insignia, the jurisdiction of military customs, and also set over the chivalric dignities').[24]

---

[21]   J. Voigt, ed., *Codex Diplomaticus Prussicus* (Königsberg, 1853), iv, no. xxxi, pp. 36–8; Selzer, *Artushöfe im Ostseeraum*, p. 36 and next; Paravicini, *Die Preussenreisen*, i, pp. 316–34; J. Voigt, *Geschichte Preussens von den ältesten Zeiten bis zum Untergange der Herrschaft des Deutschen Ordens* (Königsberg, 1832), v, pp. 712–19.

[22]   G. Oswald, *Lexikon der Heraldik* (Leipzig, 1984), p. 263; U. Arnold, 'Wigand', in *Altpreussische Biographie* (Marburg and Lahn, 1969), ii, pp. 802–3.

[23]   Bohemian chroniclers had the same attitude: T. Krejčik, 'Čeští heroldi za lucemburských panovníků', in *Heraldicka ročenka za rok 1978*, ed. Heraldický klub české numismatické společnosti (Prague, 1978), p. 44..

[24]   M. Plezia, ed., *Słownik łaciny średniowiecznej w Polsce* (Wrocław, Warsaw, Kraków and Gdańsk, 1975–7), iv, p. 728–9. See also S. Urbańczyk, ed., *Słownik staropolski* (Wrocław, Kraków and Warsaw, 1956–9), ii, p. 542; M. R. Mayenowa, ed., *Słownik polszczyzny XVI wieku* (Wrocław, Warsaw, Kraków and Gdańsk, 1974), viii, p. 323.

active period of diplomacy for the Polish heralds and kings of arms was the early years of the fifteenth century, which coincided with the drawn-out conflict between the Polish crown and the Teutonic Order. They were regularly involved in correspondence between the two bodies and frequently travelled throughout Europe on behalf of the Polish royal court: in 1402, for example, Poland King of Arms was at the grand master's court in Malbork, in connection with a visit planned by the Polish King Władysław Jagiełło.[38] In 1410, a Prussian knight, Dietrich von Logendorff, reported that Poland King of Arms was en route to London for the purposes of obtaining English support for the Poles.[39] In 1413, in the aftermath of the removal of Grand Master Henry von Plauen by the marshal, Michał Kuchmeister, a Polish knight and diplomat, Zawisza Niger of Garbowo, sent his herald to discuss a renegotiation of relations between the Order and Poland. After having no contact from his herald for some time, Zawisza Niger became concerned that he might have been drowned or killed and the knight immediately wrote to the king of Poland informing him of his herald's journey. Keen to establish the fate of the envoy, the king decided to send his own messenger to the Order, but insisted that Ulryk Zenger, the commander of Bałga, a castle of the Teutonic Knights, offer him personal protection.[40] In the autumn of 1415, a herald of the Polish king, alongside others including Zawisza Niger of Garbowo, visited the court of Ferdinand I, king of Aragon, at Perpignan. Among a series of payments made to several heralds visiting the court, the Polish herald was paid 20 florins. He was probably part of the Polish delegation accompanying the Holy Roman Emperor in the name of the Council of Constance.[41] In these sorts of circumstances

---

[38] *Das Marienburger Tresslerbuch*, p. 160; A. Nowakowski, 'The Toruń Meetings of King Władysław Jagiełło with the Great Master of the Teutonic Order Konrad von Jungingen', *Fasciculi Archaeologiae Historicae* 8 (Łódź, 1995), pp. 41–2.

[39] *Hanserecesse, I Abteilung: Die Recesse und andere Akten der Hansetage von 1256–1430* (Leipzig, 1880), v, no. 639, pp. 492–4; W. Hubatsch, ed., *Regesta Historico-Diplomatica Ordinis S. Mariae Theutonicorum* (Göttingen, 1948), i, p. 73, no. 1247. More information on the topic of the mission: J. Voigt, *Geschichte Preussens* (Königsberg, 1836), vii, pp. 61–2; Grabski, *Polska w opiniach Europy Zachodniej*, pp. 231–3; H. Zins, *Polska w oczach Anglików XIV–XVI w.* (Warsaw, 1974), pp. 33–4; Z. H. Nowak, 'Dyplomacja polska w czasach Jadwigi i Władysława Jagiełły (1382–1434)', *Historia dyplomacji polskiej*, ed. M. Biskup (Warsaw, 1980), i, p. 382; Kuczyński, 'Heroldowie króla polskiego', p. 335; Kuczyński, 'Les hérauts d'armes', pp. 655–6.

[40] A. Prochaska, ed., *Codex Epistolaris Vitoldi, Magni Ducis Lithuaniae 1376–1430* (Kraków, 1882), vi, no. 567, p. 273; B. Możejko, S. Szybkowski, and B. Śliwiński, *Zawisza Czarny z Garbowa herbu Sulima* (Gdańsk, 2003), p. 66.

[41] Barcelona, Archivo de la Corona de Aragón, Real Cancillería, Reg. 2415, fols 144v–145r. The authors are deeply grateful to Jaume Riera i Sans from the Reference Department in the Archives of the Crown of Aragon in Barcelona for his tremendous help in accessing this document. See F. Vendrell Gallostra, 'Caballeros controeuropeos en la corte aragonesa', in

Polish heralds and kings of arms represented and acted on behalf of the king and kingdom of Poland.

In addition to sending officers of arms to other courts, the Polish royal court itself hosted foreign heralds carrying routine correspondence and engaging in necessary diplomacy. For example, the register of the treasurer, Hinczka, contains an account of eight marks assigned to two English heralds who arrived in Kraków in 1394, but does not identify their business in Poland.[42] This was not the first visit by English heralds to the Polish court. In the early 1390s, Henry Bolingbroke, earl of Derby (later Henry IV of England), sent his herald to King Ladislaus II (1386–1434) to negotiate on behalf of two English knights, Thomas Rempstone and John Clifton, who had been captured by the Poles at the siege of Vilnius in Lithuania in 1391.[43] Although such occasions were steeped in the conventions of diplomacy, visits of this nature were also a good opportunity to learn about the customs and practices of officers of arms in other kingdoms and principalities. Contact and fraternity between officers of arms ensured that they had the skills necessary for international relations. Regular travel and exposure to different cultures also enabled heralds from all kingdoms to acquire additional languages and thus render themselves more useful in translation services. For example, we learn from Antoine de la Sale's romance *Le petit Jehan de Saintre* that when Jehan was jousting with a Polish knight in Paris, Brunswick Herald was allocated to the Polish knight as he did not speak French, and was charged with helping him to communicate during the event and ensuring he knew the rules of competition in jousts.[44] The

---

Miscellanea Barcinonesia, x (1971), no. xxviii, p. 30; Kuczyński, 'Heroldowie króla polskiego', p. 336; Kuczyński, 'Les hérauts d'armes', p. 656. According to Jan Długosz, during the visit to Perpignan a tournament was organised and there was a joust between Zawisza and John of Aragon. The chronicler wrote that during the first joust the Pole had unhorsed his opponent: Długosz, *Annales*, lib. XI (1413–30) (Warsaw, 2000), pp. 66, 75.

[42] F. Piekosiński, ed., *Rachunki dworu króla Władysława Jagiełły i królowej Jadwigi z lat 1388 do 1420* (Kraków, 1896), p. 193; Kuczyński, 'Heroldowie króla polskiego', p. 333; Kuczyński, 'Les hérauts d'armes', p. 654.

[43] H. Prutz, ed., *Rechnungen über Heinrich von Derby's Preussenfahrten 1390–91 und 1392* (Leipzig, 1893), pp. 100, 103, 127; L. Toulmin Smith, ed., *Expeditions to Prussia and the Holy Land Made by Henry Earl of Derby*, Camden Society, n.s. 52 (1894), pp. 108, 111, 139; E. Perory, ed., *The Diplomatic Correspondence of Richard II* (London, 1933), p. 218; Grabski, *Polska w opiniach Europy zachodniej*, pp. 189–190; H. Świderska, 'Kilka epizodów ze stosunków polsko-angielskich za panowania Władysława Jagiełły', *Teki historyczne* 8 (1956–7), p. 77.

[44] A. de la Sale, *Jehan de Saintré*, ed. J. Misrahi and C. A. Knudson (Geneva, 1965), esp. p. 144; A. Bronarski, *Le petit Jean de Saintré. Un énigme littéraire: contribution aux études sur Antoine de la Sale* (Florence, 1922), pp. 39–42; A. Sobczyk, 'Polski rycerz we francuskiej powieści (Antoine de La Sale, Jehan de Saintré)', in *Wielkopolska-Polska-Europa. Studia dedykowane pamięci Alicji Karłowskiej-Kamzowej*, ed. J. Wiesiołowski (Poznań, 2006), pp. 69–74.

fact that Brunswick Herald spoke Polish is not such a great surprise. Aside from the obvious requirement for the two neighbouring lands to converse regularly, it was not uncommon for officers of arms to be fluent in several languages. For example, Johann Holland, Bavaria Herald and the author of the poem about a tournament in Schaffhausen in 1392 (written between 1415 and 1424), spoke six languages: Italian, German, Polish, French, English and Hungarian.[45]

Diplomatic missions were not the only reason for heralds to visit the kingdom of Poland. It is well known that heralds were sent to proclaim tournaments widely throughout Europe, and they also went to Poland to do so. In the spring of 1390, for example, there was a tournament in Saint Inglevert, near Calais, well known through its inclusion by Jean Froissart in his *Chronicles*. A few months earlier, in 1389, heralds had been sent by Jean II le Meingre, Marshal Boucicaut, and two others, Renaud de Roye and Jean sire de Sempy, to England, Denmark, Germany, Bohemia and Poland to proclaim the time and place of the tournament.[46] Indeed, it would seem that some Polish knights took up the invitation. Jan Szymczak supposes that the Polish knights were invited to the tournament because of the fame of a tournament held at the Congress of Kraków in 1364, described by the well-known French poet and composer Guillaume de Machaut.[47] It seems

[45] A. Wiesend, 'Die Reime des Ehrenholds Johann Holland aus Eggenfelden', *Verhandlungen des historischen Vereins von Niederbayern* 7 (1860), p. 119. See Oswald, *Lexikon der Heraldik*, p. 206.

[46] *Chronographia Regum Francorum*, iii (Paris, 1897), pp. 97–8. See also A. F. Grabski, *Polska w opiniach Europy zachodniej XIV–XV w.* (Warsaw, 1968), p. 72; Kuczyński, 'Turnieje rycerskie', p. 304; B. W. Brzustowicz, 'Udział rycerstwa polskiego w zagranicznych turniejach w średniowieczu', *Herald* 7 (1993), p. 9.

[47] Some of the most prominent figures of Europe attended and participated in the meeting held during the Kraków Congress in 1364, including the Holy Roman Emperor and king of Bohemia Charles IV; Louis of Anjou, king of Hungary; Peter I de Lusignan, king of Cyprus; Waldemar IV, king of Denmark; Duke Bolko II of Świdnica and Jawor (Lower Silesia); Duke Siemowit III of Płock (Mazovia); Vladislas of Opole (Upper Silesia); and Otto Wittelsbach, margrave of Brandenburg. On the Kraków congress and its participants see R. Grodecki, *Kongres krakowski w roku 1364* (Warsaw, 1939), pp. 55–96; J. Wyrozumski, *Kazimierz Wielki* (Wrocław, 1986), pp. 133–9; Guillome de Machaut, *La prise d'Alexandrie*, ed. M. L. de Mas Latrie (Geneva, 1877), p. 39; S. Zajączkowski, 'Wilhelm de Machaut i jego wiadomości do dziejów Polski i Litwy w XIV w.', *Kwartalnik historyczny* 43 (1929), pp. 217–28; J. F. Böhmer, ed., *Regesta Imperii, vol. VIII: Unter Kaiser Karl IV* (Innsbruck, 1877), pp. 320–1; H. Moranvillé, ed., *Chronographia Regum Francorum* (Paris, 1893), ii, pp. 300–2; Grabski, *Polska w opiniach Europy zachodniej*, pp. 74–5. Piotr de Lusignan's victory in the Krakóẇian competition does not appear strange to us because during his diplomatic mission de Lusignan participated in many European tournaments in the years of 1361–5, winning prizes in Paris, London, Prague and Vienna: N. Jorga, 'Philippe de Meziers 1327–1405 et la croisade au XIV siecle', *Bibliotheque de l'École des hautes études* 110 (Paris, 1896; reprint London, 1973), pp. 144–201; D'A. J. D. Boulton, *The Knights of the Crown: The monarchical*

far more likely that a Polish presence at Saint Inglevert was not the direct result of a tournament twenty-five years earlier, but rather the result of Marshal Boucicaut's own connection with the Prussian crusades. Marshal Boucicaut had left for Prussia to take part in the crusades against Lithuania at least three times: in the summer of 1384 and in the winters of 1384–5 and 1390–1.[48] Thus, through his crusading expeditions Boucicaut had several opportunities to fight against Polish knights. Indeed, soon after the tournament in Saint Inglevert, a joust of war was organised between French and Polish knights over Polish support of the pagans, but the duels never took place.[49] Polish knights were evidently well-known on the tournament and jousting circuit, and Polish heralds must have acquired their knowledge of these events on their return.[50]

Likewise, in matters of local diplomacy, a challenge to Polish knights to duel might be issued. In November 1410, for example, just after the crushing defeat of the Teutonic Knights at the battle of Grunwald (Tannenberg), a Polish royal herald was sent to the defenders of the Teutonic castle of Tuchola with letters demanding that the defeated Teutonic Knights, who had fled from the battlefield, should abandon 'all their armour, horses and war symbols, especially the surcoats covering their armour'. In response, the Teutonic Knights challenged their Polish counterparts to a series of duels to defend their honour, to be held at the royal courts in France, Spain, England and Naples. In the event, the challenge was rejected by the Poles, who indicated that they would only tourney at the court of Grand Duke

orders of knighthood in Later Medieval Europe 1325–1520 (Woodbridge, 1987), pp. 241–5; Barber and Barker, *Tournaments*, pp. 107–8. On Guillaume de Machaut see Szymczak, 'Knightly Tournaments', p. 16.

[48] Paravicini, *Die Preussenreisen*, i, plate 7, no. 135, 136, 182 and plate 23, no. 12.

[49] Długosz, *Annales*, lib. X 1370–1405 (Warsaw, 1985), pp. 187–8; 'Die Chronik Wigands von Marburg', in *Scriptores Rerum Prussicarum*, ed. T. Hirsch, M. Toeppen, and E. Strehlke (Leipzig, 1863), ii, p. 660; 'Johann's von Posilge Chronik des Landes Preussen', *Scriptores Rerum Prussicarum*, ed. T. Hirsch, M. Toeppen, and E. Strehlke, iii, p. 201. See Paravicini, *Die Preussenreisen*, i, p. 304, ii, pp. 135–136, 160; J. Szymczak, 'Pojedynki rycerskie, czyli rzecz o sądzie bożym w Polsce Jagiellonów', in *Studia z dziejów państwa i prawa polskiego*, ed. J. Matuszewski (Łódź, 1999), iii, pp. 161–2.

[50] Foreign knights were participants of the tournaments held at the Polish kings' court. The duel between Jakub of Kobylany, a Polish royal knight, and an Englishman took place between the years 1447 and 1454 on the King Kazimierz court of Wawel Castle: S. Kutrzeba, 'Przyczynek do dziejów turnieju w Polsce', *Wiadomości numizmatyczno-archeologiczne* 4 (1901), no. 3–4, pp. 382–4; A. Kamiński, 'Jakub z Kobylan, kasztelan gnieźnieński, starosta brzeski 1407–1454', in *Biblioteka Warszawska* (1860), ii, pp. 559–61. After the death of Jakub of Kobylany, Kazimierz Jagiełłon, appreciating his knightly deeds and praising his bravery, established a foundation of the sum of two marks for the Dominican convent in Brześć. The monks were also obliged to hold a memorial service four times a year: A. Sokołowski, J. Szujski and A. Lewicki, ed., *Codex Epistolaris Saeculi Decimi Quinti 1384–1492* (Kraków, 1894), iii, p. 583.

the political situation from 1398 onwards, particularly in international relations. Similarly, the fact that by the fourteenth century Sweden only contained about one hundred noble families (compared to 350 in Denmark)[8] may go some way toward explaining the apparent lack of Swedish heralds, as there was perhaps not a large enough social infrastructure to support them. It is interesting that the first king of the Kalmar Union, Erik of Pomerania (d. 1459), does not appear to have used heralds in his relations with his Norwegian kingdom, despite the fact that Erik only managed one visit to Norway himself, and this does seem to confirm the Kalmar monarch's Dano-centric view of the union. It has generally been considered that Norway and Sweden at this time were viewed as Danish provinces by the Copenhagen-based monarchy, although modern historiography has reworked this approach to the three kingdoms, proposing that they were in fact viewed as a single unit.[9]

As the main royal court was largely based at Copenhagen during the Kalmar Union, the lack of permanent courts in either Sweden or Norway meant that all royal heralds emanated from Denmark. Thus the Kalmar Union was never one of equals, despite the original conditions agreed by all three kingdoms in 1397 after Erik's coronation in Sweden. One of these conditions stated that foreign envoys would be received by Erik in whichever kingdom he found himself at the time of their arrival.[10] This agreement was never ratified and remained an unfulfilled condition for both Sweden and Norway. King Erik was rarely in Sweden during his reign and records reveal that his queen, Philippa (daughter of King Henry IV of England), played a greater role than her husband in governing Sweden, particularly between 1422 and her death in 1430.[11] Given the uncertain nature of Swedish kingship and independence, whilst uprisings and rebellions against the Kalmar monarchy gathered momentum in the 1430s, the question of royal power and authority remained a bitterly contested issue which in itself made the establishment of any kind of court hierarchy within that kingdom difficult. Indeed, Marshal Karl Knutsson Bonde (known later as Karl VIII, d. 1470) has the dubious honour of being the only man to have held the Swedish crown on three separate occasions, albeit ultimately losing it to the Danish-based Christian I (1448–81). For much of the period between 1470 and 1520

---

[8] Ibid., p. 59.
[9] Compare the view of John J. Murray in 'The Peasant Revolt of Engelbrekt Engelbrektsson and the Birth of Modern Sweden', *Journal of Modern History* 19:3 (1947), p. 194, with the view of Biörn Tjällén in *Church and Nation, the Discourse on Authority in Ericus Olai's Chronica Regni Gothorum* (c.1471) (Stockholm, 2007), p. 10.
[10] Carl-Georg Starbäck and Per Olof Bäckström, *Berättelser ur svenska historien* (Stockholm, 1865), ii, p. 17.
[11] Ibid., pp. 73–4.

the ruling authority in Sweden vacillated between regent and council,[12] and it would appear that those who travelled to see the king were either members of the council or representatives of the regent, rather than any herald. The turbulence within royal houses and their fluctuations in power probably lie behind the lack of parity across the three kingdoms in terms of the development of their heraldic institutions.

Tournaments and the Emergence of Scandinavian Heralds

MAURICE KEEN maintains that the earliest heralds 'are not distinguishable by dignity or even entirely by function from [hangers-on at tournaments]', indicating their rather modest, almost inconspicuous, origins.[13] However, heralds soon became vital to the successful holding of tournaments in the Middle Ages and it is there we might look to discover the first Scandinavian heralds.[14] Although evidence is limited, contemporary accounts do indicate that tournaments were known to some members of the upper ruling echelons in Scandinavia from as early as the twelfth century.[15] The earliest surviving 'history' from Sweden is *Erikskrönikan* (The Eric Chronicle), which dates from the 1320s, and it mentions tournaments taking place between 1250 and 1313.[16] Surviving records indicate that Scandinavian kings attended tournaments outwith their kingdoms, particularly in the Baltic region, as much as they held them within their own borders, and this might indicate a greater likelihood of heralds being involved (as heralds were known to be active at this time in the Netherlands and parts of Germany).[17] King Erik Menved of Denmark (1286–1319), for

[12]   Harald Gustafsson, 'A State that Failed? On the Union of Kalmar, Especially its Dissolution', *Scandinavian Journal of History* 31:3/4 (2006), p. 208.

[13]   Maurice Keen, *Chivalry* (New Haven and London, 1984), p. 136.

[14]   Anthony Wagner states: 'Almost all these [early] mentions link [heralds] with tournaments, of which the conduct seems to have been their special providence', in *Heralds and Heraldry in the Middle Ages: An Inquiry into the Growth of the Armorial Function of Heralds* (Oxford, 1956), p. 25.

[15]   Hans H. Ronge and Finn Hødnebo, 'Turnering', in *Kulturhistorisk leksikon for nordisk middelalder*, xix (Copenhagen, 1975), p. 72. The concept of 'rida i turniment' appears in connection with the 1113 meeting between the two Norwegian kings Øystein and Sigurd and the 1181 confrontation between Magnus Erlingsson and Sverre. Similarly when King Magnus Birgerson of Sweden met King Erik Glipping of Denmark in 1275 a tournament was held where many knights competed.

[16]   See Jesper Wasling, 'Torneringar i Erikskrönikan' at <http://www.heraldik.se/artiklar/artiklar.htm>.

[17]   Michel Pastoreau, *Heraldry: Its Origins and Meaning* (London, 1997), p. 74. King Valdemar IV of Denmark attended a gathering at Lübeck in 1356 where tournaments were held; and the Swedish king Albreckt of Mecklenburg held a tournament at Wismar in 1386: Niels Saxtorph, 'Turnering', in *Kulurhistorisk leksikon for nordisk middelalder*, xix

example, is said to have presided over a two-day tournament at Rostock in 1311 at festivities held in honour of Waldemar of Brandenburg, where many lances were broken through jousting.[18] A late fourteenth-century German chronicle describes how at this event a herald served both as tournament referee and as the scribe who recorded the winners. Further, in the post-tournament festivities a herald was employed to announce the arrival of each of the knights to the celebration and describe their arms.[19] Neither the nationality of these particular heralds nor the identity of their masters is known. However, it seems probable that the herald was a local German herald rather than a Danish herald, whereas perhaps the earliest Scandinavian herald recorded in northern European sources engaged in ceremonial can be dated no earlier than 1404. That year an unnamed herald of King Erik of Pomerania was remunerated by the town of Regensburg for service at an unspecified festivity held there.[20]

Other tournaments were known to have been held in Kalmar (1337), Roskilde (1355) and Lund (1406) as part of the festivities to mark the wedding of Erik of Pomerania to the English princess Philippa, and at Stockholm (1438); tournaments were also included as part of the coronation festivities in Trondheim in 1449 (for Karl Knutson Bonde) and 1450 and 1457 (both for coronations of Christian I), and finally, also at the coronation of King Hans (1481–1513) in Copenhagen in 1483.[21] We lack descriptions of these events and thus whether the combatants in these tournaments employed heraldic shields, crests, horse trappings and the like remains unknown, but images from contemporary tombstones and equestrian seals reveal an awareness of this kind of apparel in both Sweden and Norway. A tournament-shield survives in Sweden which belonged to Karl Laurentsson Björnlår, who was known to be alive in the years 1497–1504, indicating that Björnlår had participated in a tournament at some point.[22] Depictions of

---

(Copenhagen, 1975), p. 71, and Ellen Jørgensen, *Valdemar Atterdag* (Copenhagen, 1911), pp. 39, 129–30.

[18] Verwohlt, 'Valdemar Atterdags og Erik af Pommerns herolder', p. 27, and Verwohlt, 'Kongelige danske herolder', p. 205. See also Saxtorph, 'Turnering', xix, p. 71.

[19] Noted by Verwohlt in 'Herold', p. 483.

[20] 19 December, 1404, Lübeck, *Diplomatarium Danicum*, 4th series, ix, no. 504, published online at <http://dd.dsl.dk>. The original document came from Regensburg Stadtarchiv, although it was already noted as 'missing' in 2001.

[21] See Saxtorph, 'Turnering', p. 71, Jørgensen, *Valdemar Atterdag*, p. 37, and <http://www.heraldik.org/oldl>, article on 'Norwegian heraldry' by Harald Nissen. It is also known that knightings occurred at the 1449 and 1450 coronations, which could indicate the presence of heralds, although knighting was usually the king's prerogative.

[22] An image of this shield can be seen in Göran Tegner's article 'Begravningssköld, 1500-talets början', in *Riddarlek och Tornerspel: The Dream of Chivalry*, ed. L. Rangström (Stockholm, 1992), pp. 55 and 325.

tournaments or at least of jousting can be found in Sweden; unfortunately one of these was in the now destroyed early-fourteenth-century church of Södra Råda, but another survives in Väte church on Gotland, which dates from 1350–1400.[23]

Despite this evidence that tournaments were not only a familiar concept but were also held in Scandinavia, it was a long time before the modern word for tournament, *tornering*, came into use in Sweden. It does not appear in the few surviving Swedish documents from the era; instead words such as *dust* (*dystløb* in Danish), *lek* and even *karusell* are used, and this may in itself be representative of the different pace of developement in Sweden as regards certain rites and rituals that were commonplace elsewhere. If there were Scandinavian heralds present at just one or even some of these afore-mentioned tournaments then the variety of locations involved and thus the range of languages required to perform a herald's duties must have been considerable. A rare record survives which details the abilities required by a herald: in 1580 a priest, who was present at the hand-over of Schleswig and Femern to the dukes of Schleswig-Holstein, noted in his journal that heralds had to be fluent in seven languages (without specifying which ones) and that heralds were always dressed in expensive and fine materials such as silk.[24] That heralds were fluent in so many languages is rarely mentioned explicitly in other accounts, but explains how their deployment as inter-national envoys became part of their remit. Whether the language skills developed as a result of being sent abroad, or whether heralds first became multi-lingual and then served as foreign agents is probably a moot point. The breadth of knowledge and exposure to foreign influences along with the ability to recognise different coats of arms and name the individuals who bore them implied that skills in communication, learning and adapting to new circumstances were fundamental to a herald's success.

Scandinavian Heraldic Hierarchy

UNLIKE THE KNOWN INSTANCES IN FRANCE AND ENGLAND, there is no evidence of the establishment of a formal heraldic hierarchy or col-lege in Scandinavia, nor is there a surviving example of a Scandinavian her-ald committing his lore to writing.[25] The essence of a heraldic institution

[23] The Södra Råda image was a depiction of a boar and a goat jousting, revealing that the concept was familiar enough to be treated as parody. My thanks to Dr Thomas Småberg for bringing this to my attention.

[24] Oluf Nielsen, *Kjøbenhavns Historie indtil Reformationens Indførelse* (Copenhagen, 1879), p. 193.

[25] Compare the royal grant on 2 March 1484 to John Writhe, Garter King of Arms, and all his fellow heralds and pursuivants for the establishment of a college of heralds in England.

did, however, emerge in Denmark when the oldest Nordic order of chivalry, the Order of the Elephant, was established during the reign of Christian I (1448–81). The Order found a home in the chapel of Hellig Tre Konger at Roskilde cathedral, which came to house not only the tomb of Christian and his queen, but also, until the Reformation, the knights' hall and their heraldic shields. A hierarchical division of heralds was determined by the king, comprising the *våbenkong* (king of arms) followed by the herald, and finally by the *persevant* (pursuivant).[26] There were two *våbenkonger*, one named Denmark King of Arms, the other Norway King of Arms. Given that the Kalmar Union also included Sweden this invites the question of why there was no Sweden King of Arms (apart from the one exception discussed below).[27] The situation was similar for the subordinate heralds and pursuivants: Danish regional names occur but no Swedish or even Norwegian ones. There were three heralds, known as Sjælland (Zealand), Jylland (Jutland) and Sverige (Sweden), whilst the pursuivants were similarly named Sjælland, Jylland and Lolland.[28] Once again the Dano-centric bias of the Kalmar monarchy becomes apparent. Ernst Verwohlt further informs us that it took a seven-year apprenticeship for a pursuivant to become a herald, at which point he was named after a particular region of the kingdom, whose colours he would wear. Unfortunately Verwohlt does not provide sources for this information.

Only two records of the title Sweden King of Arms have emerged, in what appears to be a highly charged use of the title for political gain. The first instance dates to 1504 and is mentioned by Birger Gunnersøn, the archbishop of Lund (then part of Denmark), in a letter to King Hans.[29] The following year this same Sweden King of Arms spent three days in Kalmar summoning Hans's Swedish rivals and enemies, including the regent Svante Nilsson, to a royal meeting regarding the cessation of the Danish-Swedish truce in June 1505. However, Nilsson and his Swedish gentlemen, fearing capture, never entered the town of Kalmar while King

---

Calendar of Patent Rolls, Edward IV, Edward V, Richard III (London, 1981), p. 422. French heralds had already formed a *collegium* in 1407; see the entry for 'Herald' in *Medieval France: An Encyclopedia*, ed. William Westcott Kibler and Grover A. Zinn (New York, 1995).

[26] See Verwohlt, 'Herold', p. 483.

[27] Interestingly, in medieval Sweden the use of the title of *vapenkung* (the Swedish equivalent of Danish *våbenkong*) only appears to have occurred between the mid-1450s and the early 1500s, precisely the period when the Danish-based monarchy was reasserting its dominance over the Kalmar Union. It seems that there never was a heraldic hierarchy established in Sweden at the time.

[28] Verwohlt, 'Herold', p. 484. Unfortunately Verwohlt does not describe how this hierarchy developed, but simply lists the names given to the heralds and pursuivants, who unusually shared the same titles.

[29] Verwohlt, 'Kongelige danske herolder', p. 213.

Hans was there with his retinue, which included his herald, the archbishops of Lund and Trondheim and some German and Scottish soldiers. Hans was further supported by eleven warships, a three-thousand-strong army and his Danish and Norwegian councillors, and it is hardly surprising that the Swedes chose to stay away. King Hans then turned the arranged meeting into a tribunal and sent his herald and another royal representative to wander the streets of Kalmar proclaiming the names of those Swedes now charged with rebellion against the king and condemned to death.[30] This appears to have been a purely political use of the name Sweden King of Arms, occurring as it did during a prolonged period of Swedish rebellion, where King Hans would have been emphasising his right to the kingdom as part of the Kalmar Union, partly by appointing a Sweden King of Arms as his servant. At no point did any individual bearing the title Sweden King of Arms undertake royal missions outside Scandinavia, which we will see was common practice for both Norway King of Arms and Denmark King of Arms.

These ongoing intra-Scandinavian struggles proved no obstacle to the Danish-based monarchy in deploying its heralds on international missions, and even from the time of the earliest known Scandinavian herald these duties involved engaging in actual mediation on behalf of their masters. Their financial rewards for their services, not only from their own but also from foreign monarchs, their increasingly ornate dress, and entitlement to land were all marks of their elevated status in society.

The Duties of Scandinavian Heralds

THE NATURE of heraldic duties performed by Scandinavian heralds was varied: they were proclaimers, trumpeters and masters of ceremonies at tournaments, and also performed ceremonial roles at funerals, weddings and coronations. It would be natural to assume that the founding of the Kalmar Union provided ample opportunity for the use of heralds in royal ceremonies, but the few surviving records of the two coronations of Erik of Pomerania (one in Norway and one in Sweden) are not detailed accounts.[31] Furthermore, and perhaps more surprisingly, no records have yet been found of either a Scandinavian (Kalmar Union) or an English herald being involved in the the 1400–4 marriage negotiations between the English and Danish royal houses, when Princess Philippa of England

---

[30] Starbäck and Bäckström, *Berättelser ur svenska historien*, ii, p. 561.

[31] And this is despite the recent view that the office of a common herald was introduced to consolidate the Union between the three Scandinavian kingdoms, see J. E. Olesen, 'Erik av Pommern og Kalmarunionen: regeringssystemetsutformning 1389–1439', in *Danmark i senmiddelalderen*, ed. P. Ingesman and J. V. Jensen (Aarhus, 1994), pp. 145–9, 165.

we have such records, and granting of arms does not appear to be common practice amongst the Scandinavian heralds at this time.[59]

Thomas Young was the next Dane officially to be named as visiting Scotland. His first two visits were in September and October 1488, when he was simply described as 'Dens', and he was paid a combination of gold coins – unicorns – totalling varying amounts of just over £3 to £4 Scots.[60] When he returned two years later as Sjælland Pursuivant, his reward was significantly higher – 15 'angels' or £19.[61] The exact nature of his missions, as with so many others, remains unclear.[62] There seems to have been a drop in the amounts paid out in the following years, as exemplified when an unspecified herald of Denmark (possibly David Cochrane, see below) came to the Scottish court in 1496 and he was awarded £13 6s. 9d., which is noticeably less than the pursuivant had obtained.[63] Sjælland Pursuivant was also with the herald and again his payment was a lot lower than before, totalling £4 10s.[64] This apparent drop in payment may represent the impoverished state of the Scottish crown at the time. The Scottish connection to Scandinavian heralds was about to become much stronger.

Scottish Heralds in Danish Service

IT WAS AT THE END of the fifteenth century that the first Scotsman is definitively known to have become a herald for Denmark. This is hardly surprising, coinciding as it does with the renewal in 1492 of the Scottish-Danish treaty of alliance guaranteeing mutual military aid between the two royal houses, although this was to prove difficult to enforce, even with the best of royal intentions.[65] Continued unrest within the Kalmar Union led to constant trouble for the Copenhagen-based monarch and at times it must have seemed that the Scottish court was under siege by Danish heralds, as hardly a year passed from 1500 onwards when at least one herald did not make a visit. However, the close connections between the two kingdoms, particularly after the 1468 marriage treaty which resulted in James III's wedding to Princess Margaret of Denmark, did produce the long and

[59] Jesper Wasling, 'Medeltida svenska sköldebrev', at <http://www.heraldik.se/artiklar/artiklar.htm>.

[60] *TA*, i, pp. 94, 96.

[61] *TA*, i, p. 132.

[62] T. Riis, *Should auld acquaintance be forgot* (Odense, 1988), ii, p. 81.

[63] *TA*, i, p. 325.

[64] *ER*, xi, p. 55.

[65] One example of this dates from 1501, when Hans was suffering rebellion at the hands of some of his Swedish and Norwegian subjects: James IV wanted to send a large force of armed men to Denmark, but this 'Scottish naval expedition' ended in failure. See Norman Macdougall, *James IV* (Edinburgh, 2006), pp. 149–50, 191–2 and 229–30.

loyal service of two Scots in particular. It could only function to Danish advantage when engaging in formal relations with Scotland to have heralds who were not only natives, and therefore knew the languages and customs of the kingdom, but who had their own networks and contacts in Scotland, thereby facilitating their tasks as Danish envoys. Heralds' tabards even came to be known as 'Scottish jackets' in Danish, presumably in reference to their frequent use by Scotsmen who embodied that role.[66] The careers of two of these Scots – David Cochrane and Thomas Lumsden – spanned the reign of two Danish kings, Hans and Christian II (1513–23). As the records so rarely include personal names in their references to heralds it is sometimes difficult to determine who precisely is meant by 'herald of Denmark', but generally Cochrane held the title of Denmark Herald or Denmark King of Arms and Norway Herald or Norway King of Arms, whilst Lumsden was Sjælland Herald.

David Cochrane is believed to have entered Danish service before 1492, and may have been in English royal service prior to that.[67] He quickly began to undertake regular missions abroad – to the British Isles, Poland and Muscovy in particular – in the years 1496, 1502, 1505, 1506, 1513–14, 1517, 1519 and 1521, and his service continued during the early years of King Christian's exile until 1528.[68] Cochrane's first master, King Hans, was keen to strengthen ties with Muscovy as a means of gaining a stranglehold on the Swedes, who remained factionalised by the Kalmar Union.[69] Hans also sought Russian support in his fight to stop the Hansa from trading with Sweden, again as a means of controlling his Swedish subjects.[70] As a part of these machinations Hans sent supplies for canon-founding to Muscovy with Cochrane in 1507. These activities led to complaints from the Stockholm council about Cochrane's missions, which the council believed were directly related to the regular attacks Sweden suffered from the Russians.[71]

---

[66] Verwohlt, 'Kongelige danske herolder', p. 219.

[67] See *Dansk biografisk lexikon*, ix, p. 319, and C. F. Allen, ed., *Breve og Aktstykker til Oplysning af Christiern den Andens og Frederik den Førstes Historie* (Copenhagen, 1854), i, p. 483. Riis lists him as entering Danish service from English service, in *Should auld acquaintance be forgot*, ii, p. 57. See also Landbohistorisk selskab, Adkomstregistrering 1513–50, at <http://webarkiv.hum.ku.dk/navneforskning/adkomst/a/a000/a156.htm> (the database is, however, about to move to <http://nfi.ku.dk/databaser/>).

[68] See *Dansk biografisk lexicon*, ix, p. 319. See also William Christensen, ed., *Missiver fra Kongerne Christiern I's og Hans' Tid* (Copenhagen, 1912–14), p. 212.

[69] Indeed Hans's foreign policy has been described as solely focused on regaining control of Sweden; see G. Karlsson, *Iceland's 1100 Years: The History of a Marginal Society* (London, 2000), p. 124.

[70] Waldemar Westergaard, 'The Hansa Towns and Scandinavia on the Eve of Swedish Independence', *Journal of Modern History* 4:3 (1932), p. 354. Westergaard seems to use the term 'envoy' and 'herald' synonymously.

[71] Allen, ed., *Breve og Akstykker*, i, p. 483, n. 1.

Indeed, in 1510 'master David' was credited with successfully bringing Muscovy into a pro-Danish alliance.[72] Cochrane did not only receive handsome payments from foreign kings; King Hans also apparently rewarded him with the rental from St Jørgens Hospital outside Visby as a regular income,[73] and he certainly became wealthy through his heraldic profession.

However, in one situation it was exactly Cochrane's extravagant dress and manner of travelling that landed him in trouble.[74] When 'Master Davy' met Sir Richard Jerningham, governor of Tournai, in Antwerp in February 1518, the governor took special note of how the herald changed into a 'cloth of gold' before going to see the mayor of Antwerp in request of a loan – presumably on behalf of Christian II.[75] Cochrane was accompanied by unnamed heralds 'in livery of green camlet' when he called on the mayor of Antwerp, and the whole retinue must have presented quite an impressive sight as it entered the civic chambers; it was not enough to persuade the mayor to lend Christian II money and Cochrane soon found himself heading empty-handed to Mechelen. The Danish herald was then subject to a kidnap attempt organised by Jerningham, in the hopes of obtaining his letters to better inform King Henry VIII on Denmark's affairs, but a servant who was actually carrying the letters on *his* person escaped with them.[76] However, the 'kind treatment' shown to the herald ensured that the Englishmen became privy to his mission, as Cochrane claimed to have formerly been in Henry VII's service and to still be favourable to England (although this may of course have been a clever ruse by the herald).

Cochrane's long years of Danish service continued when King Christian II was forced to flee Denmark, and despite the herald's already significantly advanced age, he continued to be employed as one of the exiled king's envoys to England in 1524 and Scotland in 1525. Maturity finally caught up with the herald, and in 1527 Cochrane refused Christian II's request for him to go back to Muscovy to secure the release of the Danish nobleman and loyal supporter of Christian (and infamous pirate) Søren Norby, on the grounds that he was too old to travel. It is generally thought that Cochrane made one last visit to Christian II in September 1527, although a letter dated 30 August 1528 reveals that the herald still intended to see the king as soon as

---

[72] Westergaard, 'The Hansa Towns and Scandinavia', p. 357.
[73] Allen, ed., *Breve og Aktstykker*, i, p. 483, n. 1.
[74] Verwohlt, 'Kongelige danske herolder', p. 212.
[75] See letter from Jerningham to Henry VIII, February, c. 1518, Tournai, R. H. Brodie, ed., *Letters and Papers, Foreign and Domestic of the Reign of Henry VIII, Preserved in the Public Record Office, the British Museum and Elsewhere*, ii:2 (London, 1920), pp. 1235–6. The herald was also accompanied by two Scottish noblemen, Alexander Hay and Lord 'Bukyuell' (presumably Bothwell), further highlighting the strong ties between Denmark and Scotland, or at least between Cochrane and his native kingdom.
[76] Brodie, ed., *Letters and Papers*, ii:2, pp. 1235–6.

he could obtain the means for it.[77] It remains unclear whether a final meeting did occur between Cochrane and Christian, as by the next reference to the herald in 1529 he was dead.

Thomas Lumsden was the second Scotsman known to have served as herald at the Danish court and he too was frequently used for diplomatic contacts with Scotland, England and France during the reigns of both King Hans and King Christian II.[78] Nothing is known of Lumsden's earlier life, but he was already in Danish service, as Sjælland Herald, on a mission to Scotland in May 1503. In that year he received ten French crowns, or £7 from the Scottish treasury.[79] Thomas Riis believes this Thomas Lumsden to be the same man as the eponymous Copenhagen-based Scottish merchant who became embroiled in an inheritance case concerning David Morton, another Scottish merchant based in the Danish capital.[80] If this is accurate it would present an interesting social leap from foreign merchant to royal servant.

In between his foreign travel, Lumsden settled into family life in Roskilde, where he married Dorothea Boesen, a daughter of Jens Boesen, the mayor of Roskilde, gaining access through the marriage to Dorothea's grandfather's property. Although it is known that the position of Sjælland Herald was associated with the chapel of Hellig Tre Konger in Roskilde, it remains to be clarified whether Lumsden was already settled in Roskilde before he became a herald or did so as a consequence of his appointment. Lumsden and Dorothea became members of the St Lucius guild in Roskilde, where they lived on land donated to them by the Danish king – just as Gerhard Grundis had done at the end of the fourteenth century. Further, as was practice elsewhere, Lumsden is known to have received a French herald, François de Bordeaux, in his home at Roskilde in 1512 and this is the only record we have of a Danish herald socialising with another herald, although it was probably the norm for heralds to lodge with other heralds when sent abroad on their missions.[81] What François's exact mission to Denmark was at the time is unclear, although he returned to Copenhagen in 1518 to sign a treaty on behalf of the French king and was knighted by Christian II at this time.[82]

---

[77] Allen, ed., *Breve og Akstykker*, i, pp. 483, n.1. and 484. See *Diplomatarium Norvegicum*, xiii, no. 492, Hans Hansson to Christian II, 30 August 1528, Weimar.

[78] Oluf Nielsen, *Kjøbenhavn* (Copenhagen, 1887), p. 126.

[79] *TA*, ii, p. 373.

[80] Mackie, ed., *The Letters of James the Fourth*, p.164, and Riis, *Should auld acquaintance be forgot*, ii, p. 67. Intriguingly, King James IV had met Lumsden in 1505 and knew he was King Hans's herald, yet in this letter the Scottish king merely described Lumsden as an inhabitant of Copenhagen without reference to his title.

[81] Verwohlt, 'Kongelige danske herolder', p. 214.

[82] M. Champollion, ed., *Bulletin des sciences historiques, antiquités, philologie* (Paris, 1879),

archbishop of Glasgow and Scottish chancellor, from whom he returned to Copenhagen in April 1522. Although the surviving letter states that Christian was to get his news straight from the herald, the archbishop also asked Christian to use his influence in Rome against the machinations of Gavin Douglas, archbishop of Dunkeld.[107] This request probably fell on deaf ears as Christian was about to lose control of his kingdoms, and Lumsden was next sent to France in March 1523, where he appears as an officer of arms, presumably seeking foreign aid for his beleaguered king.[108] In 1525 the ship *Gallion* was prepared awaiting Christian's use in an attempt to regain his kingdom(s).[109] In these instances the records simply note that Denmark King of Arms, probably Cochrane, was present at the Scottish court. It is unknown precisely how John Elgin weathered the royal crisis in Copenhagen, but it is likely that he simply spent it in Scotland, or elsewhere. Certainly in 1526 Elgin appeared to have served as a Scottish ambassador to Brandenburg, as he brought a request from Scotland to Marquis Albert that Scots be allowed free travel and 'traffic' in the marquis's domains.[110] He must soon have returned to Danish service, however, as in June 1527 Elgin was in Scotland, where he was noted as 'the king of Denmark's ambassador' and was paid £40 for his services to the Scottish Crown.[111] That year another of Christian II's Scottish supporters, Doctor Alexander Kinghorn, dean of Roskilde and sometime ambassador, referred to Elgin as 'that maladroit young man' who had used bribery to obtain Scottish favour toward his new master, so he was obviously successful in achieving Frederik's aims.[112] When Elgin next returned to Scotland, two years later, it was to counteract the many ongoing visits by Christian's loyal heralds and followers to the Scottish court, still seeking military and financial aid on the exiled king's behalf.

Obviously, not all the Danish heralds at this time were Scotsmen. Hans, Jylland Herald, first appears in British sources when he was sent to England in 1516 and where he was referred to as pursuivant. Herald Hans, much like his Scottish colleague David Cochrane, led an international life in the first two decades of the sixteenth century. In 1521 he accompanied Christian

---

[107] Hay, ed., *The Letters of James V*, p. 90, James, archbishop of Glasgow and chancellor to Christian II, 8 April 1522, Edinburgh.

[108] Riis, *Should auld acquaintance be forgot*, i, p. 21 and ii, p. 67.

[109] *Diplomatarium Norvegicum*, xiv, no. 499, Jørgen Hansson to Christian II, 14 June 1525, Amsterdam. See also R. H. Brodie, ed., *Letters and Papers, Foreign and Domestic of the Reign of Henry VIII*, iv:1 (London, 1870), p. 395, and Hay, ed., *The Letters of James V*, p. 120.

[110] Brodie, ed., *Letters and Papers*, iv:1, p. 1034.

[111] *TA*, v, p. 322. That same day Elgin also received £50 for a horse which King James V bought from him.

[112] Letter of Alexander Kinghorn to Christian II, 25 September 1527, Leith, in Hay, ed., *The Letters of James V*, p. 142.

through the Netherlands to Brussels where the king was received at his brother-in-law Charles V's court. Jylland also spent time in Sweden. During the first twenty-three years of the sixteenth century Stockholm was under siege either from the Danish-based Kalmar king or from Swedish rebels, or even from the man who would become Sweden's first post-Union independent king.[113] The Stockholm town records of this period highlight the many-sided role a herald could play in society. Herald Hans was in Stockholm for Christian II's coronation in 1520,[114] so was probably also present when the king ordered the execution of at least eighty people, including many of the leading Swedish nobles, shortly after the celebration (an event now known as the 'Stockholm Bloodbath'). Hans remained in the town for about half a year, perhaps as a visible symbol of Christian's authority, and reported regularly on events in the Swedish capital.[115] One of Jylland's activities in January 1521 involved a thorough search of Stockholm's royal treasury with the governor and other royal representatives, presumably to learn what wealth the town controlled. Hans appeared to have assumed a quasi-judicial role in Stockholm, as when he informed Christian II that all was well at the end of March, Hans specified that he was keeping order with his local associates and punishing any wrongdoers.[116] The herald must have returned to Denmark not long after, as by July the Stockholm council had to send representatives and a letter to Copenhagen in order to communicate with the king.[117] This was just the time when the man who became Gustav I Vasa of Sweden (1523–60) began to besiege the town, which heralded the beginning of the end for Christian II.

Herald Hans's peripatetic lifestyle continued when Christian fled Denmark. Jylland not only accompanied the king into exile but was forced to leave his wife behind in Copenhagen. There appear to be no accounts of her life, although she was awarded special protection upon the capitulation of the town to Frederik I's forces, just as had happened to Thomas Lumsden.[118] The high social status enjoyed by heralds apparently applied equally to their wives. Hans owned several properties and was also a member of the merchants' guild in Flensborg. One of the few insights we have into a herald's private domain is in the inventory of Hans's personal belong-

---

[113] See Lars Ericson, *Stockholms historia under 750 år* (Falun, 2001), pp. 117–24.

[114] Herald Jan van Udeken from Mechelen was also present at Christian's coronation, after which the Imperial herald presented Christian with the Order of the Golden Fleece. The city of Stockholm rewarded van Udeken with Herald Hans's tankard, noted as worth 19 weights of silver. See J. A. Almquist, ed., *Stockholmsstadsskottebok 1516–1525* (Stockholm, 1935), p. 192. Many thanks to Ardis Grosjean Dreisbach for this reference.

[115] *Stockholms stadsböcker från äldre tid*, 2nd series (Stockholm, 1933), v, pp. 292 and 293.

[116] Ibid., p. 321.

[117] Ibid., p. 348.

[118] Verwohlt, 'Kongelige danske herolder', p. 216.

ings, made in 1524; one wonders if he ever regained access to these items after his move to the Continent. He owned, amongst other things, a red shirt decorated with gold; eleven gold-plated silver bells; twenty-one gold-plated buttons; a gold-plated belt; four German books and one book of arms 'such as heralds tend to have'.[119] Another source highlights the amount of drinkware in the herald's possession, namely two silver beer mugs and at least twenty-one pewter jugs.[120] It would be interesting to discover the provenance of Hans's book of arms – was it imported from elsewhere, or had it been produced in Scandinavia? The resulting impression of Hans's possessions is that sixteenth-century Danish heralds enjoyed a life of affluence and high social status. As Hans was already quite aged by 1524, one can assume this list represents belongings and wealth accumulated over an extended period.

Herald Hans in Exile

IN EXILE Christian II ceaselessly sought succour and support from various foreign powers. The records reveal competing letters from Christian and his uncle Frederik, duke of Holstein, requesting support from Scotland for their opposing campaigns. James V was in his minority at this time and Scotland was ostensibly ruled by Regent Albany. James's letters show him remaining clearly in Christian's favour in the often-repeated references to the unbroken alliance and ties of blood between the two kingdoms, although the Scottish king's promises never took physical form. Regent Albany, meanwhile, maintained a relationship with Frederik, promising mutual support if the duke would provide Scotland with forces to fight against Henry VIII of England.[121] Christian also made approaches to his brother-in-law, Emperor Charles V, and even to Henry VIII. The latter found it hard to trust the Danish king, particularly given his close relations with Scotland; more importantly rumours had been rife in early 1523 that Christian intended to invade England.[122]

Intriguingly, it was the aforementioned Doctor Alexander Kinghorn who served as Christian's official envoy in the spring of 1523, visiting both James Beaton, the archbishop of Glasgow and chancellor of Scotland, and James

[119]   Ibid., p. 216.
[120]   Tr. Fr. Troels-Lund, *Dagligt Liv i Norden i det sekstende Aarhundrede* (Copenhagen, 1914), v, p. 203.
[121]   See Hay, ed., *The Letters of James V*, passim.
[122]   G. Mattingly, ed., *Further Supplement to Letters, Despatches and State Papers Relating to the Negotiations between England and Spain Preserved in the Archives at Vienna and Elsewhere* [1513–1542] (London, 1947), p. 175.

V in quest of aid for the exiled king.[123] The only reply they offered the beleaguered king was emotional support and asylum in Scotland due to the ongoing threats from England. Christian was then forced to look elsewhere for more solid sustenance. In June 1523 Hans was sent to England to seek royal safe-conduct for his ships, and the following month the herald went to Brussels to convey Christian's hope that Charles and Henry would cooperate and arbitrate on the exiled king's behalf to help him regain his throne.[124] At the end of November 1523, Hans was in Mechelen, as the letter of chancellor Klaus Pedersson states, when he wrote to alert King Christian II to the arrival there of the Imperial envoy, Hannart, on his return from England. This tantalisingly short letter merely reveals that according to the herald 'things were well'.[125]

A more awkward role was exerted by Hans in Mechelen in the early part of 1524. In January that year Christian II was in Berlin and had written to his chancellor about the English envoy John Baker's news that Henry VIII was willing to lend Christian a large amount of money in return for some of the Danish king's islands.[126] Christian thus asked his chancellor to send Antonius von Metz to England and obtain the funds in order that the exiled king could pay off his creditors. The chancellor replied to this request by updating Christian on his conversations with Margaret, regent of the Netherlands, regarding the exiled king's intended removal there. The chancellor also highlighted Hans's direct input concerning the king's wishes, which completely negated what Baker had told him, and stopped the king's desired mission to England. This chain of events implies that the herald was perceived to have almost the final say on Christian's actual wishes: the chancellor seemed prepared to give greater weight to the herald's advice over both what a foreign envoy had said and over what his own king had indicated.[127] The chancellor even appears to complain that he simply had not been kept informed by Christian, either as to his pecuniary state, or as to unfolding developments, and thus had to rely on the herald. This misunderstanding was

[123] Hay, ed., *The Letters of James V*, pp. 92–3.

[124] Louis de Praet and Jean Marnix to Charles V, 1 June 1523. Mattingly, ed., *Further Supplement to Letters, Despatches and State Papers*, p. 240.

[125] *Diplomatarium Norvegicum*, x, no. 381 Klaus Pedersson to Christian II, 27 November 1523, Mechelen.

[126] 'Sir John Baker, [...] was bred to the law, and became eminent in that profession, as well as in his promotion to different high posts of trust and honour in the service of the crown and state; being in several parts of his life recorder of London, attorney general, chancellor of the exchequer, and privy counsellor in king Henry VIII. and the three following reigns, and ambassador to the court of Denmark in 1526': 'Parishes: Cranbrooke', *The History and Topographical Survey of the County of Kent* vii (1798), pp. 90–113.

[127] *Diplomatarium Norvegicum*, x, no. 384 Christian II to Klaus Pedersson, 11 January 1524, Berlin; no. 393 Klaus Pedersson to Christian II, 18 February 1524, Mechelen.

Appendix 1.
Table of Scandinavian heralds in the late medieval period[163]

The following table of Scandinavian heralds from 1360 to 1550 is my own compilation of information gathered from various sources, and is by no means definitive. In many cases it has been impossible to conclusively determine the names and nationalities of the individuals involved, or even trace documentary evidence of their activities, despite the varied nature of their tasks.

Name	Dates	Title	Nationality
Gerhard Grundis	1362–77	Herald of Danish king, at Lübeck 1363; prob. at Brussels 1366, Avignon 1375	?
?	1390–93	Sjælland Herald	Danish?
?	1404	'Herald' (trumpeter) of Danish king at Regensburg	Danish?
? (same as next two?)	1404–07	Herald of Queen Margaret of Denmark in Hungary	Danish?
Simon Tennemark (cf. below)	1411	Herald at King Sigismund of Hungary's court (in Margaret's service?)	Danish?
Simon Hendel (cf. above)	1418–23	Herald of three realms; also known as Norway Herald	German
?	1452	Denmark Herald	Danish?
?	1453–67	Denmark King of Arms in England	?
?	1458–61	Lolland Pursuivant in Portugal	?
?	1462	Sjælland Herald	?
Christian Hendel	1464–74	Sjælland Pursuivant	Danish
?	1473	Denmark King of Arms	Danish?
Thomas Young	1488–90	Sjælland Pursuivant	?
David Cochrane (Kock)	1492–1529	King of Arms of Denmark	Scot
Hans Frolegh	1490–3	Pursuivant, in England	Danish
Johannes Broke	1490–3	Pursuivant, in England	Danish
? (Bengt Svensk? Cf.below)	1504–5	Sweden Herald at Kalmar	?
?	1508	Norway King of Arms at Brussels	?
Johannes Gotschalk	1508	Pursuivant	Danish?
Bengt Svensk	1510	Sweden? Herald	Swedish
? (Thomas Scott?)	1510, 1515, 1519	Norway Herald	?

---

[163] Information from various printed primary sources: see Jesper Wasling, 'Skandinaviska härolder', <http://www.heraldik.se/artiklar/artiklar.htm>, and Riis, *Should auld acquaintance be forgot*, ii, pp. 57, 67, 81, 284, 285, 286, 291, 292, 297.

?	1510	Two pursuivants with David Cochrane in France	?
Thomas Lumsden	1505–28	Sjælland Herald	Scottish
Thomas 'Puncium' (same as above?)	1521	Herald in Danish service	Danish?
Hans Jylland	1516–30	Jylland Herald	Danish
John Elgin (Hans Illingen/ Johannes Hylgen)	1515–29	Sjælland Herald	Scottish
Frederik	1528	Sjælland Herald / King of Arms	Danish?
?	1529	Herald (in Swedish service) sent to Low Countries	Swedish?
Francisco de Medina	1529–53	Herald in Danish service	Spanish
Alexander Mure/Muir	1531–3	(Denmark?) Herald (formerly Conservator of Scots in Flanders)	Scottish
?	1545	Herald	Danish?
?	1551	Herald	Danish?
Nicolaus	1559	Herald (in Danish service)	?
Carolus Skotte	1559	Herald (in Danish service)	Scottish